D0992332

REBUILDING CITIES

REBUILDING CITIES

The Effects of Displacement and Relocation on Small Business

by
BASIL G. ZIMMER
Professor of Sociology
Brown University

Chicago QUADRANGLE BOOKS *1964*

 For information, address the publisher at 180 North Wacker Drive, Chicago 6. Library of Congress Catalog Card Number: 64-14135. Designed by Joan Stoliar. Manufactured in the United States of America.

This volume is dedicated to my wife
JANET
and to our children
BASIL JR. *and* LINDA JEAN

ACKNOWLEDGMENTS

THE present study was supported through funds provided by the Small Business Administration under the Research Grant Program for Management Research. It is a tribute to this agency that it perceived the importance of this problem in respect to small businesses in urban areas throughout the country. The findings of the study fully justify the agency's concern.

The writer wishes to express his appreciation to Dr. Wilford White, Director, Office of Management and Research Assistance and to Dr. Weston R. Clark, Research Studies Division, for their interest and sympathetic encouragement throughout the long analysis.

The writer is particularly indebted to the hundreds of displaced business owners who cooperated in the study by responding to a rather lengthy interview. Without their help we could not have recorded their experiences.

The assistance provided by Mr. James F. Reynolds, Executive Director, Providence Redevelopment Agency, and Mr. David Joyce, Director, The Family and Business Relocation Service, is deeply appreciated. Both agencies cooperated fully.

A note of thanks and appreciation is also due to the three conscientious and faithful interviewers who turned detective many times in their efforts to trace the missing and the difficult to find. The very high proportion of successful returns is a tribute to their efficiency. Thus a special indebtedness is owed to Mr. Stephen Finner and Mr. Richard Osborn, advanced graduate students in the Department of Sociology, and to Mr. Edward F. Tully, an experienced professional interviewer. Mr. Finner and Mr. Osborn also assisted at many other stages of the study. They were completely responsible for coding the responses and preparing the data on IBM cards.

I wish also to thank Mr. Alvin Dorse, a research assistant during the past two years, who competently carried out the tabulations and helped with much of the statistical analysis, and Mr. Melvin Feldman, who helped with the preparation of the index.

A special debt is owed my wife, Janet, whose work on the project at all stages likely exceeded my own efforts.

B.G.Z.

CONTENTS

REBUILDING CITIES

CHAPTER 1

INTRODUCTION

THERE are few problems of more immediate and pressing concern in urban areas than those pertaining to urban renewal and expressway construction. Such programs are essential, as well as inevitable, if cities of the future are to be viable social systems. However, both types of projects are wrought with problems of displacement and relocation of residential and non-residential units. Consequently in the execution of these programs, established social, economic and institutional relationships are disrupted. These programs are still in their early stages; the full impact will not be experienced for many years to come.

The problems of dislocation resulting from such programs are of a type and of a magnitude which have been largely unknown to urban centers of the past. Even to the casual observer, it is evident that American cities are entering a new stage in their historical development. We are currently in the midst of a new wave of programs the purposes of which are to rebuild our cities. As a consequence of aging, as well as neglect and exploitation, large sections of our cities have already reached advanced stages of decay and deterioration. Widespread blight is a common feature of our urban centers. Congestion and traffic strangulation are commonplace. It is the task of the last half of the present century to clear our cities of these areas in order to maintain the vitality of our urban way of life. The problems of urban renewal and rehabilitation are major undertakings of serious proportions, but superimposed on all of this is the further task of constructing major expressways, often through densely settled congested areas, in an attempt to provide adequate transportation routes leading into, and providing circulation patterns within, urban centers so as to accommodate the heavy traffic flow that presently threatens to strangle our cities. Thus the programs for the reconstruction of the urban environment include major downtown rebuilding projects as well as neighborhood renewal efforts and projects for the construction of major transportation routes.[1]

For urban sociologists and for other students of the city, a study of the effects of displacement and relocation is an important area for research since it provides an opportunity to contribute to our knowledge of a new dimension in the growth and development of the urban community. Whereas in the past, change in city areas has largely been due to expansion[2] and "natural" or "laissez-faire" development, cities are now entering a stage of planned rebuilding of the deteriorated, and perhaps obsolescent, physical environment. At the same time, many of the larger cities are experiencing an absolute decline in population size.[3] What effect the redevelopment process will have on the structure and functioning of the city will necessarily become a focus of concern in the formulation of, or in tests of, theories of city growth and development. This study proposes to contribute to the existing but limited knowledge of the effects of displacement and relocation on the distribution and function of selected institutional structures, that is, small nonresidential establishments. There are, of course, several dimensions to the problem but we are concerned primarily with the human aspects as well as the economic implications for the community

1 George S. Duggar, "The Relations of Local Government Structure to Urban Renewal," *Law and Contemporary Problems,* Vol. XXVI, No. 1, Winter 1961, pp. 49-69.

2 "The Growth of the City: An Introduction to a Research Problem," in R. E. Park and E. W. Burgess (eds.), *The City,* Chicago; University of Chicago Press, 1925, pp. 47-63.

3 United States Department of Commerce, Bureau of the Census, *1960 Census of Population,* "Preliminary Reports," PC (P3)-4.

and the individual business enterprise. Essentially this is a study of the ability of certain kinds of institutional structures to withstand the disruptive effects of change and of how such structures adapt to changes in the social system of which they are a part. We are concerned also with how these changes affect the form and development of the community.[4]

If urban centers are to effectively execute urban renewal and highway construction programs on the scale which is essential for the survival of such centers, it is important that we gain additional knowledge concerning some of the consequences of these programs. The agencies, planners and public administrators responsible for the rebuilding of our cities must be aware of the social and economic problems associated with displacement and relocation if they are to cope effectively with this aspect of public improvement programs. From the point of view of the displaced occupants, an account of the experiences of business establishments which have already faced the problems associated with displacement may serve to alert future displacees to some of the consequences of being forced to move from their established sites. It is only through the systematic accumulation of knowledge concerning the problems of dislocation that more effective programs can be developed.[5] From a practical point of view, if the problems associated with displacement and relocation can be effectively resolved, the rate at which renewal and highway construction proj-

4 This of course is the core of ecological theory. See A. H. Hawley, *Human Ecology: A Theory of Community Structure,* Ronald Press, 1950.

5 For example, the Small Business Agency could utilize such information in the development of a program to provide assistance to small business concerns that are displaced by various public improvement projects. That this is a concern of the SBA is evident from its recent instructions to its Regional Directors to appoint representatives for the purpose of maintaining liaison with local, state and federal authorities connected with urban renewal. It is the function of these representatives to meet and counsel with the owners and managers of individual small business concerns who may require technical and financial aid, and to inform them of the types of assistance available from the Small Business Agency. These are (1) technical and management advice, (2) special consideration in obtaining small business loans, and (3) occupational and vocational retraining for proprietors who fail to relocate, and for their employees. See: Martin Millspaugh, "Problems and Opportunities of Relocation," *Law and Contemporary Problems,* Vol. XXVI, No. 1, Winter 1961, p. 27.

ects can proceed will be increased. However, this dimension of rebuilding our cities may well prove to be one of the major obstacles governing the future of such projects.

PURPOSE AND SIGNIFICANCE OF THE STUDY

This is a report on the experiences of more than 350 small business establishments which were displaced either through urban renewal or highway construction programs within the city of Providence, Rhode Island, during the five-year period 1954 through 1959. Although these two programs differ in purpose and in procedure, the one common feature is that they both displace the occupants of an area and disrupt established patterns of behavior. The purpose of the study is to determine some of the salient consequences of displacement both in respect to what it means to the individual business firm and to the community at large.[6] Specifically we are concerned with what happens to business establishments when they have been forced to vacate their established sites. Attention will be focused on the effect displacement and relocation has on the operation of the business unit and the kinds of problems associated with relocation. Of particular interest is the extent to which dislocation leads to business failures for the individual firms and to business losses to the central city and to the larger community through either suburbanization or discontinuation of the business operation. Our analysis will include a comparison of those businesses that did not survive the move with those that successfully relocated. For example, we are interested in how these differ by type and size of business, and by the characteristics of the owners. Other areas of interest include the fol-

6 Little systematic research has been done in this area. Most of the information available to date on what relocation means to the displaced businesses has been based on non-representative reports obtained through letters from local redevelopment officials, agency records or on mail questionnaire surveys. See for example: Daniel Chill, *Business Relocation: A Moving Problem*, (Divisional Paper, Yale Law School, New Haven, March, 1960). This study is reported on extensively in William N. Kinnard, Jr. and Zenon S. Malinowksi, *The Impact of Dislocation From Urban Renewal Areas on Small Business*, University of Connecticut, Storrs, 1960; and James H. Saalberg, *A Study of Business Dislocations Caused by the Central Artery*, (Unpublished Master's Thesis in city planning, Massachusetts Institute of Technology). A summary of this work has been published by the Greater Boston Economic Study Committee as Economic Base Report Number 6, April, 1960.

lowing kinds of questions: What are the changing distribution patterns of businesses resulting from displacements and what are the selective factors in the suburbanization movement? What leads to a decision to relocate in the central city or to move to the suburban area? What are the major problems encountered by businesses when they attempt to relocate? What factors are involved in selecting a new site? An attempt will also be made to determine the general reaction of the businessmen to displacement and the type of adjustment realized at the new location. In order to measure some of the consequences of relocation, comparisons before and after the move will be presented for a number of selected variables, such as rents, sales, physical features of the business location, and the type of area served. Special attention will be focused on some of the financial aspects of the move.

Due to the rapid growth of urban renewal and highway construction projects in the execution stage in urban centers, cities are coming face to face, for the first time, with the magnitude of the relocation load that will be generated when these projects get underway full scale. Business dislocations to date have been largely incidental to the objectives of urban renewal or highway construction programs, in that displaced businesses have been largely those that happened to be in areas to be cleared. Even in the case of renewal projects, attention has been focused primarily on residential developments. Consequently business displacements have not reached the relative proportions of residential dislocations. In the first ten years of urban renewal, the annual rate of displacement of non-residential establishments has been about 3700.[7] However, it is estimated that the total amount of displacement occurring in cities may be three times that caused by urban renewal alone, due to other public improvement programs. And this ratio is expected to increase "as the Interstate Highway program is completed in rural spaces between cities and begins carving swathes through densely populated urban areas."[8] Also in the fu-

7 Urban Renewal Administration Statistics (Unpublished) quoted in "Problems and Opportunities of Relocation," M. Millspaugh, *Law and Contemporary Problems,* Winter 1961, Vol. XXVI, No. 1, p. 24.

8 *Ibid.,* p. 7, Statement of Albert M. Cole, Administrator, Housing and Home Financing Agency, in *Hearings Before a Subcommittee of the Senate Committee on Banking and Currency on the Housing Act of 1958,* 85th Congress, 2nd session 73 (1958).

ture we can expect business displacements to increase when the full impact of the Housing Act of 1959 is realized, since this provides that 20 per cent of the federal renewal grants may be spent on purely non-residential areas, regardless of whether new housing is created after the blight has been cleared. Thus localities are now able to initiate projects in which the relocation load will be almost totally composed of commercial and industrial establishments.[9] The study area typifies these experiences, for all of the businesses displaced in the city of Providence during the period of study were incidental to other objectives, but more recently a predominantly non-residential project has been approved. This is a business area (Weybossett Hill) on the fringes of the Central Business District.[10]

The problems of relocation of business firms are very real and will increase in importance in the future. But relocation has too often been treated as a minor problem of secondary importance.[1] Both in renewal and in highway construction, attention has been focused predominantly on the physical aspects of the programs, that is, the merits of a new expressway for moving traffic and the need for the redevelopment of an area to eliminate slums and blight. Not enough attention has been given to what clearance of an area means to the displaced residents or business establishments.[2] Thus when several of our urban renewal programs were observed by a British sociologist planner, the evaluative statement was made that in the United States urban renewal was

9 *Ibid.*, p. 24.

10 See Annual Report of Redevelopment Agency, 1961. This is the first "predominantly non-residential" project the Redevelopment Agency has ever undertaken.

1 Richard H. Leach, "The Federal Urban Renewal Program: A Ten Year Critique," *Law and Contemporary Problems*, Vol. XXV, Autumn 1960, No. 4, p. 788.

2 For a particularly devastating appraisal of this dimension see: Herbert J. Gans "The Human Implication of Current Redevelopment and Relocation Planning," *The Journal of the American Institute of Planners*, February, 1959, Vol. XXV, No. 1. For further dimensions of renewal programs see: Peter H. Rossi and Robert A. Dentler, *The Politics of Urban Renewal*, The Free Press of Glencoe, Inc., 1961; Julia Abrahamson, *A Neighborhood Finds Itself*, New York: Harper & Bros., 1950; and Hearings Before the Subcommittee on Involuntary Relocation of the Elderly of the Special Committee on Aging, United States Senate, 87th Congress, second session, 1962.

viewed as being "primarily for the benefit of the redeveloper and his tenants, whereas British renewal tries to aid mainly the present residents of the slum area."[3] However, this apparent neglect regarding relocation has not gone entirely unnoticed in the American literature. From a practical long-range point of view, one writer observes that, "if the relocation phase is not managed successfully, urban renewal can do enough damage to families and businesses to create a new wave of reaction (negative), a reaction that might be sufficient to stop the momentum of the urban renewal process itself."[4] More salient, however, is the general welfare of the displaced occupants.

That relocation has been largely neglected is evident from a brief reference to the relative amount of urban renewal resources that have been devoted to this aspect of the program. Before doing so, however, it is noted that more is provided for urban renewal relocations than in most other public improvement programs including highway relocations. In a recent report on urban renewal activities throughout the country, costs were given for more than 500 projects by major project activity.[5] An inspection of these data showed that only 0.6 per cent of the gross project costs were allocated to relocation costs. A further analysis showed that this expenditure was only three-fourths of the amount spent on property management and land disposition expenses. Relocation costs were approximately equal to the expenditures for legal services which were grouped under "project administration and overhead." A similar neglect is found in the present study area. For example, during 1961 the amount spent by the Redevelopment Agency for relocation services was only equal to the amount expended for real estate appraisal services or negotiation services. Only 4 per cent of the services rendered or contracted for by the Redevelopment Agency was for relocation.[6] Even if relocation

3 *Ibid.,* p. 23.

4 Martin Millspaugh, "Problems and Opportunities of Relocation," *Law and Contemporary Problems,* Winter 1961, No. 1, p. 6.

5 "Urban Renewal Project Characteristics," Housing and Home Finance Agency, Urban Renewal Administration, Washington 25, D.C., Table 8, p. 17.

6 The Redevelopment Agency purchased this service from the City Family and Business Relocation Service.

services are expressed as a per cent of the Redevelopment Agency's salaries and overhead, it accounts for only 12 per cent.[7]

The need for an expansion of urban renewal activity is apparent from two recent reports. In 1960, ACTION estimated that a total of $100 billion a year should be spent on urban renewal for the next ten years if the spread of urban blight is to be halted and overcome.[8] Experience in Boston shows the needs for speeding up the program. In that area, which has been active in renewal, the rate of renewal activity has apparently been outstripped by the rate of decay. It is reported that between 1950 and 1960 there were 22,000 dwelling units that had fallen into the sub-standard category, which is nearly three times the amount of poor housing eliminated during the same period.[9] This experience is not considered atypical.[10] It is this type of differential between renewal and decay that led the American Municipal Association and the United States Conference of Mayors to estimate that $3,618 million in federal grants for urban renewal would be needed between now and 1970.[1] Thus the magnitude of the relocation problem will increase with time as the pressure for available sites increases in the future due to the accumulation of displaced units over the years from additional clearance projects. As available sites are occupied by previously displaced units, competition for sites will necessarily increase. Accordingly the problems of relocation will become more acute, and the need for relocation services will increase. The magnitude of the problem of rebuilding our cities, both present and future, is evident from the following discussion

7 Computed from data presented in Annual Report for 1961, Providence Redevelopment Agency, 410 Howard Building, Providence, Rhode Island. Ordinarily one would admire economy in governmental expenditures; however, it seems to the writer that there are other aspects of the renewal program more worthy of economy than relocation services, for the brunt of the program falls on the displaced occupants, and more particularly on tenants.

8 "ACTION Puts Costs of Total Urban Renewal at $42 Billion A Year Over Current Spending," *Architectural Forum*, May, 1960, p. 5.

9 Boston Municipal Research Bureau, *Charting the Future of Urban Renewal*, 12, 1959.

10 Richard H. Leach, "The Federal Urban Renewal Program: A Ten Year Critique," *Law and Contemporary Problems*, Vol. XXV, Autumn 1960, No. 4.

1 *Ibid.*, p. 789.

of urban renewal and highway construction programs and needs, nationally as well as locally.

SCOPE OF THE PROBLEM

Urban Renewal Programs Nationally. The urban renewal program nationally is in the very early stages of development. It is claimed that even in New York City where the need is possibly the greatest, the urban renewal program is essentially only in the planning stage and cannot be expected to move beyond the pilot stage for several years.[2] As a federal program, urban renewal started in 1949 and has been emphasized only since 1954 when the housing act converted slum clearance and redevelopment to "urban renewal," and made possible the creation of an Urban Renewal Administration in the Housing and Home Finance Agency. This change permitted an attack on the whole problem of urban decay. The urban renewal concept was extended further by the Housing Act of 1959. This introduced a new program to assist localities in the preparation of "Community Renewal Programs." Under this provision, communities could obtain federal funds to undertake an appraisal of the community's total need for all types of renewal measures and its total resources for putting these measures into effect.[3]

The favorable legislation of recent years has encouraged a number of communities to participate in the federal program. By early 1962, some 1200 renewal projects of various sizes and types had been approved and funds reserved by the federal agency. And the rate of entrance into the program is likely to increase in the future, as is evident from the proportion of projects started during the past two years. Of the total projects reported in the March 1962 Urban Renewal Directory, 445 of the 1,129 projects (39.4 per cent) had been approved, at the planning stage, during 1960 or later.[4] Only 11 per cent of the urban renewal projects under-

2 Leach, *op. cit.*, p. 790.

3 Millspaugh, *op. cit.*, p. 10.

4 Community renewal programs and demonstration projects are excluded.

taken since passage of the 1949 Housing Act had been completed at the time of this report.

Since 1960 there have also been 48 Community Renewal Programs and 15 Demonstration Projects approved.[5] Still another index of the relative newness of the urban renewal program is that only about one-fifth of the funds ever committed to local communities have been disbursed. Thus, even among the projects underway, only a small proportion has reached advanced stages of execution. Two-fifths of the projects have only been approved at the planning stage.

Participation in urban renewal programs is disproportionately concentrated among the larger urban aggregates, as is shown in Table 1-1. Of the communities with projects underway, only 1 per cent are in the million-and-over category, but this population size class accounts for 10 per cent of the projects and 22 per cent of the federal grant reservations. When we combine the 41 localities with 250,000 or more population, we find that, while they account for only 8 per cent of the participating communities, they include 27 per cent of the projects and 54 per cent of the grant reservations. These communities also contain 70 per cent of the funds disbursed for completed urban renewal projects.[6] On the other extreme, the 220 communities under 25,000 constitute 43 per cent of the participating localities, but only 27 per cent of the projects, and 8 per cent of the grant reservations. The more than 200 communities in this size class contain less than 5 per cent of the federal grants for completed projects. Thus it is abundantly clear that it is the communities in the program with populations 250,000 and over that have a high disproportionate share of the projects and the grant reservations, while those in the population size groups of 50,000 or less are underrepresented.

5 To date 42 demonstration projects have been approved.

6 These are the projects under Title I of the Housing Act of 1949, and Title III of the Housing Act of 1954.

TABLE 1-1

NUMBER AND PER CENT DISTRIBUTION OF LOCALITIES, PROJECTS, GRANT RESERVATIONS AND CONTRACTS COMPLETED BY POPULATION SIZE GROUP

Population Size Group	Number of:		Percentage Distribution of:			
	Localities	Projects	Localities	Projects	Grant Reservations (000)	Completed Contracts (000)
Total Number	520	944	520	944	2,294,678	37,915
1,000,000 and Over	5	94	1.0	10.0	21.6	26.9
500,000 – 1,000,000	12	61	2.3	6.5	18.4	25.3
250,000 – 500,000	24	96	4.6	10.2	14.1	17.6
100,000 – 250,000	57	143	11.0	15.1	17.5	10.1
50,000 – 100,000	93	154	17.9	16.3	12.5	7.8
25,000 – 50,000	109	146	21.0	15.5	7.7	7.6
10,000 – 25,000	125	148	24.0	15.7	5.8	2.4
Under 10,000	95	102	18.3	10.8	2.3	2.3
Total Per Cent	...	...	100.0	100.0	100.0	100.0

Source: "Urban Renewal Project Characteristics," **Housing and Home Finance Agency, Urban Renewal Administration,** December 31, 1961.

Other significant differentials by community size are also evident from the data presented in Table 2-1. The average size of the federal grant per community for all projects underway is $4.4 million. Since there are slightly less than two projects per participating community, the average grant per renewal project nationally is $2.4 million. However, the average amount reserved for each community varies markedly by population size. Average grants range from a high of nearly 99 million for the five communities in the million and over category, but fall continuously and rapidly as size of population decreases. In the contiguous population-size class, the average grant is reduced to 35 million. Thus the average grant received by the twelve cities in the half million to 1 million class is only one-third the size of the grant in the five cities with a population in excess of 1 million, but is nearly three times the average grant received by the 24 cities with one-fourth to one-half million population. The average size grant is substantially less for the smaller communities.

The same kind of pattern by population size is found in respect to the average grant per urban renewal project. As expected, the larger communities have the largest renewal projects underway. This is likely a function of both need and resources available. Grants per project range from less than $500,000 for communities with less than 10,000 population to approximately $6 million in communities with 500,000 or more. It is abundantly clear from these data that urban renewal in the early stages has been essentially a big-city program. This is further shown by the average number of projects per participating community by population size class. The participating communities under 50,000 population have an average of 1.2 projects, but the number increases continuously by size of community and reaches its peak in the 1 million and over category, where we find an average of nearly nineteen projects.

The proportion of communities participating in the federal urban renewal program varies by population-size class. Of all the local units with a population of 10,000 or more according to the 1960 Census, nearly one in four has at least one project underway. The participation rate ranges, however, from a low of only 12 per cent among communities in the 10,000 to 25,000 population-size class to a high of 100 per cent participation among the five units

TABLE 2-1

COMMUNITY PARTICIPATION IN URBAN RENEWAL PROGRAM BY POPULATION SIZE

Population Size	Number of Localities:		Per Cent of Localities	Average Size of Grant Per:		Average No. of Projects
Group	In Size Class[b]	With Projects[b]	with Projects	Locality[c] (000)	Project[c] (000)	per Locality[c]
Total	1802	425	23.6[a]	$ 4,413	$2,431	1.8
1,000,000 and Over	5	5	100.0	98,937	5,263	18.8
500,000 – 1,000,000	16	12	75.0	35,233	6,931	5.1
250,000 – 500,000	31	24	77.4	13,521	3,380	4.0
100,000 – 250,000	81	57	73.4	7,033	2,803	2.5
50,000 – 100,000	190	93	48.9	3,087	1,864	1.6
25,000 – 50,000	394	109	27.7	1,621	1,210	1.3
10,000 – 25,000	1085	125	11.5	1,074	907	1.2
Under 10,000	a	a	a	566	527	1.1

Source: "Urban Renewal Project Characteristics," December 31, 1961.

(a) Localities under 10,000 excluded. In this category the Urban Renewal Administration reports 16,496 localities and 95 projects.

(b) According to the URA the total number of units in each size class was derived by adding the Census Bureau figures for "incorporated places" and "urban towns and townships" for the United States and Puerto Rico. The URA definition of "unit" is not strictly comparable to the Census Bureau's because the URA includes a few counties, operating for unincorporated territory within their boundaries, and a few towns that do not meet the Census Bureau's criteria to be classified as urban towns. Letter to the writer from **Housing and Home Finance Agency**, Washington 25, D.C., dated August 3, 1963.

(c) Includes only the participating Communities.

with 1 million or more population. Sharp differences are found at various levels in the population size classification. The break points are worthy of note. Apart from the five very large units, decreases in population size do not seem to affect the rate of participation until the size of the unit falls below 100,000. Above this level approximately three localities out of four have projects underway. But in the next smaller population group, that is, 50,000 to 100,000, the participation rate drops to less than half of the units in the category, and the rate declines substantially again in the next population group where only slightly more than one-fourth of the units are participating in the federal urban renewal program. The smaller communities have the lowest participation rate, as already noted. Thus it is apparent that urban renewal pertains predominantly to the larger urban centers.

A substantial majority of the communities with a population of 50,000 or more have at least started the rebuilding program. Three-fifths of the localities of this size have had at least one project approved. But viewed from a different perspective, the urban renewal program is only in the beginning stages, for we find that four communities out of ten in the 50,000 and over group have not developed a project to the planning stage. Only in a very few cases do we find that projects have been completed. There is every indication, however, that renewal programs will expand rapidly in the future as more communities enter the program and as more projects are undertaken by the communities that have already reached the stage of limited participation. It is quite likely that the ground-work required from a community to get approval from the urban renewal administration for the first project is such that it would be done only if the local community planned to participate on a broader scale in the future. Thus the problems of displacement and relocation nationally are still in the early stages, and will increase in scope in the near future.

Urban Renewal Programs in the Study Area. When the study area is compared with the national averages, it is readily apparent that this area has been more active in urban renewal than other participating communities of comparable size. In this population size category, as was shown in Table 2-1, the average number of projects per participating community nationally was 2.5, and the average grant to each community was approximately $7 million. In the same Urban Renewal Agency report, Providence had four major projects[7] and one test case project[8] underway and had grants reserved which amounted to nearly $12 million.[9] In a report issued by the Urban Renewal Administration three months later,[10] in addition to a Community Renewal Program and two Demonstration Projects, Providence had three new major projects underway with additional grant reservations amounting to $35 million.[1] Thus, since the Providence renewal program effectively got underway in late 1953, the Redevelopment Agency has obtained commitments from the federal agency for nearly $47 million. During the eight-year period ending in December, 1961, the city of Providence has averaged approximately $6 million per year in federal grant reservations. This average annual rate is only slightly less than the total average amount reserved for communities in the same population size class for their total participation in the renewal program since its inception. It is apparent that Providence is one of the leaders in the nation in its size class in renewal acitivity. However, even in this area the renewal program is still largely in the early stages, for not many of the projects approved at the federal level have reached the displacement and relocation stage. Thus the bulk of the problems of rehousing the population and the major problems of relocating non-residential establishments that will be displaced are yet to be faced by the community. That these problems will reach serious proportions in the near future is evident from the magnitude of the projects to be undertaken.

7 Central-Classical $4.3 million, Lippitt Hill $3.2 million, West River $2.8 million and Willard Center $1.5 million. "Urban Renewal Project Characteristics," December 31, 1961.

8 Point Street $113,960, a test case to confirm the constitutionality of the Community Redevelopment Act. *Providence Redevelopment 1945-61,* mimeographed report p. 4, *Redevelopment Agency.*

9 "Urban Renewal Project Characteristics," Housing and Home Finance Agency, Urban Renewal Administration, Washington 25, D.C., December 31, 1961.

10 Urban Renewal Project Directory, March 31, 1962, Housing and Home Finance Agency, Washington 25, D.C.

1 Weybosset Hill ($10.5 million), Railroad Relocation ($11 million), and East Side Renewal Project ($13 million).

This brief review of urban renewal activities at both the national and local level makes it abundantly clear that such programs are developing at a rapid pace and that renewal projects have been, and will continue to be, of a magnitude to effect profound changes in our urban centers. It is also evident that these programs will cause tremendous dislocations of both residential and non-residential units and that these will be faced with the task of relocation. Thus an inquiry into the problems of displacement and relocation needs no further justification. But apart from the disruptions of urban renewal, cities must also accommodate the displacements resulting from highway construction programs. The significance of this is suggested by the following brief review of highway needs in and around urban areas, both nationally and locally.

Factors Contributing to Urban Expressway Needs Nationally. Increased need for urban highways which will result in widespread commercial and residential displacements is seen in population growth figures, in changing population distribution and in increases in automobile ownership and travel during recent years. In order to get some notion of the magnitude of the problem of displacements that are likely to be due to highway construction, each of these dimensions will be considered further. Looking first at population increase, we note that during the 1950 to 1960 decade the population of the United States experienced a larger numerical growth than during any other census decade in history. Even the rate of increase exceeded the growth of the past four decades. Projections of the future population indicate that substantial growth will also be experienced in the years ahead.[2] However, it has been suggested by the chairman of the special committee on urban transportation of the Highway Research Board of the National Academy of Sciences that the sweeping changes in population distribution that have taken place during recent years are far more significant in respect to the problems of

2 Projections of future populations vary according to assumptions regarding future fertility. However, the most recent projections show a population for 1980 of between 245 million and 259 million. See *Current Population Reports*, "Interim Revised Projections of the Population of the United States, By Age and Sex: 1975 and 1980," Series P-25, No. 251, July 6, 1962.

urban transportation than are the changes in total population.[3]

It is the concentration of population in urban centers, and more particularly the suburbanization of population around the larger urban aggregates, that have created and aggravated the need for improvements in highways within and around urban centers. That the population is becoming increasingly concentrated in metropolitan areas is evident from the changes during the last decennial period.[4] For the decade 1950 to 1960, the census reports a total population increase of approximately 28 million, but of this increase 23.6 million were added in the 212 metropolitan areas. Thus, of the population increase, 84.3 per cent took place in these metropolitan areas. But of even more significance, from the point of view of future urban expressway needs, is the differential growth pattern within metropolitan areas. Of the population increase in such areas, 18 million of the increase was outside of the central cities. This represents a doubling of the population in the fringes of cities during a single decade. In the 212 metropolitan areas in the United States, the growth rate outside exceeded central city growth rates five-fold and was seven times the rate of growth outside metropolitan areas.[5] Even these data understate the growth on the fringes of central cities in metropolitan areas, for most of the increase in population in central cities was due to annexation of suburban territories.[6] Of the 5.6 million increase in population in central cities, 4.9 million or 87.5 per cent was gained through annexation.[7] Thus, from the point of view of

3 Highway Research Board, Special Report 69, "A Key to Change, Urban Transportation Research," National Academy of Sciences, National Research Council, Publication 965, p. 2.

4 For definition of Standard Metropolitan Statistical Area, see United States Census of Population, 1960, United States Summary, "General Social and Economic Characteristics," U. S. Dept. of Commerce, PC (1)-1A U. S.

5 See: U. S. Department of Commerce, Bureau of the Census, *Population of Standard Metropolitan Statistical Areas 1960 and 1950, Preliminary Reports, Population Summaries,* Series PC (P3)-4, October, 1960 (Washington, D.C.).

6 Leo F. Schnore, "Municipal Annexations and the Growth of Metropolitan Suburbs, 1950-60," *The American Journal of Sociology,* Vol. LXVII, No. 4, January, 1962, pp. 406-417.

7 U. S. Summary, 1960 Census of Population, Tables P and R, p. XXVI (Introduction).

transportation, it is significant that another 5 million of the growth, in addition to the 18 million, is on the outer ring of the city.

This pattern of growth is not new, but rather is an acceleration of past trends.[8] During the first half of the present century, the population of the United States doubled in size, but the areas outside of metropolitan areas increased by only 50 per cent while metropolitan areas more than tripled in size.[9] At the same time that the population was becoming increasingly concentrated in metropolitan communities, it was also becoming more decentralized within such areas. During each decade since 1920, the rate of growth in population in the rings of metropolitan areas exceeded the growth rate of central cities. In the 1940 to 1950 decade, the ring increased two and one-half times faster than the central cities, and during the last census period, 1950 to 1960, as already noted, the growth rate differentials increased to a five-fold excess in the outside area. Central cities increased by 9.4 per cent, much of which was due to an expansion of boundaries, while the remaining portion of metropolitan areas increased by 47.7 per cent.

The rapid expansion of the urban area has greatly increased the mileage of express highways necessary to serve the dispersed population and community activities – social, cultural, and economic. The suburbanization of population has to a large extent been dependent on highway transportation facilities and subsequently has increased the burden on the highways. As the population outside of central cities increases, the need for expressways in cities increases proportionately. In this widespread settlement pattern, the private automobile becomes the almost exclusive mode of travel, thus placing heavy demands on the road system.[10] For example, as the distance to work increases, a larger proportion of the trips are by private automobile. Beyond ten miles, more than eight out of every ten trips are by automobile.[1]

8 Donald J. Bogue, *Population Growth in Standard Metropolitan Areas, 1900-1950: With an Explantory Analysis of Urbanized Areas,* Washington, D.C., Housing and Home Finance Agency.

9 Philip Hauser, *Population Perspectives,* Rutgers University Press, New Brunswick, New Jersey, 1960, p. 97.

10 B. G. Zimmer and A. H. Hawley, "Suburbanization and Some of its Consequences," *Land Economics,* Volume 37, No. 1, February, 1961, pp. 88-93.

1 Thurley A. Bostic, Roy T. Messer, Clarance A. Steele, "Motor-Vehicle-Use Studies in Six States," *Public Roads,* December, 1954, p. 111.

The total vehicle-miles of travel in the United States has increased some 200 per cent since the end of World War II.[2] Of the 720 billion vehicle-miles of travel in the United States in 1960, nearly 50 per cent occurred within our rapidly expanding urban areas.[3] Within the next fifteen years, it is estimated that vehicle-miles traveled in the United States will increase by approximately two-thirds.[4]

In the past, expressways and toll roads have been constructed predominantly in rural areas while urban areas have been largely neglected. For example, originally the Pennsylvania Turnpike terminated ten miles from Philadelphia at the eastern end, and at the western end it stopped well outside the limits of Pittsburgh. This was not an isolated example, but rather was typical of the conventional highway practice.[5] Consequently as highways were improved in rural areas, increased traffic was dumped at the city limits to make its way along antiquated streets where the need for highway modernization was more obvious.[6] The problems of moving traffic and the need for an entire system of expressways in urban centers is obvious, and this type of construction will expand increasingly in the near future. Some notion of the magnitude of the problem is evident from an appraisal of the San Francisco Bay Area. It has been estimated that passenger movements in 1970, under the present pattern of regional transportation, will require 48 lanes of freeway to handle the peak hour volumes at the principal gateways to the central metropolitan area. At the same time, ten or twelve lanes would be needed to handle passenger cars

2 *Statistical Abstract of the United States,* Table 755, p. 557 (1961).

3 *Highway Statistics,* Table VM-1, U. S. Bureau of Public Roads (1960).

4 *U. S. Bureau of Public Roads,* "Third Progress Report of the Highway Cost Allocation Study," February, 1959.

5 Wilfred Owen, *The Metropolitan Transportation Problem,* The Brookings Institution, 722 Jackson Place, N.W., Washington 6, D.C., 1956.

6 *Ibid.* Early federal legislation did not generally make funds available to cities. The Federal-Aid Road Act of 1916 provided that no federal funds could be spent in cities of more than 2,500 population "except that portion of any such street or road along which the houses average more than 200 feet apart." It was not until 1944 that federal-aid legislation specifically authorized federal funds for urban streets. (In the 1930's federal help was given to cities for highway work, but the primary objective was to provide employment.)

crossing the Bay.[7] The cost of such construction would of course be astronomical.

A further indication of the increased demands that have developed in recent years for the expansion of our highway system is found in the historical changes in vehicle ownership. During the past half-century, motor vehicle registrations have increased from less than one-half million to nearly 74 million.[8] During the past seven years, the annual percentage increase in motor vehicle registrations has been 1.7 per cent or more. But a preliminary estimate of the increase in 1960 over 1959 was 2.4 million vehicles or 3.3 per cent.[9] Within the next twenty years as projections prepared by the states for the Bureau of Public Roads indicate, the total number of motor vehicle registrations will reach from 115 to 120 million.

Motor vehicle registrations have increased at a more rapid rate than population during recent years and will likely continue to do so in the future. In 1958 there were 38.9 vehicles per 100 population, but two years later this had increased to 42.5.[10] It has been estimated that this rate will increase to 49.5 per 100 persons in 1976.[1] This increase is also reflected in the proportion of families that own cars. From 1951 to 1959 the proportion of families owning cars increased from 65 per cent to 74 per cent.[2] Multiple car ownership increased from 8.8 per cent in 1954 to 13.5 per cent five years later. From the point of view of the burden placed on urban transportation facilities, it is highly significant that multiple ownerships are predominantly in suburban areas. Car ownership

7 The successful development of a rapid transit system would of course reduce the problem immeasurably. For a full discussion of transportation problems and rapid transits in urban areas in particular, see: *Ibid.*

8 The 1960 figure is an estimate reported in "Motor Vehicle Registration Estimates for 1960," *U. S. Bureau of Public Roads Release 60-20* (September 25, 1960).

9 *Ibid.*

10 C. A. Steele, "Characteristics of Motor Vehicle Ownership and Use," Highway Research Board, Proc. 40, 1961, pp. 95-110.

1 T. R. Todd, "Forecasts of Population Motor Vehicle Registrations, Travel, and Fuel Consumption," Public Roads, 30:12, 261-274 (February, 1960).

2 "Survey of Consumer Finances," Federal Reserve Board and Survey Research Center, University of Michigan.

is higher in the metropolitan suburbs than in any other area. Nearly nine suburban households out of ten have at least one car while one in five has two or more cars. Suburban areas account for about one-third of the households but more than two-fifths (42.3 per cent) of the multiple car owners.[3]

The demand for transportation facilities tends to increase at a faster rate than the population. This is due in part to the continued shift to the use of the automobile as the predominant mode of travel.[4] It is also due, as already noted, to the changing distribution of population, particularly in and around urban areas. Another factor is the change in the age composition of the population resulting in an increased proportion in the driver age group, that is, those 15 to 74 years.[5] Rising incomes also increase vehicle ownership. There has also been a change in the cultural pattern regarding driving in that women are increasingly learning to drive and, as each new age group enters the driving age, the proportion of women who have learned to drive will increase.

In the opinion of one expert, the traffic problem is worsening much more rapidly than the highway program can hope to furnish relief.[6] Others have concluded that the future highway problems in the rapidly growing metropolitan areas will surpass even the complex ones that are now facing highway administrators. The urban transportation problem will continue to mount as the population continues to shift to expanding urban areas.[7]

There is abundant evidence at the national level to show that future highway construction will be accelerated and that a major portion of this will occur in urban areas. Consequently vast sections in our cities will have to be cleared through displacement to make room for the highways that are needed. The changes wrought by this in the distribution of commercial and other-type establish-

3 *Automobile Facts and Figures,* 1959-60 Edition, p. 33.

4 T. J. Seburn, and B. L. Maush, "Urban Transportation Administration," Bureau of Highway Traffic, Yale University (1959), pp. 4-16.

5 C. A. Steele, *op. cit.*

6 Wilfred Owen, *op. cit.*

7 E. L. Kanwit and T. R. Todd, "Recent Population Trends and Their Highway Implications," Highway Research Board, Proc. 40, 1961, pp. 1-29.

ments is not an idle issue; rather, the consequences of displacement and relocation are a problem of major concern.

Factors Contributing to Urban Expressway Needs in the Study Area. The Providence area reflects the national scene but in many respects the same patterns are found in more advanced stages. The central city in this area has already suffered a substantial population loss. Patterns of population change and distribution for the past 30 years are shown in Table 3-1. The rate of growth in the state has been uneven and below the national rate, but during each decade the population did increase.

TABLE 3-1

RATE OF POPULATION CHANGE 1930-1960 BY SELECTED AREAS

Selected Areas	1930 to 1940	1940 to 1950	1950 to 1960	1930 to 1960
State	3.8	11.0	8.5	25.0
Metropolitan Area	2.9	7.5	16.5	32.4
City of Providence	0.2	– 1.9	–16.6	–18.0
Remainder of Metropolitan Area	4.8	13.8	40.5	67.4

During the last thirty years the population increased by one-fourth. It is worthy of note that only during the last decade did the metropolitan area population exceed the rate of growth of the state. Of particular interest, however, are the comparative changes in population in the central city and in the outside part of the metropolitan area. During the 1930 decade, the population of the city remained stable while the outside area increased by 5 per cent. It was during the 1940 decade that the city first experienced a decline in size. While the city had a net loss of nearly 2 per cent, the outside area increased by nearly 14 per cent. The last decade shows the pattern of suburbanization to have reached advanced stages, for the central city declined by 17 per cent while the outside area increased by 40 per cent.[8] Thus, while the rate of growth in the total area in recent years has been lower than the national average, the changing distribution of population has nonetheless reached serious dimensions. During the past thirty years the central city has declined in size by nearly one-fifth but the remaining part of the metropolitan area has increased by more than two-thirds. The proportion of the state population in the central city of Providence has declined from 37 per cent in 1930 to only 24 per cent in 1960. In the metropolitan area the proportion in the central city has declined from 41 per cent to 25 per cent during the same period. These data are shown in Table 4-1.

TABLE 4-1

PER CENT DISTRIBUTION OF POPULATION FOR SELECTED YEARS BY AREAS

	Metropolitan Area			State		
Years	Total	Central City	Other	Total	Central City	Other
1930	100.0	41.0	59.0	100.0	36.8	63.2
1940	100.0	40.0	60.0	100.0	35.5	64.5
1950	100.0	36.5	63.5	100.0	31.4	68.6
1960	100.0	25.4	74.6	100.0	24.1	75.9

The outward movement of population has placed heavy demands on the local road system out of proportion to the total increase in size. This is clearly a case of the traffic problem being aggravated not by population growth but by a changing distribution. The significance of the changing distribution in respect to the traffic problem exceeds the relative size of the population in the outside area, for the movement out of the city is selective of young adults, that is, that segment of the population most likely to travel by private automobile. The population in the 20-44 year

8 The city lost 41,176 persons plus a natural increase of 21,937 resulting from 53,017 births and 31,080 deaths during the decade. (Source: Research Division, Rhode Island Development Council.)

group in the city declined by one-third during the decade. It is this group that has been disproportionately attracted to the suburbs.[9]

Vehicle registrations have increased steadily during the past thirty years.[10] In the state, the number of registered vehicles increased from 136,000 in 1930 to 364,000 in 1960 – nearly a three-fold increase. However, the proportion of registrations in the city has declined since 1950 even though the absolute number has increased.[1] It is only in the last two years that the number has declined in the central city while the annual rate of increase outside has been about 3 per cent. In 1950 one-fourth of the vehicles registered in the state were in the city, but ten years later this had declined to only one-fifth. During the last five years the number of vehicles registered in the city declined by more than 1100, but in the remaining part of the state there was an increase of approximately 40,000 vehicles. It is the latter that contributes substantially to the demands for an expressway system causing widespread displacements in the central city.

The increase in vehicle availability is further evident from an analysis of population in relation to vehicle registrations as is done in Table 5-1. In 1930 there were five persons in the state for every

TABLE 5-1

NUMBER OF PERSONS PER VEHICLE FOR SELECTED YEARS BY AREAS

Year	Area		
	State	Providence	Remainder
1930	5.0	*	*
1940	3.8	*	*
1950	3.1	3.9	2.8
1960	2.4	2.9	2.2

*Data not available.

9 Slightly more than 10 per cent of the decline, however, was due to a deficit in the younger ages at the time of the previous census, due to the lower birth rates during the depression period.

10 State Motor Vehicle Registration office records.

1 Data not available separately for the city for earlier periods.

vehicle. This declined steadily and by 1960 the ratio was reduced to only 2.4. The ratio was higher in the city of Providence than in the remainder of the state; however, in both areas the ratio has declined substantially during the last census period. In 1950 there were 3.9 persons per vehicle in the city but this declined to 2.9 by 1960. In the outside area the comparable ratios were 2.8 and 2.2. Again this suggests the greater use of the private automobile in areas outside of the central city.

In a recent small sample study in Smithfield township, the geometric center of which is approximately nine miles from the Providence Central Business District, it was found that most of the open-country dwellers commuted to urban jobs in Providence. The homes were located principally along the main highways in continuous ribbons with lesser concentrations along the secondary roads. Only 4 per cent of the 28 square miles in 1950 was sufficiently densely settled to be included in the Providence urbanized area. Of the residents in the sample who had moved into the town during the preceding ten years, less than 1 per cent worked within the town. Nearly all of those employed worked in Providence, and in most cases the journey to work was made by private automobile,[2] thus placing an increased burden on the city road system.

A substantial number of the employed population in the Providence metropolitan area commutes across a political boundary in the daily journey to work. This is a very crude index of traffic flow, but it does provide some indication of the amount of movement that is recurrent on a daily basis. Place of work and place of residence are shown for selected cities in Table 6-1. These cities account for approximately three-fourths of the metropolitan population. The central city of Providence provides only half of the workers for all of the jobs held in the city. Thus half of those who work in Providence commute from another political subdivision. Only 20 per cent of the employed population in the city work outside of the city, whereas 80 per cent live and work in the central city. This is the lowest proportion of out-commuters in any of the cities included. Yet the fact that one worker in five living in the city travels out of the city daily to work adds substantially to the traffic flow in the area. In the other cities the resident population

2 Vincent Whitney, "Urban Impact on a Rural Township," in M. Suchman (editor), *Community Structure and Analysis,* New York, Cromwell (1959), pp. 413-432.

TABLE 6-1

POPULATION OF SELECTED CITIES AS PER CENT OF METROPOLITAN AREA POPULATION AND PER CENT OF WORKERS WHO ARE RESIDENTS AND COMMUTERS*

Area	Population as Percentage of Met. Area Pop.	Per Cent of Those Working in Each Place Who:		Per Cent of Employed Residents Who:	
		Reside in Place of Work	In Commute to Place of Work	Work in Place of Residence	Out Commute to Work
Providence	29.0	51.8	48.2	80.0	20.0
Pawtucket	10.7	57.2	42.8	57.0	43.0
Cranston	8.2	34.4	65.6	29.6	70.4
Warwick	7.7	54.2	45.8	24.8	75.2
Woonsocket	6.4	74.1	25.9	61.1	38.9
East Providence	5.1	41.3	58.7	31.5	68.5
Central Falls	2.8	27.9	72.1	23.5	76.5
North Providence	2.1	33.3	66.7	13.8	86.2

*Adapted from Table V-3 in A. J. Field, **An Ecological Analysis of a Mature Metropolitan Area: Providence, 1929-1958,** p. 152 (unpublished Ph.D. dissertation, Brown University, 1960).

fills from less than one-third to three-fourths of the jobs held within the city.

In only two of the seven cities, excluding Providence, do a majority of the employed residents work within the political unit in which they live, but even in these areas two out of five workers commute to another area for work. In the five remaining cities, more than two-thirds of the employed residents work outside of the city. In the case of North Providence which is contiguous to the central city, 86 per cent commute to another area for work. As the population in these areas continues to grow, the demands on the road system are likely to increase. For example, in the last ten years, the vehicle miles traveled in Rhode Island increased from 2.2 million in 1950 to 3.3 million in 1960 – a 50 per cent increase.

As a consequence of the pattern of population that is developing and the increased use of the automobile, the need for expanded highways in the Providence area is clearly evident. And these highways are needed predominantly in urban areas. In a recent state report on highway problems, it was stated that many existing highways and streets are congested and cannot handle the mounting number of automobiles – new facilities must be constructed. The same report shows that in 1953 motor vehicle travel in urban areas was more than four times that in rural areas.[3] According to this study 80 per cent of the travel in the state is in urban areas. This report concludes that traffic congestion is the largest single problem in highway transportation in Rhode Island, and that it will continue to grow in importance as a deterrent to the economic development of the state. Also, congestion is worse in and around Providence than elsewhere in the state. Relief of congestion in the metropolitan area thus becomes of the greatest urgency.[4] Expressways through the city of Providence have been given top priority. It is in these areas that displacements are greatest. Thus the need to know the consequences of displacement for all types of units becomes apparent. The present study, however, is limited only to displaced commercial establishments.

3 Governor's Highway Study Committee, "A Report to the Governor on Highway Problems," *Rhode Island Roads,* published in Providence, Rhode Island, June, 1959, p. 18.

4 *Ibid.,* p. 55.

BUSINESS ESTABLISHMENTS IN THE STUDY

The present study is based on businesses that were displaced by both urban renewal and highway construction projects which were undertaken in Providence, Rhode Island, during a five-year period, 1954 through 1959.[5] One of the major problems involved in an attempt to measure the effects of displacements on business establishments is that of finding the original businessmen for a follow-up study. Yet a complete enumeration is needed in order to give an adequate description of the consequences of dislocation. Accordingly, various methods were employed to trace the displaced units. The Providence Family and Business Relocation Agency and the Providence Redevelopment Agency provided a list of the business establishments displaced from each of the projects which were undertaken during this period.[6] In many cases these records also contained the name and residential address of some of the former business owners, if the business was no longer in operation. In both of the above instances the follow-up was easy; however, these agencies did not have any information for a substantial minority of the establishments. To find the latter units constituted a major effort, but, as noted, these units were needed if the study was to be representative. Consequently the interviewers employed a variety of techniques in order to locate the latter businesses. The telephone directories and city directories for successive years were used in an attempt to find the units. City and state licensing agencies and tax records, both current and past, were checked in order to determine the new location or to determine the name of the owner of the business at the previous location. Sales tax records were also examined. When these efforts failed, information was sought from neighboring businessmen in

5 The dates projects were undertaken by type of project are: Urban Renewal: Willard Center (1955), West River (1956), West River Extension (1958), Point Street (1958), and Lippitt Hill (1959); Highway Construction: Platt 900 (1954); Huntington Expressway (1957), North South Freeway I (1958), North South Freeway II (1959).

6 Both of these agencies cooperated fully in our efforts to locate the businesses after displacement. The directors, Mr. David Joyce of the Family and Business Relocation Agency and Mr. James Reynolds of the Redevelopment Agency, gave generously of their time and help.

the old area whom we had already found and interviewed.[7] When none of these methods provided the needed information, we contacted the real estate offices in charge of the building that had been occupied prior to displacement, and in some cases we worked through trust officers when the former building occupied had been owned by a trust. This, of course, could be used only for renters. Each of these methods resulted in finding additional businesses or at least the names of the owners which then could be traced through their place of residence. Although these tracing efforts were very time-consuming and thus costly, we successfully located a very high proportion of the units involved for a follow-up study.

Of the 363 establishments in the original list of displacements for the projects included in this study, we were unsuccessful in finding any trace of the owners of only 37 of the businesses. It would seem safe to assume that these units are no longer in business in the area. An additional 15 units were excluded after it was confirmed that the owners had moved out of the state. Thus we succeeded in locating 90 per cent of the units that had been displaced during the period, and in contacting more than 85 per cent of the businesses that had been forced to move for either urban renewal or highway construction projects.[8] Of the 311 displaced businesses which we were able to locate and contact, completed interviews were obtained for 292 establishments. This is a response rate of 94 per cent. The refusal rate did not vary significantly by type of project, that is, urban renewal or highway construction, or by present business status. Of the 69 out-of-business units contacted, the owners of only four establishments refused to be interviewed, and only 15 out of 242 relocated units did not participate in the study.[9] Approximately one-third of the businesses displaced during the five-year period covered by the study were from urban renewal projects, and the other two-thirds were

7 In some cases it was useful to obtain the name of the owner, when this was not known, from the name of the business. We could then search for the person in terms of his home address.

8 No attempt was made to contact the businessmen who had moved out of the state, nor did we determine whether or not they continued in business.

9 This very high response rate is likely due in large part to the fact that only three highly skilled, experienced and mature interviewers were used for the whole study.

displaced by highway projects. Thus, from the point of view of the community as well as the commercial establishments, the highway construction program has been more disruptive during the period than the urban renewal program.

SELECTED CHARACTERISTICS OF DISPLACED BUSINESSES

The displaced businesses were predominantly small establishments. Nearly one unit in five (18 per cent) was owner-operated, that is, it had no employees. Nearly one-third (31 per cent) had one or two employees and an approximately equal proportion (30 per cent) reported between three and nine workers. Only one unit in five employed ten or more workers. Less than one establishment in ten had twenty or more employees. Prior to displacement, the median number of employees for all establishments was 3.16. Thus it is apparent from these data that the displacements during the period of study involved primarily small businesses.

Nearly one-fourth of the establishments in our study were food-related retail units, and only a slightly larger proportion were in other-type retail businesses. About one-fifth of the units were in jewelry-related manufacturing[10] and a slightly smaller proportion were service establishments (16 per cent) and "other"-type businesses (17 per cent). The latter category includes manufacturing, wholesale, and construction activities.

As is evident from the data presented in Table 7-1, there are marked variations in number of employees by type of business. The median size of unit (number of employees) ranges from only 1.4 workers among service establishments to 9.2 employees among the businesses in the "other" category. Jewelry firms have the second highest median number with 7.6 employees. The proportion of units that are owner-operated (no employees) ranges from a low of 5 per cent of the jewelry firms to 43 per cent of the service establishments. Food-related retail units are the only other businesses where the proportion of no employees exceeds the proportion for all establishments. The larger establishments, that is, those with ten or more employees, account for 3 per cent or less

10 Providence is one of the leading costume jewelry centers in the United States, and these firms are located predominantly in the older sections of the city, not far from the Central Business District.

TABLE 7-1

SIZE OF BUSINESS BY TYPE OF BUSINESS PRIOR TO DISPLACEMENT

Type of Business	Size – Number of Employees						
	Number	None	1-2	3-9	10+	Per Cent	Median
Total	292	18.2	31.2	29.8	20.9	100.0	3.2
Food – Related Retail	65	20.0	56.9	20.0	3.1	100.0	2.1
Other Retail	74	16.2	31.1	32.4	20.3	100.0	3.6
Jewelry	56	5.3	17.9	41.1	35.7	100.0	7.6
Service	47	42.6	36.2	19.1	2.1	100.0	1.4
Other	50	10.0	8.0	36.0	46.0	100.0	9.2

of the service and food-related retail units as compared with 36 per cent of the jewelry firms and 46 per cent of the businesses classified in the "other" category. More than three-fourths of the food-related retail and service establishments have fewer than three employees. The proportion of units in this size class decreases to less than one-half of the non-food-related retail businesses and to less than one-fourth of the jewelry and "other"-type businesses.

As shown in Table 8-1, the displaced businesses had been in

TABLE 8-1

PER CENT DISTRIBUTION BY NUMBER OF YEARS IN BUSINESS AND IN SAME NEIGHBORHOOD

Length of Time	Years In Business	Years In Neighborhood
Total	292	292
Less than 5	7.0	13.8
5 to 9	16.9	20.0
10 to 19	37.9	33.9
20 and Over	38.2	32.3
Total Per Cent	100.0	100.0

operation for several years. More than 90 per cent had been in business for more than five years. Three-fourths of the units had been in business for more than ten years and two units out of five for twenty years or more. It is also evident that the businesses were firmly established at their former location in that two-thirds of the establishments had been in the same neighborhood for more than ten years. One-third of the units had been in the same neighborhood for twenty years or more prior to displacement. We also find that the displaced businesses were operated by persons who had been long-time residents of the Providence area. Less than 10 per cent of the owners or managers had lived in the area for less than 25 years, whereas nearly half had lived in the area for 45 years or more.[1] Place of residence within the metropolitan area is about equally divided between the central city and the suburban areas. Although all of the businesses were located within the central city at the time of displacement, slightly less than one-half of the owners resided within the city. Thus it is apparent that the consequences of public improvement programs within the city extend beyond the corporate limits.

Selected Characteristics of Business Owners. Differences in the characteristics of businessmen by place of residence within the metropolitan area follow the same general pattern frequently observed for central city-suburban populations. The age and educational composition of the business owners vary by place of residence. The displaced businessmen living in the suburbs tend to be younger than those living in the city. More than one-third of those in the suburban area are under 45 years of age, as compared with only one-fifth of those in the city. It is also noted that half of those in the central city are 55 years of age or over, as compared with only one-fourth of those living in the suburbs. Businessmen living in the suburbs also tend to be better educated. On the lower end of the education scale (six years or less), we find 22 per cent of those living in the city, but only 5 per cent of those in the suburbs. At the other end of the scale, the proportion with twelve or more years of education increases from 38 per cent of those in the city

1 Since less than 10 per cent of the businesses were operated by managers, henceforth for convenience and brevity the concept "owner" is used to include both owners and managers unless otherwise specified.

to 63 per cent of those living in the suburban areas. The median level of education is only 10.3 for those in the city as compared to 12.3 in the suburbs. It is evident from these data that the younger, better educated businessmen with establishments in the city live in the suburbs, while the older and less well educated reside in the city. This is further evidence of the kinds of people that are being lost by central cities as a result of the suburban movement. What this pattern of residential settlement means in terms of selecting a new site for relocation is to be considered later in our analysis. However, it is anticipated that residential suburbanization portends the suburbanization of their businesses.

The place of residence of owners also varies markedly by size and type of business. The owners of the smaller establishments are disproportionately concentrated in the central city. These data are presented in Table 9-1. Nearly two-thirds of those living in

TABLE 9-1

SIZE AND TYPE OF BUSINESSES DISPLACED BY PLACE OF RESIDENCE OF OWNERS AND PROPORTION LIVING IN SUBURBS

Size and Type of Business	Total	Place of Residence		Per Cent Living in Suburbs
		Central City	Suburbs	
Total	291*	139	152	52.2
Number of Employees	100.0	100.0	100.0	....
None	18.3	25.9	11.3	32.1
1-2	31.0	38.9	23.8	40.0
3-9	29.7	22.3	36.4	64.0
10 and Over	21.0	12.9	28.5	70.5
Median	3.2	2.2	5.9	....
Type of Business	100.0	100.0	100.0	....
Food – Related Retail	22.3	29.5	15.8	36.9
Other Retail	25.1	15.8	33.6	69.9
Jewelry	19.2	23.7	15.1	41.1
Service	16.2	22.4	10.5	34.0
Other	17.2	8.6	25.0	76.0

*One owner lives out of state.

the city employed fewer than three workers prior to displacement, as compared with only one-third of those whose residence is in the suburbs. On the other hand, 29 per cent of those in the latter area employed 10 or more workers, whereas only 13 per cent of those living in the city did so. The proportion of owners in each size class that lives in the suburban area increases continuously from 32 per cent of those with no employees to 71 per cent of those with ten or more. The median number of employees of those who live in the city is 2.2 as compared with 5.9 for those in the suburbs.

Not only are the suburbs selective of owners of the larger businesses but of owners of certain kinds of business also. These differences are only in part a function of size. Those in food-related retail, jewelry, and service establishments tend to disproportionately live in the central city, whereas those in non-food-related retail and in the "other" category are much more likely to live in the suburbs. Non-food-related retail owners are more than twice as likely to live in the suburbs as in the city, and those in manufacturing, wholesale and construction activities are three times as likely to live in the suburbs. Thus, although all of the disruption of businesses took place in the central city, it is evident that the consequences of urban renewal and highway construction programs rest, in large part, on suburban dwellers.

Urban Renewal Versus Highway Projects. It is expected that businesses displaced in urban renewal projects will differ from those displaced because of highway construction because of the nature and purpose of these programs. The extent to which differences do exist by type of project is considered in the following discussion.

The data presented in Table 10-1 show that renewal projects had a high disproportionate number of food-related retail and service establishments. Among the businesses displaced, 22 per cent were food-related retail units, but this proportion ranges from 41 per cent among urban renewal projects to only 12 per cent of the units displaced by highway construction. Renewal areas also had 50 per cent more service establishments than were found among the units displaced by highway projects. As will be shown later, these are the two types of businesses which experienced the highest loss rates following displacement.

Urban renewal projects also contained smaller businesses than

TABLE 10-1

TYPE AND SIZE OF BUSINESS PRIOR TO DISPLACEMENT BY TYPE OF PROJECT

Type & Size of Business	Total	Renewal Projects	Highway Projects
Total Number	292	104	188
Type of Business	100.0	100.0	100.0
Food – Related Retail	22.3	41.3	11.7
Other Retail	25.3	17.4	29.8
Jewelry	19.2	1.9	28.7
Service	16.1	20.2	13.8
Other	17.1	19.2	16.0
Size of Business	100.0	100.0	100.0
None	18.1	24.0	14.9
1-2	31.2	44.2	23.9
3-9	29.8	21.2	34.6
10 and Over	20.9	10.6	26.6

highway projects. In the former areas, 24 per cent of the establishments were owner-operated with no employees, as compared with 15 per cent of those in the latter areas and 18 per cent of the total. One-third of all the units displaced had only one or two employees, but this ranged from 44 per cent in the renewal areas to only 24 per cent in the highway projects. But 27 per cent of the establishments in the latter areas employed ten or more workers, whereas only 11 per cent in the renewal areas did so. Differences in size are, of course, closely related to variations in type of business in the different areas.

The demographic characteristics of the business owners also vary by type of project. Age differences are less marked, however, than educational differences. The business owners in the renewal areas tend to be older than those in highway projects. In the latter areas, only 34 per cent of the owners were 55 years of age and over, as compared with 42 per cent of those in the former area. Conversely, 31 per cent in the highway projects were under 45 years of age, but in this age category in the renewal areas we find only 23 per cent. The median age of owners ranges from 52.8 years in renewal areas to 50.5 years in highway projects. Slightly more than one-third of the business owners in both types of projects were between 45 and 54 years of age.

The major differences by education are found at the extremes. The proportion of owners with seven to twelve years of education is the same in both types of projects. About two out of three business owners are in these educational categories. However, in the urban renewal projects, 23 per cent of the owners have less than six years of formal training, while only 8 per cent of those displaced by the highway are found at this level. The latter have 24 per cent with some college training, as compared with only 10 per cent in the renewal areas. The median level of education of owners in the latter areas is 10.7, but this increases to 12.2 among those in highway projects.

The type of customers served and the geographical limits of the area served also vary markedly by type of project. As is shown in Table 11-1, nearly one-third of the displaced businesses catered primarily to a neighborhood market prior to the move. However, in renewal areas 55 per cent did so as compared with only 19 per

TABLE 11-1

AREA SERVED AND TYPE OF CUSTOMER SERVED AT OLD LOCATION BY TYPE OF PROJECT

Area Served and Type of Customer Served	Total	Renewal	Highway
Total Number	292	104	188
Area Served	100.0	100.0	100.0
Neighborhood	31.5	54.8	18.6
Community	43.2	27.9	51.6
Region – Other	25.3	17.3	29.8
Serve Any Particular Ethnic or Racial Group			
Yes	22.9	44.2	11.2
No	77.1	55.8	88.8

cent of the businesses in highway project areas. More than half in the latter areas served the whole community, whereas only slightly more than one-fourth of those in the renewal areas did so. Businesses in renewal areas were also much less likely to serve a non-local market. Further evidence of the more restricted market of businesses in renewal areas is found in the type of customer served. Such businesses disproportionately served a particular ethnic or racial group. We find that while 23 per cent of the total businesses were primarily dependent on a particular kind of customer, this ranged from only 11 per cent among the businesses in highway projects to 44 per cent of the establishments in renewal areas. These differences are particularly significant in that the consequences of displacement are likely to be quite different for those businesses serving a limited market than for those serving a broader area. Specific location is likely to be less important to the latter-type businesses; thus displacement may not be as disruptive. This is to be considered in detail below.

That businesses in renewal and in highway projects differ in characteristics is further evident from the data in Table 12-1 on rentals and sales. Businesses in renewal areas were generally less well-to-do than businesses displaced by highway projects. Both rentals and sales were lower in renewal areas. In these areas, 46 per cent of the business units paid less than $50 per month in rent, but among the highway displacements only 20 per cent were in this rental category. Businesses in the highway projects were concentrated disproportionately in the $150 to $299 category. Here we find 42 per cent as compared with only 15 per cent of the businesses in renewal areas. Similar differences by type of project are found in respect to average monthly sales prior to displacement. Whereas one-fourth of all businesses report sales of less than $1,000 per month, the proportion ranged from 40 per cent among the businesses in renewal projects to only 17 per cent of those in highway projects.[2] At the other extreme we find that 22 per cent of all of the displaced businesses had sales in excess of $15,000 per

2 Lower sales are likely due to the high proportion in food-related retail and service establishments. Median monthly sales prior to displacement were $2,375 and $808 respectively, as compared with $10,500 for non-food-related retail, $6,273 for jewelry, and $13,125 for the manufacturing, construction and wholesale businesses.

TABLE 12-1

REPORTED MONTHLY RENTALS AND SALES AT OLD LOCATION BY TYPE OF PROJECT

Rentals and Sales	Total	Renewal	Highway
Rentals	100.0	100.0	100.0
Under $ 50	28.1	46.3	19.5
$ 50 – $ 99	28.1	31.5	26.5
$150 – $299	33.6	14.8	42.4
$300 and Over	10.2	7.4	11.5
Sales	100.0	100.0	100.0
Under $ 1,000	25.1	40.0	16.9
$ 1,000 – $ 2,999	23.0	27.7	20.3
$ 3,000 – $ 7,499	15.8	9.2	19.5
$ 7,500 – $14,999	14.2	10.8	16.1
$15,000 and Over	21.9	12.3	27.1

month, but this declined from 27 per cent of the highway units to only 12 per cent of the establishments in renewal areas.

Businesses displaced through highway projects seem to have been much more firmly established economically at the old location than those in renewal areas. At least they were operating at a substantially higher level financially. Businesses in renewal areas were more likely to be small marginal businesses. Thus, it seems safe to expect a lower survival rate among businesses from urban renewal projects, due largely to the business composition of such areas, as compared to businesses displaced by highway construction projects. Renewal areas tend to be made up disproportionately of food-related retail and service establishments with only a few employees; from these the owners realize only a small annual income. Business owners in such areas tend to be older and less well-educated than those displaced by highway projects. The former also tend to be largely neighborhood type businesses which cater disproportionately to a particular ethnic or racial group. Rentals tend to be low, as are sales also. Financially, urban renewal businesses compare quite unfavorably with units displaced by highway projects. The significance of these characteristics will be considered in the chapters to follow.

EVALUATION OF OLD LOCATION

There is little evidence to suggest that there was any real dissatisfaction among owners with the former location as a business site. A substantial majority of the businesses reported that they would have remained at the old location indefinitely, had they not been forced to move. And even though the renewal projects presumably involved deteriorated buildings in areas of decay and poor slum-type neighborhoods, the proportion of units that would have continued to do business in the same neighborhood is even higher than is found among units displaced by the highway. Nearly 90 per cent of the units in the renewal areas would have remained in the original area indefinitely, as compared with 80 per cent of the establishments displaced by the highway program. The high proportion clearly indicates that there is a rather marked indifference about the physical deterioration on the part of the businesses in these areas. It is also quite evident that pressure for renewal would not come from the businesses in the slum neighborhoods. On the contrary, such areas appear to be attractive business locations for certain kinds of units. It is more likely that they would resist change. This is understandable when we recall that most of the businesses are small food-related retail or service establishments catering largely to a neighborhood market, and more specifically their customers come predominantly from a particular ethnic or racial group living in the slum areas that are to be displaced and renewed.

Among the small proportion of units in both types of projects that would not have remained at the old location indefinitely, the most frequently given reason was lack of space, that is, they needed more room. In many instances these units wanted to expand their business. Nearly one-fourth of the businesses that reported they would not have remained in the old area gave as their reason either the poor condition of the neighborhood (16 per cent) or of the building that the business occupied (9 per cent). This would seem to contradict our earlier observation concerning the indifference on the part of businesses regarding the poor physical condition of the area, but when these responses are viewed as a proportion of the total, they account for less than 4 per cent. In other words, only one unit out of twenty-five would not have remained at the old location indefinitely because of the decay and deterioration of either the buildings or the area.

GENERAL REACTION TO DISLOCATION

The general reaction to the forced movement at the time of displacement was predominantly negative. Only a small minority (14 per cent) of the owners gave a favorable response when asked to express their general reaction to being forced to move out of the condemned area. Those who rented the building occupied at the old location were even less likely to respond favorably than owners. In each tenure group, a majority reported an unfavorable reaction to the forced move. For nearly one business in five, the response was, in fact, quite emotional in that specific "anger" was expressed about the whole thing. The proportion responding thusly was the same for businesses in both the renewal and highway projects and did not vary by building tenure. Approximately one-fourth of the units were deeply worried and discouraged about the consequences of the move.

In general, businesses from renewal areas responded even more negatively to the move than those displaced by the highway construction program. The latter were more likely to be neutral or indifferent in their reaction or to view the whole process fatalistically. These businesses were more likely to view displacement as inevitable, that is, it had to be. Much of the unfavorable reaction to the forced move was due to the anticipated consequences of the move, whether real or imagined. When asked how they thought the move would affect their business, two firms out of five reported that they had thought that the move would prove to have a negative effect. Many were convinced that displacement would actually ruin their business. A sizable minority of the units reported that they were uncertain about the consequences of the move. Thus it seems clear that much of the unfavorable reaction to the move, at the time of dislocation, was due to uncertainty or to a deep suspicion that the move would be harmful. Only a minority (28 per cent) felt that the move would not affect their business. A much smaller proportion (12 per cent) expected the move to be beneficial. But for a majority of the establishments involved, the forced move was viewed with a great deal of apprehension. That this view was justified, in fact, is evident from the loss rates discussed below.

BUSINESS LOSSES

One of the possible consequences of displacement is that the disruption may be such as to result in a discontinuance of the business operation. From the point of view of the community, the frequency of business losses through displacement is of significance, for it may mean loss of jobs as well as the loss of taxable property. It also obviously has serious implication for the individual business owner. In Table 13-1 is shown the proportion of losses by type of business for all projects from which businesses were displaced during the five-year period covered in this study. The losses are shown as "known" and as "probable" losses. The latter includes all businesses which were successfully contacted and found not to have relocated after displacement, as well as those businesses of which no trace could be found. It is assumed in this classification that since these units had completely disappeared locally, they were no longer in business in the area. However, since we were unable to obtain any information on these units, we have recorded them only as "probable" losses. At any rate, it is very doubtful that any of these units are presently in business in the area. The "known" losses pertain only to those businesses which we were able to contact and obtain definite information to the effect that the business was no longer in operation. The businesses that relocated were actually contacted personally and all but a very small proportion were successfully interviewed. The data on probable losses pertain to all of the units that were displaced, including those who refused to complete an interview. Even in the case of refusals, however, sufficient information was obtained in all cases to permit a classification by type of business.

The probable loss rate for the central city is higher than for the

TABLE 13-1

PER CENT OF DISPLACED UNITS RELOCATED AND PER CENT OF KNOWN AND PROBABLE LOSSES TO CITY AND AREA BY TYPE OF BUSINESS

Type of Business	Total Number	Per Cent Relocated in		Known Losses to		Probable Losses to	
		City	Area	City	Area	City	Area
Total	363*	56.5	66.7	33.3	23.1	43.5	33.3
Food – Related Retail	81	45.7	49.4	42.0	38.3	54.3	50.6
Other Retail	81	56.8	71.6	32.1	17.3	43.2	28.4
Jewelry	72	70.7	73.6	15.3	12.5	29.3	26.4
Service	65	61.5	66.2	36.9	32.3	38.5	33.8
Other	61	50.8	78.7	39.3	11.5	49.2	21.3

*Includes three units for which type of business is not known.

area because many businesses successfully relocated and remained in the area, but their new location is beyond the corporate limits of the city. Thus from the point of view of the city, business losses occurred either from discontinuances or by movement out of the city. Of the total businesses displaced, the probable loss to the area was about one-third but losses to the city exceeded two-fifths. This seems to be the best estimate of the losses. We have been unable to find any evidence which would suggest that these loss proportions are not valid; however, even if we limit our discussion to the "known" losses, we note that one-fourth of the units were lost to the area and one-third were lost to the central city. However, the latter is thought to be too conservative an estimate of the number of businesses which are no longer in operation in the area.

Business losses, as is evident, vary significantly by type of business. The probable loss rate for the area ranges from a low of 21 per cent of the businesses in the "other" category (which includes manufacturing, wholesale and construction) to 51 per cent of the food-related retail units. Service establishments have the second-highest loss rate with about one-third lost to the area. Losses to the city are quite different. Although food-related retail units continue to have the largest proportion of losses, the second-highest frequency is found in the "other" businesses. This is followed closely by the losses reported among the non-food-related retail establishments. The particularly high loss rate for the latter two types of businesses reflects in large part the higher suburbanization rates of these establishments. The city loss rate is lowest for jewelry firms. The overall loss rate among these firms was relatively low but in addition to this, these units were most likely to relocate inside of the city. The known losses are smaller than the probable losses, but the differences by type of business follow the same pattern as already observed for probable losses.

When we focus our attention on the proportion of businesses that relocated after being forced to vacate their site, we find that 67 per cent of the units are still in business in the area and that 57 per cent of the original establishments relocated in the city. Thus only slightly more than half of the displaced businesses continue to do business inside the city, even though two out of three are still in business in the area. The proportion of units continuing in business in the area ranges from a low of 49 per cent of the food-related retail units to a high of 79 per cent of the "other" businesses. The second lowest survival rate is found among service units where two-thirds continued in business in the area.

From the point of view of the city, we find that less than half of the food-related retail units relocated within the corporate limits. This low proportion is largely due to a high discontinuance rate, since only a small number of units moved to the suburbs. The jewelry firms have the highest relocation rate within the city. These firms, as already noted, had a relatively low loss rate in general and infrequently relocated in the suburbs. Rather they relocated in the traditional jewelry manufacturing district. It is particularly noteworthy that only one-half of the businesses in the "other" category relocated within the city, even though nearly four-fifths of the units relocated in the area. Similarly, only 57 per cent of the non-food-related retail units relocated in the city while 72 per cent relocated in the area. Among service establishments, slightly more than three-fifths continued in business in the city following displacement. Only a very small number moved to the suburbs.

These data clearly show that displacement causes a much higher loss to the city than to the area. But it is to be noted that the loss rate to both the city and the area is substantial. This takes on added significance when we recall that the units affected had been in business for a long time and thus had survived the critical years.[3] However, these findings must be viewed with caution, for some of the units that are no longer in business may have used displacement as an opportunity to close down their businesses for purposes entirely independent of the problems connected with relocation. This is discussed more fully in Chapter II.

The loss rates vary markedly by type of project, as is shown in Table 14-1. Business losses following displacement are higher in urban renewal projects than in projects for highway construction. Among the urban renewal projects included in this study about four units in ten are probable losses to the area, while one unit in

3 For a thorough analysis of the experiences of new businesses, see: Kurt B. Mayer and Sidney Goldstein, *The First Two Years: Problems of Small Firm Growth and Survival,* Small Business Research Series No. 2, Washington, D.C., 1961.

TABLE 14-1

PER CENT OF DISPLACED UNITS RELOCATED AND PER CENT OF KNOWN AND PROBABLE LOSSES TO CITY AND AREA BY TYPE OF PROJECT

Type of Project	Total No.	Per Cent Relocated in		Known Losses to		Probable Losses to	
		City	Area	City	Area	City	Area
Total	363	56.5	66.7	33.3	23.1	43.5	33.3
Urban Renewal	127	48.8	60.6	46.5	34.6	51.2	39.4
Highway	236	60.6	69.9	26.3	16.9	39.4	30.1

two is a probable loss to the city. For displacements due to highway construction, the probable losses are 30 per cent and 39 per cent respectively. The known losses follow the same pattern. In the urban renewal projects, slightly more than one-third of the establishments were lost to the area and nearly half were lost to the city. Among highway construction projects, the comparable losses were 17 per cent and 26 per cent. Thus approximately six out of ten of the displaced businesses in urban renewal projects relocated in the area, as compared with seven out of ten of the businesses displaced by highway construction programs. However, the city retained less than half of the businesses in the urban renewal areas and three-fifths of those displaced by highway projects. A further consideration of business losses is the topic of the next chapter.

CHAPTER 2

THE NON-SURVIVORS

THE forced movement of business units from established locations is certain to have disruptive consequences. The extreme form of disruption is, of course, that which results in the discontinuance of the business operation. Yet this is the fate that awaits a significant proportion of the businesses displaced in urban renewal and highway construction programs. During recent years in the city of Providence, approximately one business unit in three has been unsuccessful in setting up and continuing business in a new location following the forced vacating of an established site. The present chapter is devoted to a comparative analysis of the establishments that moved to a new location and continued in business and those which closed their businesses following displacement.[1]

1 For a review of the experiences of 21 projects in 14 cities based on reports obtained in letters from local community redevelopment officials, see: William Kinnard and Zenon S. Malinowski, *The Impact of Dislocation From Urban Renewal Areas on Small Business*, University of Connecticut, Storrs, July, 1960. Of the non-survivors included in this discussion, 15 per cent had attempted to continue at a new location prior to closing down their businesses. This ranged from one-tenth of the renewal losses to one-fifth of the losses in highway project areas.

TYPE OF BUSINESS

It is evident from the data presented in Table 1-2 that the non-survival rate varies markedly by type of business.[2] The discontinuance rate is particularly high for certain kinds of retail activities and service establishments. Food-related retail units constitute less than one-fifth of the establishments which remained in business following the move, but account for two-fifths of the units

TABLE 1-2

PER CENT DISTRIBUTION BY TYPE OF BUSINESS BY PRESENT STATUS

Type of Business	Survivors		Non-Survivors	
	Number	Per Cent	Number	Per Cent
Total	227	100.0	65	100.0
Food – Related Retail	39	17.2	26	40.0
Other Retail	57	25.1	10	15.4
Jewelry	49	21.6	7	10.8
Service	38	16.7	16	24.6
Other	44	19.4	6	9.2

that went out of business. Similarly, service establishments account for only one in six of the in-business units but one in four of the units that discontinued after being forced to move. Jewelry, non-food-related retail and "other" businesses, which are largely man-

2 The findings in this chapter are likely to be conservative because of the bias of the out-of-business sample, since we were unable to find any trace of nearly one-third of the units presumed to have gone out of business. Thus while the business losses (including the units that disappeared) have been estimated to be approximately one in three, the non-survival rate declines to slightly less than one in four when limited only to those units successfully contacted. The present chapter is necessarily limited to the businesses which could be located. It is doubtful that any of the differences would change even if the disappeared businesses were included; however, the magnitude of the differences would likely be larger. Approximately 10 per cent of the original list of businesses disappeared.

ufacturing, wholesale and construction units, are underrepresented in the non-survival category. While these business types account for more than two-thirds of the units that continued in business, they make up only one-third of the failures. Thus, it is clear that the forced move is not equally disruptive of all types of businesses, but rather that hardships seem to be concentrated only among certain kinds of units.

CUSTOMER RELATIONSHIPS

Discontinuance rates are highest among the kinds of units that are most likely to draw customers from a small geographical area. High frequency use retail and service functions are largely neighborhood-type businesses and it is these units that have the highest out-of-business rates. This observation is supported by the data presented in Table 2-2, which shows the different business-customer relationships that existed prior to displacement by present business status. Business units which did not survive the move disproportionately depended on the immediate neighborhood for customers. At the original location, more than two-fifths of the out-of-business units drew their customers from the immediate neighborhood, whereas only slightly more than one-fourth of the in-business units did so. Further, two-thirds of the out-of-business units depended on the immediate neighborhood or the same side of town for their customers, whereas only one-third of those who continued in business after the move were dependent on the same limited local trade area.

We find that one-third of the surviving business units catered to customers throughout the Greater Providence area while at the old location, but only one-fourth of the failures reached such a large market area. The difference between the businesses that survived and those that did not is even more marked in respect to the proportion that reached a non-local market area. Here we find that 18 per cent of the relocated business units served the New England area and 12 per cent a more widespread geographical market, but the proportion of out-of-business units catering to the same areas was only 6 per cent and 5 per cent respectively. Thus,

TABLE 2-2

CUSTOMER RELATIONSHIPS AND NUMBER OF EMPLOYEES PRIOR TO DISPLACEMENT BY PRESENT STATUS

Customers Served and Number of Employees	Present Status	
	Survivors	Non-Survivors
Area Served	100.0	100.0
Neighborhood	28.2	43.2
Same Side of Town	8.8	21.5
Greater Providence Area	33.5	24.6
New England Area	17.6	6.1
Other	11.9	4.6
Served Special Ethnic or Racial Group	100.0	100.0
Yes	19.4	33.8
No	80.6	66.2
Number of Employees	100.0	100.0
None	14.1	32.4
1-2	27.3	44.6
3-9	34.4	13.8
10 and Over	24.2	9.2

of those that survived, about three businesses out of ten were geared to a non-local market, as compared with only one in ten of the non-survivors.

Further evidence of a different kind of business-customer relationship between those who successfully moved and the units that failed following displacement is found in the proportion of business operators who "knew most of their customers" while at the old location. The out-of-business units report more frequently that they "knew most of their customers." This suggests that these units probably had more personal and direct contact with their customers. This is likely due to the smaller area served and the higher frequency of contact. Since these units were predominantly dependent on a local neighborhood area for support, the forced movement was particularly disruptive and in a high, disproportionate number of cases resulted in a "failure" of the business to continue in operation.

Our data also show that business units catering to a particular ethnic or racial group are the ones most likely to go out of business. A move out of the area cuts them off from their customers, and in many instances where they remained in the same general area, their customers moved. Consequently such businesses had a failure rate which was more than 50 per cent higher than that experienced by business units which did not draw customers from a particular racial or ethnic group. One-third of the units that failed had drawn their customers from a particular type of group, but less than one-fifth of the units that survived did so. This is further evidence that the units hardest hit by the move are those which are dependent upon a highly localized market, since the particular racial or ethnic groups served were predominantly from segregated or concentrated neighborhoods.

SIZE OF BUSINESS

The chances of surviving the move also vary directly with size of business unit when measured in terms of number of employees. This is shown by the data presented in the lower portion of Table 2-2. Among those which went out of business following displacement, one-third were owner-operated units with no employees other than perhaps unpaid family help, as compared with less than one-seventh of those who survived. The failure rate is also disproportionately high among units with only one or two employees. Business units of this size account for 45 per cent of the out-of-business units but only 27 per cent of the units still in business. The largest business units, that is, those with ten or more employees, constitute one-fourth of the survivors but less than one-tenth of those who failed. Nearly three-fifths of those who continued in business had employed three or more workers while at the old location, but of those who discontinued in business less than one-fourth were in this size class.

When non-survival rates are computed by size, the proportion out of business ranges from 10 per cent among those with ten or more employees to 40 per cent of those with no employees. Thus, it seems quite evident that displacement works a particular hardship on the smaller business establishments.[3] It is likely that many of the smaller units were somewhat marginal businesses at the old location, operating at a minimal level. The displacement jeopardized this balance and with conditions changed the units could not survive. Such was the case of the fruit and grocery store, displaced by the urban renewal program in the Lippitt Hill area, which was run by a 75-year-old Russian immigrant, with no schooling, who had been in business for more than a half century and had occupied the same location for 27 years. He catered to the immediate neighborhood. His weekly income from the business was only $30 but he was making a living, since, according to his own account, this was sufficient to meet his needs. When he was displaced, he was too old to start over and did not have the resources to do so anyway. He had no choice but to retire. His present income is $58 per month. In this case, however, as in many others, the loss was more than a financial one, for in losing his business he lost his job. The business provided him with something to do in addition to a small income. He was forced into retirement and of this he says, "I'm going crazy with nothing to do. It's highway robbery." This loss of a job as something to do, apart from the loss of income, is a frequent theme among those who "retired."

A similar reaction is clearly expressed by a former junk dealer who was unable to relocate and had to retire since, as he put it, "One cannot get work at 64 years of age." He hates retirement. He states his feelings thusly, "It makes me nervous just hanging around." Here again the financial loss is not emphasized but rather the important loss is that he no longer has anything to do. Regarding his junk business he says, "It was my whole life. I had a radio in my shack there and could even cook simple meals there if I had to." He had no employees. It was a small operation with sales averaging only slightly more than $500 per month, but he found the business very satisfying. It also provided him with a "good place to go and get away from home for a while." In this, as in other cases, the financial loss was not great but the other losses were of serious proportions. This type of business loss ob-

3 This likely understates the losses in the small categories since the units that disappeared would likely be disproportionately concentrated in these categories also.

viously has little, if any, effect on the community, but to the individual concerned, it destroys a "way of life."

Perhaps a low level of operation for many of the marginal establishments could have continued for years if the population and business composition of the affected areas had remained unchanged or continued to develop consistent with the historical trend, but the complete disruption of the area placed a strain on such units which was beyond their capacity to absorb. Consequently the business operation was closed. Still further evidence of this is found in a comparative analysis of sales and rentals for business units by present status, while at the old location.

SALES AND RENTALS

Businesses that survived the move were paying higher rental in the old location than were those units that went out of business following displacement. As is shown in Table 3-2, the difference is particularly marked in the top rental group, that is, those in the $150 and over category. At this rental level we find one-fourth of the units that survived, but only one-twelfth of those who discontinued in business. When we note the amount of taxes paid annually by the units that owned the building they occupied prior to the move, the differences are even more marked. Of those which discontinued in business, 37 per cent paid less than $300 per year in taxes on their property, as compared with 28 per cent of those which survived the move. At the other extreme, 36 per cent of the survivors were in the top tax category, that is, they paid more than $750, but only 16 per cent of the out-of-business units were in this tax category.

Sales at the old location also indicate that the small business units experienced the highest non-survivor rate. Of the units that discontinued, two-fifths reported sales of less than $1,000 per month at the old location, as compared with only one-fifth of those that survived relocation. Among the units that successfully moved, 45 per cent reported sales of $7,500 or more per month, but only 15 per cent of the out-of-business units had sales of this amount. Stated differently the median monthly sales at the old location of the units that went out-of-business were considerably less than

TABLE 3-2

MONTHLY RENT, TAXES, AND AVERAGE MONTHLY SALES PRIOR TO DISPLACEMENT BY PRESENT STATUS

Rent, Taxes and Sales	Present Status	
	Survivors	Non-Survivors
Monthly Rent	100.0	100.0
Under $ 50	29.7	25.7
$ 50 – $ 99	25.8	40.0
$100 – $149	19.5	25.7
$150 and Over	25.0	8.6
Taxes (Annual)	100.0	100.0
Under $300	28.2	36.8
$300 – $749	35.9	47.4
$750 and Over	35.9	15.8
Monthly Sales	100.0	100.0
Under $ 1,000	19.1	40.4
$ 1,000 – $ 2,999	20.6	28.8
$ 3,000 – $ 7,499	16.0	15.4
$ 7,500 – $14,999	17.6	5.8
$15,000 and Over	26.7	9.6

$2,000, but were nearly $6,000 among those which continued in business after displacement. These data suggest that displacement is particularly damaging to those business units that have been operating close to a subsistence level. It may well be, as noted earlier, that these businessmen could have made a living at this level of operation over an extended period of time, since many had no employees and either owned their building or paid low rentals. But since financial resources were very limited, the strains of displacement and the costs of relocation made continuance in business impossible.

This interpretation finds partial support from the responses to the question: Would you have remained in business at that location indefinitely if no change had taken place in the area and you had not been forced to move? Nearly all of the non-survivors claimed that they would have remained in business at the old location indefinitely. These units apparently were aware of the fact that they were marginal and could not withstand the disruption of a move, but nonetheless they felt that the business could have continued in operation under conditions as they existed in the old area prior to the disruption caused by the urban renewal or highway construction program. The point worthy of note is that 97 per cent of the non-survivors claimed that they would have continued in business indefinitely at the old location. Whether or not the failures could have survived at the old location over a long period of time is open to question, but at least retrospectively most of them thought that they could have and that they would have been better off if conditions had remained unchanged.[4]

In some cases, even though displacement may have caused the business to discontinue, this did not result in a hardship for the owners. One such case was that of the 77-year-old Russian immigrant tailor displaced from the Lippitt Hill renewal area who did not even attempt to relocate. Rather he used this as an opportunity to get out. This man had no schooling and had started his business more than 40 years ago with only $7.50 in his pocket, which he had saved while working in a tailor shop in a local department store. Of this, $7 reportedly went for his rent the first day. He said, with pride, that "within two years I was making more than my salary at the department store and I was my own boss." He reports that his business has provided him with a good living and he is very happy about his life in America. Although he probably would have continued indefinitely at the old location, he reported that he had very little business left and he was "glad to give the whole thing up." He said that he wasn't making much money anymore, but that he was very pleased with how he had been handled. In short, he felt that the state had been good to him. It even cut his rent near the end when his business was very bad since his customers had nearly all moved out. In his opinion, if one "cooperates with the state they would be nice to you." His appraisal of the whole thing is summed up in his own words thusly, "No one bothered me for 41 years – I am not sorry about anything."

4 At any rate 94 per cent had been in business for more than five years and 91 per cent had occupied the same location for more than five years. More than one-third had been at the same location for fifteen years or more.

Quite a different reaction, however, is reported by an owner of a jewelry electroplating and polishing firm who had been in business at the same location for 26 years. This business had been displaced by one of the highway projects. The firm wanted to relocate, but the cost of the move was thought to be prohibitive. Even prior to displacement, this business was faced with many problems due to the extended illness of the former owner and his eventual death. The wife had tried to continue the business but was deeply in debt at the time of displacement. Her reaction to the forced move was a violent one. She claimed that "we lost everything – it was a very terrible thing – I can't understand how the city of Providence would permit it. The whole idea of forcing anyone out of a tax-paying business is like communism to me. The whole thing is un-American." A very similar opinion was expressed by a former bar owner. The latter unequivocally stated that as a result of being forced to move he was now "flat on his back." His reaction is evident from his remark that "it's a dirty lousy deal. The condemnation proceedings are communistic." In his opinion the government has no right to move a business. The forced move apparently was costly to him. This old Italian immigrant, who had lived in Providence for fifty years, had entered business nineteen years ago from a manual labor background. Just prior to displacement, he had averaged $70 per week from his business, but now he reports that he has only a veteran's pension of less than $1,000 per year.

Businesses that did not survive the move were in a much less favorable position economically at the old location than the units that continued in business by moving to a new location. This is further evident from the data on rentals and sales as presented in Table 4-2. For all dislocated businesses the median monthly rent paid at the old location was $86, and median monthly sales amounted to slightly more than $3,500. Thus rental costs were approximately 2.4 per cent of gross median sales. However, marked variations in this ratio are observed by type of project and present business status. Businesses displaced by the highway program were better off at the old location than the establishments displaced from renewal areas. Rentals were considerably higher but sales were proportionately even larger, consequently the rent-to-sales ratio was lower. Among the relocated businesses from both types of projects, rents were 1.5 per cent of sales as compared with the ratio of 4.8 per cent among the non-survivors. Thus the latter carried more than three times the relative rent burden of the former. Among the relocated businesses and the non-survivors, the rent-to-sales ratio was higher in renewal areas than in highway projects.

When we focus on present business status, we find that median rents paid by relocated businesses from renewal areas were approximately half the amount paid by the relocated businesses from highway project areas; however, median sales were less than one-third the volume reported for the latter areas. Thus, while rents were substantially lower in the renewal areas, the relative rent burden was substantially higher. The same pattern, but a less marked difference by type of project, is observed among the non-survivors. The rent burden of the relocated businesses in renewal areas as a ratio of sales was 70 per cent higher than in highway project areas (2.4 and 1.4 respectively). Among the non-survivors the burden was 16 per cent higher (5.0 and 4.3 respectively).

However, the most meaningful difference in the rent-to-sales ratio is found between the businesses that relocated and those that did not survive the move from both types of projects. Even though different kinds of public improvements are involved, there

TABLE 4-2

MEDIAN RENTS AND SALES PRIOR TO DISPLACEMENT AND PROPORTION OF SALES IN SELECTED CATEGORIES BY PRESENT STATUS AND TYPE OF PROJECT

Present Status and Type of Project	Median		Ratio	Proportion of Sales	
	Rent	Sales		Under $1,000	Over $7,500
Total	86	$3,543	2.4	25.1	36.1
Survivors	88	5,893	1.5	19.1	44.3
Renewal Projects	55	2,300	2.4	32.4	29.7
Highway Projects	105	7,500	1.4	13.8	50.0
Non-Survivors	80	1,666	4.8	40.4	15.4
Renewal Projects	50	1,000	5.0	50.0	14.2
Highway Projects	104	2,429	4.3	29.2	16.7

is a marked similarity in the selective process in relocation, and even though the renewal businesses operated at a much lower level than those in the highway project areas prior to displacement, the businesses that survived the move from both types of areas were in a more favorable position economically than the non-survivors.

Focusing first on displacements from renewal areas, we find that median monthly rents paid at the old location by establishments that continued in business after the move were only 10 per cent higher ($55 vs. $50), but median monthly sales were 130 per cent more. Thus the rent burden of the non-survivors was more than double that of the establishments that relocated. The rent-sales ratios were 5.0 per cent and 2.4 per cent respectively. It is apparent from these data that the typical non-survivor from renewal projects was operating at a minimum level prior to displacement. Although rents were low in absolute dollars, the burden was a heavy one in relation to volume of sales. When we look at the proportion of sales at the extremes as shown in the righthand part of Table 4-2, we note that among the survivors less than one-third had sales of less than $1,000 per month, as compared with half of the non-survivors. On the other hand, the survivors had double the proportion of units in the top sales category.

Similar but even larger differences are found between those that relocated and the non-survivors among the businesses displaced by the highway program. While both paid approximately the same median rent at the old location, large differences by present business status are found in the volume of sales. Median sales of the non-survivors were less than one-third of the sales of the relocated units. Consequently the rent burden of the non-survivors exceeded the relocated businesses three-fold. The units that continued in business after displacement had median sales of $7,500 per month with a rent burden amounting to 1.4 per cent. Non-survivors, however, report monthly sales of less than $2,500 and a rent load of 4.3 per cent. Among the non-survivors, 29 per cent report sales of less than $1,000 per month at the old location, as compared to 14 per cent of the units that continued in business. Of the latter, one-half report sales of $7,500 or more per month, but among the non-survivors this drops to only 17 per cent. It is apparent that the units that relocated were largely those which were in a relatively strong financial position prior to displacement.

A point worthy of note is that the businesses that successfully relocated from renewal areas averaged a slightly lower sales volume than the non-survivors from highway projects; however, rents were significantly lower in the former areas. This difference is likely due in large part to the kinds of businesses involved in each type of project. Renewal areas contained a high, disproportionate number of food-related retail and service establishments. These businesses are more likely to pay lower rents than other-type businesses and also are more likely to have a lower sales volume. And even though rents may be substantial in relation to sales, these businesses can apparently continue to function at this level and relocate accordingly. Thus, while the survivors from renewal areas may appear in the aggregate to be similar to the non-survivors from highway projects, different kinds of businesses are involved and the absolute dollar value of sales has a different meaning.

At any rate, these data clearly demonstrate, in both types of areas, that it is the businesses functioning at the lower levels that are unable to survive the disruptive effects of the move. However, the breaking point may vary according to the quality of the area from which the units are moved, as well as the type of businesses displaced.

TENURE AND COMPENSATION

Contrary to expectation, we find that the non-survivors had a higher proportion who owned the building occupied at the old location than is found among the businesses that moved to a new location. The proportion who owned was 40 per cent and 32 per cent respectively. This may be due to age differences. The reactions concerning the price received from the government for their building differ markedly by present business status. A much larger proportion of the business units surviving the move are satisfied with the price received than are found among those who have gone out of business. Only 38 per cent of the survivors reported that they had not received a fair price, as compared with 62 per cent among those who went out of business following displacement. However, it is not that they were compensated differently; rather, it was their expectation as to what the government should pay for that differed. The major complaint, expressed by nearly half of the non-survivors who felt that they had not received a fair price, was that they should have been compensated for the "value of the business," and not just for the value of the building (and land) occupied. However, one-third of the non-survivors reported that their business was worth more than the price received. It is apparent from these data that when units cannot successfully relocate, there is a widespread belief among such businessmen that the government in such programs should compensate the owner for the value of the business as an operation. To this group, "businesses should be bought" (by the government) as though on the open market where complete transfer of ownership would be effected. They feel that they should have been compensated not only for the building but the "worth" of the business as a business. It is not only a matter of displacement to this group. Rather, they view the whole process as the equivalent of confiscation of their property and their long years of investment in building up a business. In short, they feel that they have been deprived of their business operation without due compensation for the losses incurred.

This type of reaction was also frequently expressed by renters who were unsuccessful in relocation. Renters frequently stated that there should be a compensation for loss of business for tenants comparable to the consideration that is given to owners of buildings in the area. In the latter instance, renters claim that a fair, objectively determined price is paid to the owner, but the renter is forced to vacate and relocate without any adjustments except moving costs, if in a renewal project, being provided. There is a general belief that owners are compensated in part through being given an inflated price for their building.[5]

This interpretation, however, is not shared by owners. This is clearly illustrated by the owner of a foundry who had employed 100 workers and was displaced by a highway project. He had owned the business for 14 years at the same location. During the last regular year in business prior to dislocation, he had paid approximately $6,000 in city taxes and had a payroll which averaged $20,000 per month. Although he had received $400,000 for his building, he claims that he decided to go out of business be-

5 This topic is considered more fully in Chapter III.

cause it would have cost too much to replace the structure and move his equipment. In his words, "They didn't give me nearly enough so I could replace my business and stay in production." In his opinion, and this is shared by many of the displaced businessmen, the government "should pay moving costs and should give replacement value on property." His general reaction to the whole process is summed up in his comment, "If they are going to condemn businesses and make them move, the condemnation board should be *experts*. They should know what the business is worth and what is would cost to replace it. They didn't know much here, so we were not in a position to try to stay in business."

This same opinion, expressed somewhat differently, is shared by the owner of an auto body shop who had been in business for twelve years in the same neighborhood. He also claimed that he could not replace his building for the price received; thus he didn't even attempt to find a new location but took a job working for someone else in the same line of work but at a salary somewhat lower than his income from his growing business. His reaction is expressed thusly, "The set-up for determining the value of a man's business is unfair. I was trapped as far as having a choice about the price finally given me. It is useless to hire a lawyer and fight for more money – only the big men can afford this." This former businessman, a resident of the city for fifty years, is quite suspicious of the state's purchasing program. This is evident by his comment, "People on the political inside made money by buying land cheap on North Main and in the path of the East Providence Expressway and sold it to the state for a good profit."

Further evidence of dissatisfaction with appraisals is found in the near-violent reaction of a former owner of a millworks and home building firm who claimed that he had received only $15,-000 for his property but it would cost him $65,000 to replace it. He feels that the whole condemnation process is "rotten" and that the government should "have a more decent appraisal set-up – it's crooked now." He elaborates as follows: "They had men appraise my property who worked for the state and therefore were not neutral or honest either. I would be fighting yet, but my lawyers talked me into giving up." In short, this man feels that he took "a terrible beating." Incidentally, he also feels that "lawyers are not very bright and do not have the courage to really fight in court."

It is apparent that considerable bitterness has developed over the prices received for property. Also there is considerable confusion, particularly among the displaced businesses that did not relocate, as to just what the government should pay for when a business is forced to move.[6] Renters are likely to be particularly resentful in highway construction projects since no provisions are made to help cover the costs of the move. In such cases, they are forced to move without any compensation, regardless of the costs or inconvenience. This is a real problem, particularly for those units whose existence is at best marginal and whose financial resources, managerial and administrative skills are too limited to survive the displacement. From a practical point of view this is perhaps an issue that merits careful consideration by policy-determining and administrative officials.

The response to the forced movement varies by present business status. When business owners were asked how they felt about being forced to move, the out-of-business units were more likely than the in-business units to respond emotionally. In some cases this reaction was carried to an extreme. This is illustrated by the sixty-five-year-old shoemaker, an Italian immigrant with six years of education, who had occupied the same location during his thirty-five years in business. His complaint was that "the loss was more than just a building – my work is gone forever too. All of my customers have moved away." He said that the forced move "shook my confidence in my city and country – I never thought they would do such a thing." This man's reaction to the move was a very violent one. At the time of displacement, he said he "blew his top and still considers the whole thing a nightmare." Actually this man is going blind and could not have continued in business under any circumstances, although he said he would have continued indefinitely at the old location if he had not been forced to move. However, he blames all of his problems on the trouble he has had with the state. This is evident from his comment, "All the strain near the end is what I blame for my partial blindness." Along with many others he feels that the government does not consider

6 "When the government condemns property it is required to pay only for what it *acquires* for itself and not for what it *takes* from the owner. The government is *not* in condemnation acquiring a business but only the premises." Jane Jacobs. *The Death and Life of Great American Cities,* Random House, 1961, p. 312.

all the things when it takes one's property. It "should consider paying me for my job loss too." He gave away his equipment and is now retired. In short, he is very bitter about the whole thing.

A similar reaction was expressed by a sixty-nine-year-old Polish immigrant who had operated a variety store at the same location for forty-five years, and had catered largely to a neighborhood market. In this case the owner reported having been treated "rotten." He claims that he had become sick and had to spend five months in the hospital as a result of the treatment received from the state. He had started the business with savings accumulated while working in the mills. In his opinion, he did not receive a fair price for his building nor his home which was also in the condemned area. He reports that "They made one offer – take it or leave it – and it wasn't enough. We didn't have a lawyer to fight them, so they beat us. They told us to get out and we didn't like it. They acted as though they could tell us to do anything." If this person had it to do over again he feels that one should "fight them in court – get a lawyer – and squeeze them so they would be honest."

Another aged businessman blamed the forced move for the death of his wife.[7] With the help of his wife he had operated a small neighborhood grocery store at the same location for thirty-seven years. It is his firm belief that the state has no right to force businesses out and that "they" have no consideration for the small businessman. Following displacement he retired without even trying to find another location. When asked why he decided to go out of business he said that "my wife died because they forced me out, so I got disgusted and sick, so I just quit. The whole thing still makes me sick." In this instance also, if he had to do it over he would fight the state with a good lawyer.

Among the businessmen who relocated, only 15 per cent report they were angry or emotionally disturbed by the forced move, as

7 This is not an uncommon response. A similar reaction is reported in an appraisal of West End Urban Renewal Project in Boston. Gans points out that, "several deaths among residents at the time that West Enders realized the area would be cleared were attributed by informants to the shock of this recognition." "Human Implications of Renewal and Relocation," *Journal of American Institute of Planners,* Vol. XXV, No. 1, February, 1959, p. 19.

compared with 22 per cent of the non-survivors. Two-fifths of the latter but only one-fifth of the former reported that they were worried, discouraged or confused by the whole process of displacement. Thus approximately two-thirds of the non-survivors had viewed the move with anxiety, while only one-third of those who continued in business did so. The survivors were more likely to be fatalistic when they learned about the forced move. A frequent response was that nothing could be done about it; that improvements are necessary and that this is one type of price that has to be paid for progress. According to these businessmen – nearly one in ten of the survivors – urban renewal and highway construction programs are in the best interests of the community, and in order to get them the consequences must be accepted even though some are hurt. About one-fourth of both the survivors and non-survivors reported that they were either quite neutral or favored the forced movement. Altogether, nearly three-fourths of the units that discontinued in business but less than half of the successful movers responded unfavorably to the forced movement.

PROBLEMS OF RELOCATION AMONG NON-SURVIVORS

While nearly all of the non-survivors claimed that they would have continued in business indefinitely at the old location if they had not been forced to move, one-third made the decision to go out of business without any effort to move to a new location. However, a majority had apparently originally planned to continue their business operation at a new location, for more than two-thirds of the units reported that they had tried to find a new site prior to their decision to discontinue in business. Among the latter, nearly one-fifth reported that the major problem they had to face in trying to relocate was the high cost of buildings or rentals of alternative locations. One businessman, who was unable to relocate and went out of business because prices for a new site were too high, views the problem of cost thusly, "Prices of real estate are going up anyway and on top of that, all these businesses being pushed out and looking for new places send all the commercial buildings up some more" He feels that "if they can force us out then it would have been fair to force people selling us other places not to jump their prices so much." He was not alone in his belief that displacement of businesses in one area led to price increases. Some businesses encourage others faced with dislocation to "get out early before they run up land values in the areas you are moving to."

Nearly one-tenth of the non-survivors reported that, when they attempted to relocate, they found that they couldn't afford to start business over again in a new location because of a lack of capital. However, the most frequently mentioned problem in finding a new site pertained to the problem of zoning or licensing of the business at a new location. Three businesses out of ten specifically reported this as their major problem in their efforts to move to a new site. Liquor stores and junk yards were the types of businesses that were particularly faced with this problem.

The special problems encountered by junk dealers are worthy of note. It is among these businesses that the non-survival rate is high and particular bitterness is expressed, due largely to problems of zoning and licensing in their attempts to move to a new location. Without exception, all of the junk dealers who went out of business following displacement expressed very strong resentment over how they had been treated. In no other group is as much resentment apparent. Over and over again they recount their futile attempts to find a new location. A general theme expressed by these businesses is that they are not wanted in the community, that people look down their noses at this type of business and that displacement is used as an opportunity to get rid of them. This is cogently expressed by a forty-seven-year-old dealer who had occupied the same location for twenty-five years, thusly, "They deliberately forced us out. They say they don't want our kind of junk business around." He reports that he was unable to relocate because of zoning restrictions. Thus he feels that "the city would not let us relocate." Consequently he had to sell his inventory to an iron works, and according to his account he lost heavily on the sales. He claims, for example, that "cars I paid $60 for I had to sell for $20." He is now a part-time welder and makes only a fraction of what he made while in business. This is a case where a fair price had been received for his building, but the real damage and loss were due to the inability to find another location. He feels that "when businesses are forced to move the government should rezone an area into which such activities could move." This is an opinion shared by many.

The same problem is expressed by still another dealer who had occupied the same location for seven years. In his opinion, "The major problem when trying to find a new location is the zoning problem. I have tried three times to get a junking license, but haven't been able to do so." In a different context he continues, "I never dreamed licenses for a scrap yard would be so difficult to get." Although he had received a fair price for his building, he found the whole thing "quite disheartening when I was denied a new license for a yard." He is presently not working but hopes to go back into business in the near future ("as soon as I can get a license"). His general comment concerning his position is rather typical. "My problem is wanting to get back into a business that is considered dirty and therefore wrong. It is just as respectable as any other enterprise and with proper fencing restrictions not an eyesore at all."

A similar opinion is expressed even more emphatically by a forty-three-year-old dealer who had operated a business for ten years at the same location and whose father, from whom he obtained the business, had occupied the same location for twenty additional years. When this man was forced to move, he tried to find a new location but could not do so because he could not find an area zoned for "junk yards." He claimed that he had "put money down on seven different locations, even in areas zoned M-2 Industrial, but could not get proper zoning or a license to operate." It was obvious in talking with this man and his wife that they were desperate and very bitter about the whole thing. Since he could not find a location into which he could move, after looking for more than eighteen months, he was forced to go out of business. He says, "I had no choice – there was no place to go." Consequently he was forced to sell his inventory and equipment and abandon the old location. He reports that he "took a terrific loss." Regarding displacement he said, "It ruined me because I couldn't relocate. If the government is going to force you to move they should set up areas so businesses could move into them. They should provide by zoning for all types of business. Individual cases should be investigated and something worked out for them before forcing them to move." This man shared with others the opinion that junk yards are needed and they can be attractively camouflaged so as not to be a blight on an area. He bitterly resents the fact that there is strong resistance to zoning for this type of function. He is very dissatisfied with how he had been handled and claims that no one had tried to help him find a new location. According to him, the only concern on the part of the state was to get him out of the area. The bitterness of this man is evident from the following comment regarding what one should do when forced to move, "Get the best possible lawyer. You need one who is a real fighter for justice." But he was quite disillusioned regarding the legal help he had received, as is evident from his statement that "incompetent lawyers have made a lot of money on victims but really do not do anything for business." At any rate, this man had a successful operation prior to displacement; he had a monthly salary of $1,400 and paid approximately $2,000 in wages, but he no longer is in business. However, he too hopes to re-enter the same type of business soon if he can find a location zoned properly and can get a license.

One of the other dealers, who could not relocate and went out of business because he couldn't get a license at a new location, shares many of the opinions expressed in the above illustrations. This dealer claims that prior to displacement "we used to have meetings with the state people and everything was rosy – they made many promises to us which they never kept." In his opinion, "all of the 'junkies' should get together and see what is the mystery, why it is getting so hard to get a license."

One-fourth of the non-survivors who attempted to relocate reported that they were unable to find an adequate site where they could continue to operate their business. This was due either to their inability to find selected site characteristics or to the costs involved. At any rate they could not find anything that suited them. Slightly more than one-tenth wanted to continue in business in the same general neighborhood in which they had been located prior to displacement, but they could not find a place in the area.

REASONS FOR GOING OUT OF BUSINESS

The problem of finding a new location was given in a majority of cases as the reason for deciding to discontinue in business.

About one business in six decided to go out of business either because a suitable site for relocation could not be found or insurmountable problems of licensing or zoning were encountered. In several instances, units could not get a license transfer or could not find a site that was, or could be, zoned for their type of operation. Consequently the only apparent alternative was to discontinue the business. One-fourth of the units decided to go out of business because they could not afford the costs of relocation. Not only is there the cost of moving equipment and inventory, but there is the problem of preparing the new building for occupancy. For some types of businesses, this can be a major undertaking. Such businesses did not have the resources to "start over" which they felt they would have to do when they moved to a new location. Another 9 per cent decided to go out of business, since in the move they would lose contact with their usual customers. This response also implies that a move would require building up new customers.[8] In fact, this would be the case for several units, since in the old location, as noted above, they had catered primarily to customers living in the general neighborhood. Movement out of the area would sever these contacts. Even to remain in or near the original area would be fruitless, for many, if not most, of their customers would have also been forced to move from the area.

Only a small minority of the business owners (12 per cent) decided to go out of business because of age. They reported that they were too old to start over again, thus when forced to move they decided not to relocate. Such was the case of the sixty-seven-year-old jewelry manufacturer who had been in business at the same location for twenty-two years. He had a small electroplating operation, which he ran by himself with the part-time help of his wife. The latter was unpaid, but together they averaged around $350 per month. He felt that a move would upset everything and he was too old to change. Also, his heart wasn't in it because of the high rents that would be necessary in a new location. He said, "I was mad for a while, then calmed down." He was about ready to

8 When the non-survivors were asked how they thought a move to a new location would affect their business, more than two-fifths reported that they would lose all of their old customers and would thus have to build up a new trade. Consequently, moving to a new location would be tantamount to starting all over again. Another 15 per cent said a move would be too costly and would ruin them. Only 3 per cent said a move would have helped them if they could have found the right spot.

retire in a few years anyway, so when he was displaced he decided that he had had enough. He used this as an opportunity to retire. In his opinion this was the only sensible move since a new start was out of the question. So he just sold a few things and gave the rest away. Although he has mixed feelings on how he made out financially, he says that he has "no hard feelings" now. Regarding business conditions, he expressed the same concern as many other jewelry owners on how the cheap foreign labor and imports were hurting local businesses. The future of his business did not appear bright. He and his wife now live on his pension and some small investments. He sums up his present position thusly, "I'm enjoying myself but have very little money."

Another small minority closed down their business at the time of displacement because the owners had job offers which appeared to provide more attractive opportunities. This type of case is illustrated by the forty-two-year-old barber who had built up a good steady business from the immediate neighborhood during the nine years that he had been in business at the same location. He liked being in business because it gave him a good feeling to be able to run his own life and be his own boss; however, being in business did demand long hours and hard work. He employed one other barber in his shop. At the time of displacement, he had an opportunity to take a barbering job at one of the state institutions where the pay was approximately the same as he had been making with his own business. At first he planned to relocate and attempted to find a new location, but in so doing he came to the conclusion that there were too many other barber shops, and that in any location it would take a long time to build up customers again. So he decided that there would be "less headaches" working for someone else than in trying to get resettled in a new location. Thus he sold his equipment and discontinued his business. A decision, which in his opinion, was a wise one since "I am very happy here and glad I don't have to worry about business so much. I have a lot more free time now."

A similar reaction was expressed by a forty-six-year-old owner of a jewelry polishing firm who had been in business for eight years at the same location. The high cost of relocation and the general decline in business caused him to seek a buyer for his business. He claimed that he had put a lot of hard work into his business but sold out very cheaply; thus he was not at all satisfied with how he had made out financially. Being in business proved disillusioning to him. This is evident from his comment that "thirty years ago being in business made you a privileged, well-to-do person, but this is no longer true." He used the displacement as an opportunity to sell out and accept a job as a salesman for a large local manufacturing firm for which he had worked previously as a foreman. Actually he experienced an increase in income and of his present job he says, "I am all through at five and I don't have to take my worries home with me."

Thus the reasons for going out of business are many and varied and in many instances quite independent of any negative effects related to the forced move. On the contrary, displacement provided some of the establishments with a convenient opportunity to discontinue their business which they would have done anyway, but the timing would have been different.

It is apparent from these data that all of the non-survivors could not be classfied as business failures resulting from the move, since the decision to go out of business in many cases was only indirectly related to the forced move. The businesses did not fail in the traditional sense. It will be recalled that one-third of the non-survivors did not even attempt to find a new location. Nonetheless there was widespread dissatisfaction expressed concerning the financial outcome of the forced move and the discontinuance of the business operation. Dissatisfaction was adamantly reported by a majority of the non-survivors. However, nearly two-fifths of the units reported that they were satisfied with how they had made out financially in closing down their business. A point worthy of note is that only a small minority (20 per cent) felt that they had not been given adequate time to settle their affairs before they were forced to vacate their site.

For a large majority, this experience put an end to their business aspirations. Seven out of ten of the non-survivors reported that they did not expect to enter business again. For these businessmen, this was the end and they would either retire (21 per cent) or enter some other occupation. However, for three units out of ten, out-of-business was only a temporary circumstance, for they expected to re-enter business in the future. One-third planned to do so within a year, but the other two-thirds did not know when they would do so. Of those who plan to re-enter business sometime in the future, only one-fourth reported that they had obtained enough for their business following displacement to finance another business venture. But three-fourths of the businessmen replied in the negative, that is, in disposing of their business they had not realized enough to go into business again. Other resources would be needed. In the meantime, these former businessmen entered other-type jobs. When asked how they liked their present work as compared with being in business, a substantial majority (65 per cent) reported that they liked being in business better, whereas less than one-fifth preferred their present work.

DEMOGRAPHIC CHARACTERISTICS

We have already observed that the units which went out of business following displacement were selective by both type and size of business. The present discussion focuses on some of the demographic characteristics of the owners of the businesses that discontinued as compared with those that moved to a new location. Although the median age of the owners of both the "in" and "out" business units is very similar, 50.8 years and 52.8 years respectively, an inspection of the age distribution indicates that the age composition of the two groups differs significantly. There is little difference by present business status in the proportions under forty-five years of age. Slightly more than one-fourth in both groups are of this age. However, the relocated establishments have a high, disproportionate number of owners in the forty-five-year to fifty-four-year category. Even though this is the modal age for both survivors and those who discontinued in business, the proportion is higher among those who stayed in business following displacement. Similarly, the in-business units have a slightly higher proportion in the fifty-five-year to sixty-four-year group. On the other hand, the owners of the out-of-business units are concentrated disproportionately in the sixty-five years of age and over category. Here we find one-fourth of the owners who discontinued in business as compared with only slightly more than one-tenth of the in-business owners. It is apparent that a substantial number of out-of-business owners were of retirement age and many decided to retire rather than attempt relocation. It will be recalled that at least half this proportion, (12.3 per cent) when asked why they decided to go out of business, reported that they felt that they were too old to start over again.

The importance of age is further evident when we compare survival rates by age groups. For persons under sixty-five years of age, the proportion continuing in business was approximately eight out of ten, but among those over sixty-five years of age the survival rate dropped to only six out of ten owners. It is strikingly clear that the older persons are the ones who are hardest hit by displacement. For they must give up a long-established business operation and are too old to start over again in a new location. Nearly half of the non-survivors are fifty-five years of age and over. Alternative job opportunities are very limited or even non-existent for persons of this age as compared with the opportunities available for those who are younger.[9]

The non-survival rate is particularly high among business owners with limited education. We find that 31 per cent of the non-survivors had completed six years or less of formal schooling, as compared with only 8 per cent of the survivors. At the other extreme, 23 per cent of the owners of businesses that successfully relocated had some college training, as compared with only 5 per cent of those in the out-of-business group. The median level of education of the out-of-business group is only 10.6 years as compared with 12.1 years for those still in-business. The median conceals much of the difference, however. In this case an arithmetic average would show a much larger difference, because the two groups are concentrated at different extremes of the educational distribution. Another way of viewing the influence of education is to note the survival rate at different educational levels. Among those at the lowest level of education, only 47 per cent survived the move, whereas 95 per cent at the college level did so. However, this is likely an overstatement of the role of the education variable, for some of this difference is probably due to age as well

9 Gans point out that many small businessmen in displaced areas will lose their incomes and livelihood – many are too old to be hired by employers, so both economically and psychologically their future is grim. This, he claims, is one of the hidden costs of redevelopment and relocation. See: Herbert J. Gans, *op. cit.*

as to differences in size and type of business in relation to education. Older persons are concentrated at the lower educational level, and it is this age group that experienced the lowest survival rate also. Similarly this age group and educational level make up a high, disproportionate number of the owners of food-related retail and service establishments, both of which have a high non-survivor rate.

PREVIOUS EXPERIENCE

Apparently the ability to relocate following displacement is related to the occupational experience of the business owners prior to entering business. Among the non-survivors, 26 per cent had entered business from the craftsmen-foremen occupational level, but only 12 per cent of the survivors had originated from this occupational category. These occupations generally represent a high degree of manual skill but ordinarily provide little administrative or managerial experience. The latter, of course, is necessary for the successful operation of a business, and is particularly needed when a disruption of routine occurs, and a major adjustment or change is forced on the business unit. Some of this difference again reflects age and educational differences, as well as differences in size and types of businesses, but these account for only part of the variation in survival.

These data suggest that persons best equipped by experience to run a business are the ones most likely to make the transition from one area to another. Evidence in support of this is provided by a close inspection of the previous occupational experience of the survivors. While less than two-thirds at the craftsmen-foremen level survived the move, all of those who were previously in professional-managerial occupations did so. Of those who survived the move, approximately one-fifth were not in the labor force prior to entering business, as compared with less than one-tenth of those who went out of business. The survival rate of persons who had no previous occupational experience was more than 80 per cent. Since most of those in this category were students prior to entering business, this high rate reflects two factors – special training for operating a business and entering family businesses which were already established. Both appear to provide real advantages. The survival rate is lower for those who entered business directly from the armed forces. This group constituted 15 per cent of the out-of-business group but only 9 per cent of those still in business. About one-third of this group did not survive the move, which is approximately 40 per cent above the average for this sample of respondents. This is particularly high, since persons in this group are concentrated in the age groups where the survival rates are highest. This again likely reflects a lack of preparation for business through training or experience, since many of these entered business due to the lack of alternative job opportunities following demobilization after the war.

We have already indicated that the ability to survive displacement and relocation varies with the qualifications of the owners to manage a business operation. Further evidence of this is found in the responses to the question regarding where persons learned to run a business. More than half (54 per cent) of those who did not survive the move reported that they had learned to operate a business by "picking it up on their own," as compared with slightly more than two-fifths (43 per cent) of those who continued in business following the move. Those who learned the business while working for someone else account for 14 per cent of the non-survivors but only 10 per cent of those who continued in business. Nearly 30 per cent of those who learned to operate a business by "working for someone else or by picking it up on their own" did not survive the move.

Owners who learned to operate the business from their own family constitute 24 per cent of the survivors, as compared with 15 per cent of those who went out of business. For persons who learned the business from their family, approximately 85 per cent successfully relocated, which is substantially higher than the average for the total sample. A similar high survival rate is found among those businessmen who had special training for operating a business. Of this group, only 14 per cent went out of business following the move. The same survival rate is found among those who reported that they had learned to operate a business from other businessmen.

The non-survival rate of those who learned to operate a business while working for someone else or by picking it up on their own was nearly twice as high as the rate experienced by those who learned through their family, from other businessmen, or had special training. It is likely that the former group constituted the more marginal business operations which could have continued under existing circumstances at the old location, but the forced movement disrupted this minimum balance and placed on them the burden of an adjustment that was beyond their business skills or resources. Consequently they had to abandon their business operation and enter other-type jobs.

LENGTH OF TIME IN BUSINESS

One would expect to find at least a partial explanation to the differential survival rates in the length of time the unit had been in operation and the reasons for entering business. However, when both the survivors and non-survivors are classified by year entered business, significant differences emerge by period entered business but none seems to be a function of length of time in business. Those entering business during the years immediately following the second world war, that is, between 1945 and 1949, have the highest non-survival rate. These are likely businesses started by war veterans upon demobilization. This finding is consistent with our earlier observation that those who entered business from the armed forces had the highest failure rate. It is not difficult to assume that these people lacked both business training and experience and entered business due to the lack of alternative opportunities for employment. The non-survival rate of those who entered business during the war (1940 to 1944) was less than half (13.5 per cent versus 31.5 per cent) the rate experienced by those entering business in the early postwar period. Apparently the unusual opportunities of the war years, if the establishment survived the initial phase of getting started, must have provided the owners with a sound foundation for their business operation. When they were forced to move some fifteen to twenty years later, they had acquired both the business acumen and the necessary resources to be able to successfully absorb the disruption.

Also during the war years (1940-44), there was an unusually high loss rate among businesses. For example, the number of discontinued businesses in 1942, the first full year of our participation in the war, was 604.4 thousand as compared with only 360.5 thousand two years earlier.[9] Perhaps the unusually high business losses at this time selected out the "weaker" businesses; consequently the businesses in our sample that were organized during this period are the ones that had already successfully survived a period when the casualty rate was very high. Apparently they were sturdy at the time and were still sturdy enough at the time of displacement to survive the disruption of the move. At any rate, the loss rate following displacement was exceptionally low. This does not seem to be a function of length of time in business, for establishments which had been in operation for longer periods had higher loss rates.

Contrary to expectation, the units with the highest survival rates were those which had only recently entered business. The failure rate of businesses organized after 1955 was less than 10 per cent. This is less than half the total rate in our sample. However, this may well be a superfluous observation, for the absolute failure rate of this group would have been much higher, but those who failed to survive the early stages of setting up a business would have discontinued prior to the condemnation of the area, and before the forced move, since most failures occur early.[10] Consequently the failures were not included among the businesses that were displaced, therefore they did not fall within the scope of this study. However, the point to be emphasized is that of those who did survive up to the point of displacement, a high proportion was also able to absorb the disruptive effect of the move.

Apparently the particular time period when the business was

9 Survey of Current Business, May, 1946, June, 1946, and January, 1952, presented in Kurt Mayer, "Business Enterprise: Traditional Symbol of Opportunity," *The British Journal of Sociology,* Vol. IV, No. 2, June, 1953, p. 172.

10 In a recent study of 81 new businesses in the Providence area, it was found that four firms closed within two months of their opening, 13 firms did not survive the first six months, and an additional 15 closed during the second half of the first year. The authors report that this closure rate of 34 per cent during the first year conforms closely to the findings of other studies of the longevity of retail and service businesses. By the end of the second year, 12 more firms closed. Thus after a two-year period, 40 of the original 81 firms were no longer in business. Kurt Mayer and Sidney Goldstein, *The First Two Years: Problems of Small Firm Growth and Survival,* Small Business Administration, Research Series No. 2, Washington, D. C. 1961, p. 56.

organized and originated is more important in the ability of the establishment to survive displacement than length of time in business. The major differences of significance are between the war years and the immediate postwar period. It is likely that more than economic conditions at the time the business was started is important. During the two time periods, different kinds of persons were likely attracted to enter businesses, and the number of business openings varied markedly.[1] During the early postwar years, many businesses were started without proper preparation on the part of the owner and without adequate financial resources. Ex-servicemen went into business merely as a means of providing a job for themselves.[2] Consequently the failure rate was abnormally high and even many of those who managed to survive ten or more years, up to the time of displacement, apparently were not sufficiently established nor had they accumulated the necessary resources or business experience to withstand the disruptive effects of the move. Many had apparently reached only a tenuous equilibrium at the old location, and the level of operations was such that they did not have the reserve needed to set up their business operation at a new location.

The reported motivational factors for entering business differ by present business status.[3] Among the units that went out of busi-

1 The immediate postwar years witnessed a very high rate of new business openings. Whereas only 143.4 thousand new businesses were started in 1943, this increased to 429.8 thousand in 1945 and to a high of 619.2 thousand in 1946. By 1950 the number had dropped to 397.5 thousand per year. *Survey of Current Business,* May, 1946, June, 1949, and January, 1952 (Quoted in Mayer, *British Journal of Sociology,* p. 172, Vol. IV, No. 2, June, 1953.)

2 This is not particularly atypical in that in many instances the motivation for entering business is "the immediate need for a job." See: Mayer and Goldstein, *op. cit.,* p. 29. Following the war this differed mainly in magnitude or degree. At that particular time this reason likely would have accounted for a larger than average proportion of the reasons for entering business. Also many of those entering business immediately following the war had learned new skills in the service which may have prepared them for the "craftsmanship" or "technical competence" in respect to a given product or service, but this experience would not have provided them with the administrative skills needed to run an efficient business operation. For example, it's one thing to be able to repair a radio but quite another to run a radio sales and services business.

3 For an interesting discussion of why people enter business, see: Kurt Mayer, *op. cit.*

ness following the move, we find a slightly larger proportion of owners emphasizing "negative" reasons for entering business such as "not wanting to work for someone else," "no other job available," or "dissatisfaction with former job." One-third of the non-survivors cited reasons for this type, as compared with less than one-fourth of those who successfully relocated. Non-survivors were also more likely to emphasize the desire "to make money" as the reason for entering business; 38 per cent report this as the main factor which motivated them to enter business, but only 30 per cent of the in-business units gave this as their reason. The latter, however, were much more likely to enter business because the business was already in the family. This group had a distinct advantage since they entered already established businesses and were thus in a much more secure position. This apparently made them less sensitive to the disruptive effects of relocation.

Perceptions of the advantages and disadvantages of being in business also differ by present business status. More than half of those who survived the move, but only about one-fourth of the non-survivors, reported that it was the independence provided by business that was the main advantage. However, the opportunity to make more money or to get ahead was stressed as the advantage by 55 per cent of the out-of-business units but by only 26 per cent of those still in business. Viewing these data from a different perspective, we noted that of those who stressed independence as the main advantage of being in business, 87 per cent survived the move, as compared with only 62 per cent of those who viewed business primarily as a way to make more money or to get ahead. The survival rate drops to only 50 per cent among those who claim that the advantage of being in business is that it requires "less time and work."

The non-survival rate is lowest among the business owners who reported "responsibility" as the main disadvantage of being in business. Only 9 per cent giving this response did not successfully relocate; however, the proportion increases to 26 per cent of those who stressed the hard work involved in running a business or the difficulties of trying to make a profit. Among the owners who view "being too dependent on customers" as the disadvantage of being in business, nearly half (45 per cent) did not survive displacement.

Whether or not perception of business is an important factor in successful relocation, or whether successful relocation determines one's attitudes toward business, is an unanswered question, but, regardless of the priority of variables, the different evaluations by present business status are worthy of note. Also the differential survival rates in relation to the psychological interpretation of the advantages and disadvantages of operating a business are clearly discernible. In short, it seems that those business owners who view business in a positive way, that is, as affording satisfactions other than only a money-making opportunity, are more likely to be able to survive the disruptive effects of a forced move. Seeking the advantages of independence and a readiness to assume the disadvantage of responsibility seem to be psychological states that make for persistence[4] and hence, success in adjusting to change. Business owners of this type had the highest survival rates.

OCCUPATION AND INCOME OF NON-SURVIVORS

In the preceding discussion, we have been concerned primarily with the differences between the business units that survived the forced move and the units that discontinued in business following displacement. Attention in Table 5-2 is, however, focused on what happened to the business owners who did not survive the move. A related question of interest concerns the relative position this group now occupies in the regular non-business occupational structure, as compared with the type of work they engaged in prior to entering business originally. It is noted that nearly one-fifth of the former business owners entered the ranks of the unemployed when they closed down their business. This proportion likely represents a temporary condition for many. At any rate, for a substantial number, unemployment is at least a stage of undetermined duration in the transition from business to some other type of economic activity. More than one-fifth of the displaced owners who discontinued in business went into retirement. It will be recalled that, of the units that did not relocate, many owners reported that

4 In a recent study of new businesses, it was reported that "persistence" is a crucial factor in survival. Even "marginal" businesses were able to survive if the owners had "persistence and a low level of expectations." Mayer and Goldstein, *op. cit.*, p. 134.

TABLE 5-2

PRESENT OCCUPATION OF NON-SURVIVORS AND OCCUPATION PRIOR TO ENTERING BUSINESS

Occupation	Present	Previous
Total	100.0	100.0
Professional	3.1	....
Managerial – Official	15.4	....
Clerical – Sales	12.3	15.4
Craftsmen	15.4	26.2
Operatives – Laborers	12.3	30.8
Unemployed	18.5	....
Retired	21.5	....
Not in Labor Force	1.5	24.6*
Farm	....	1.5
No Answer	....	1.5

*Armed Forces and Students.

they were "too old to start over again"; however, our data show that they would have continued in business indefinitely had they not been displaced. Actually the choices available for this group were limited, since they were too old to find other jobs. Thus the inability to relocate and continue in business had the effect of forcing them out of the labor force into retirement or into part-time work.

This is illustrated by the sixty-six-year-old owner of a welding business displaced by one of the highway projects, who had been in business in the same location for forty-five years. He claims that he did not receive enough for his property to replace it at a new location. He resents the fact that he was only paid for the land and building and not for the business. In his opinion he would have had to go $30,000 in debt to start again, but he states, "I didn't want to go into debt at my age." It may very well be that this is a very unrealistic figure. For one thing it is based on starting with nothing in that he gave his equipment to his son. It is certain that he could have relocated in rented quarters with his old equipment at little expense other than moving costs. This is not to say that he would not have been hurt by the move, but the hurt would be less extensive than his claim. At any rate his perception of the consequences is reflected in his remarks. Now he finds himself in a position where no one will hire him because insurance companies won't accept him, that is, he cannot be protected on the job. However, he does work part-time for his son, which he resents, as is evident from his remark, "I used to have four men working for me, now I'm working for someone else – it's no good," and in another context he states, "I was making good money then and I was my own boss – now I'm broke." He says that the government should pay for the businesses they destroy. In his opinion he was not handled properly. He claims that "the appraiser didn't even look at my shop – all he did was walk in and walk out. I don't mind highways – we need them – but they took away my business and now I got nothing – it's not right."

For many of the owners, the business experience apparently equipped them for better jobs than they had held formerly. Either the business experience or the passing of time made upward mobility possible. For while none of the non-survivors had entered business from the professional-managerial occupational levels, nearly one-fifth of the total re-entered the occupational structure at this level when they closed their business. While nearly three-fifths of the owners had entered business from blue collar occupations, that is, at the skilled and semi-skilled levels, only one-fourth returned to this level after leaving business. If we view only those currently working, we find nearly one-third in professional-managerial positions and another one-fifth in clerical or sales positions. Thus more than half of the former business owners currently working entered white collar occupations after going out of business.[5] It is noted further that three-fifths of those working entered the same type of work as they were engaged in while in business.

The type of activity engaged in after going out of business differs by the size of the business operation prior to displacement, measured in terms of number of employees. Of those entering

5 This high rate is due mainly to those who entered business from the armed forces and those who were not previously in the labor force before entering business. Approximately one-third of the blue collar workers entered white collar positions after being in business.

white collar positions, only 10 per cent had businesses which were single-person operations, as compared with 28 per cent among those who entered blue collar occupations, and 46 per cent of those not currently working. Among those who retired, nearly three-fifths (57 per cent) operated businesses which did not employ any workers. None of those who retired had operated businesses with three or more employees. Apparently older persons with larger businesses continued their operation and successfully relocated. But to the owners of smaller units, relocation following displacement did not seem to be worth the effort, cost or risk of trying to get established at a new location. Thus the owners took advantage of the disruption as an opportunity to retire even though they would have continued to operate their small businesses indefinitely if they had not been forced to move.

Viewing the relationship between size of business and subsequent activity from a different perspective, we find a consistent increase in the proportion entering white collar positions as the size of unit increases. Thus, among units which were single-person operations, only 10 per cent of the non-survivors entered white collar positions, but this proportion increased to 38 per cent among those with one or two employees, and to 47 per cent of those who had three or more employees. It is observed further that among the units with no employees, two-fifths went into retirement, as compared with one-fifth of those with one or two employees, and none of those with three or more workers.[6]

The reaction to the change in status varies by the type of activity in which the former business owner is currently engaged. Nearly one-fourth of those in both white collar positions or blue collar jobs reported they liked their present activity better than being in business. Likewise nearly one-fourth of those who retired preferred their present status. But the significant difference by present activity is found in the proportion who expressed a strong negative opinion concerning their present status. While only one-third of the white collar workers liked business better than

6 These differences are in part a function of age by size of unit. One-third of those with no employees are 65 years of age or over, as compared with one-fifth of those in the two larger unit categories. Similarly the proportion approaching retirement age is larger in the "no employees" group than in the other two size classes.

their present job, more than two-thirds of the blue collar workers and the retired preferred being in business. About two-fifths of the while collar workers equated their present jobs with being in business, while only 5.6 per cent of the blue collar workers and 7.7 per cent of the retired did so. The unanimous negative opinion expressed by the unemployed group is so obvious and expected as to make elaboration unnecessary.

Of the total businesses that did not survive the move, 29 per cent expect to re-enter business at some future date. Conversely, 71 per cent have no such plans. The proportion expecting to re-enter business is highest among those who are currently not working. Of this group, more than half expect to go back into business at some unspecified future date. However, two-thirds of the blue collar workers and three-fourths of the white collar workers do not plan to re-enter business. And among the retired, 93 per cent do not have any future business plans.

The present income of those who remained in business is significantly larger than for those who did not relocate. According to the data presented in Table 6-2, more than half of the former owners in the out-of-business category report a current annual income

TABLE 6-2

PRESENT INCOME AND INCOME COMPARED WITH BEFORE DISPLACEMENT BY PRESENT STATUS

Income	Present Status	
	Survivors	Non-Survivors
Present Income	100.0	100.0
Under $2,000	12.0	26.2
$2,000 – $3,999	14.9	29.2
$4,000 – $7,499	28.6	41.6
$7,500 and Over	44.5	3.0
Compared With Before Displacement	100.0	100.0
Present Income Higher	23.0	4.6
Same	33.6	9.2
Present Income Lower	43.4	86.1

of less than $4,000, but only one-fourth of those still in business are at this income level. More than two-fifths of the persons who did not survive the move report an income between $4,000 and $7,500, as compared with slightly more than one-fourth of those who successfully relocated. The really significant difference, however, is found at the top income level. Here we find 44 per cent of those who are still in business, but only 3 per cent of the non-survivors. These differences must be viewed with caution, however, for the differences cannot all be attributed to the consequences of displacement; the income of the two groups also differed markedly when all were still in business at the old locations. It will be recalled that the units that did not survive following displacement were small units, many of which were operating at a minimum level. The relative difference between the two groups may not have changed with the forced move, but the size of the income in both groups has likely decreased for many. It is noted that only 5 per cent of those out of business, but 23 per cent of those in business, report that their present income is higher than it was prior to the move. One-third of those still in business, but less than one-tenth of the non-survivors, report that their income has remained unchanged. But 86 per cent of the former business owners claim that their present income is less than they were making prior to displacement. Slightly more than two-fifths (43 per cent) of those still in business make the same claim. One point to be emphasized here is that more than half of those who relocated are in the same or better income position than while at the old location, as compared with less than one-seventh of those who went out of business following the move.

The present income of the non-survivors varies according to the type of activity entered after closing down their business operations. As shown in Table 7-2, those entering blue collar work have the smallest proportion in the lowest income category. Slightly more than one-tenth of the blue collar workers, but one-fourth of the white collar workers, are found at this income level. The latter high proportion is likely due largely to the former business owners who entered sales and clerical positions. The overall position of white collar workers is, however, more favorable, as is evident from the higher proportions at the top level. Also, when asked how present income compares with income while in business, nearly twice as many in white collar positions as in blue collar jobs report no change or a higher income. We find that 70 per cent of the white collar workers, as compared with 83 per cent of the blue collar workers, report that they are making less now than when they were in business.

TABLE 7-2

PRESENT INCOME AND INCOME COMPARED WITH BEFORE DISPLACEMENT BY PRESENT OCCUPATION OF NON-SURVIVORS

Income	Present Occupation				
	Total	White Collar	Blue Collar	Not Working	Retired
Present Income	100.0	100.0	100.0	100.0	100.0
Under $3,000	46.2	25.0	11.1	76.9	92.9
$3,000 – $4,999	32.3	40.0	61.1	15.4	.....
$5,000 and Over	21.5	35.0	27.8	7.7	7.1
Compared With Before	100.0	100.0	100.0	100.0	100.0
Present Income Higher	4.6	10.0	5.6	.....	.....
Same	9.2	20.0	11.1	.....	.....
Present Income Lower	86.2	70.0	83.3	100.0	100.0

What has happened to those "not working" and retired is particularly noteworthy. While only 46 per cent of the non-survivors report an income of less than $3,000, we find 77 per cent of those not working[7] and 93 per cent of the retired at this income level. All of the former business owners in the "not working" and "retired" categories report that they are making less now than when they were in business. It is evident that one of the consequences of displacement for nearly nine out of ten of the former business-

7 The "not-working" category is a confused one, since it includes persons who are not in business or not holding any other regular job; however, in some instances persons in this category are actively engaged in managing their own investments in stocks and property but claim that they are "not working." This accounts for the "high" proportion in the top income levels. For example, a former junk dealer reports his present income in the $15,000 and over category, but claims that he is "not working."

men who did not relocate was a decrease in income. The average decrease was least for those who entered white collar positions and largest for those who retired.

REACTION TO DISPLACEMENT

The general reaction to the move varies by present business status. Responses to the question – In the whole process of condemning and cleaning out the old area, how do you feel about the way you were handled? – by present business status are shown in Table 8-2. Favorable or neutral responses come disproportionately from those who successfully relocated. Thus, of those in business 27 per cent report that they feel "fine" about how they were treated, as compared to 18 per cent of those who are no longer in business. The proportion indifferent to how they were handled is 34 per cent and 26 per cent respectively. The out-of-business units are more likely to feel that they had been hurried, that is,

TABLE 8-2

REACTION TO MOVE BY PRESENT STATUS

Reaction to Move	Present Status	
	Survivors	Non-Survivors
How Feel About Way Handled	100.0	100.0
Fine – Positive	27.3	18.5
Neutral	34.4	26.1
Took too long to get project underway	3.1	.....
Hurried – not given sufficient time	3.1	7.7
Not Good – Bad – Negative	21.1	46.2
Other	6.6	.....
No Answer	4.4	1.5
Would Be Better Off if Not Moved	100.0	100.0
Yes	35.7	73.8
Uncertain	19.4	12.3
No	44.9	13.9

they were not given enough time before they had to vacate their site. Also the out-of-business establishments disproportionately responded unfavorably to the move. Nearly half of the units reported that they were badly treated. The high-emotional negative feelings are seen in the frequent response "like hell" that was given by those who went out of business following displacement, and are perhaps illustrated further by the more colorful, but not atypical, reaction expressed by a forty-five-year-old bar owner, who had only a fifth grade education and had averaged $60 per week from his business. He said, "It was a real kick in the ass."

Further evidence of the negative attitude of the out-of-business units is found in the responses to the question on whether or not they would be better off if they had not been forced to move. Three-fourths of the former business owners report that they would be better off if still at the old location, while only one-third of the in-business units respond thusly. On the other hand, 45 per cent of the relocated units report that they would not be better off if they had not been forced to move, while 19 per cent are uncertain, but among the out-of-business units the proportion giving comparable responses are 14 per cent and 12 per cent respectively. Thus it is evident that a substantial number of the out-of-business units have very negative feelings about how they were handled in being displaced, and most of them feel that they would be better off if no change had taken place. The reactions of those who relocated are quite different. They are more satisfied with how they were treated, and only a minority feel that they would be better off if they had not been displaced. Responses are approximately the same whether the businesses were displaced by highway projects or by urban renewal areas.

The negative reaction, particularly among those who went out of business, is also evident in the replies from owners when asked if they had received a fair price for their building at the old location. These data apply only to the one-third of the units that owned the building occupied. Although nearly two-fifths of the establishments report that a fair price was received, the responses vary from only 38 per cent of the out-of-business units to 65 per cent of those still in business. The high proportion of out-of-business units reporting that they had not received a fair price for their building is worthy of note. A substantial majority view the settlement negatively. Their major complaint, which was frequently expressed, was that they should have been compensated for their business or at least for the cost of the move as well as their building.[8] For example, the owner of a used machinery business who sold motors predominantly to local mills and factories was perfectly satisfied with the price received for his building, but nonetheless his response to displacement was a very negative one. He was forced out of business, he claimed, because the cost of moving was prohibitive. He stated his problem thusly, "They gave me a fair price for my building but I had to go out of business since it would have cost me a fortune to move my heavy machinery." He elaborates further, "I had just got 500 surplus government motors, big ones weighing tons, when they told me to move. It was impossible for me to move and they forced me to sell in a hurry, so I had to sell everything for scrap instead of piece by piece. I had to take a big loss on everything." He went into retirement but he hates it even though he is eighty-seven years of age. Had he not been displaced, he claims that he would have had no notions whatsoever of quitting business. In his opinion, "Government trucks should be used to move everything free when they force you to move to another location."

A forty-five-year-old former bar owner, who had been in business in the same neighborhood for eleven years, expressed strong dissatisfaction with the price received for his building, but when asked why he felt that way he responded, "They should have paid me for the business." This man had tried to relocate but could not find a licensable location in the same neighborhood, so he sold his license and equipment at a big loss and now works in a restaurant. And even though he made only $60 per week while in business, his present income is much lower.

The same kind of reaction is expressed by a grocery store owner who had been in business for thirty-four years and had served a neighborhood market. In his opinion "they" have no consideration for the small businessman. He feels that "the government should pay for all loss of business and relocation costs until you

8 This view is also expressed in a recent appraisal of urban renewal programs. The author proposed that liquidation funds in lieu of moving allowances should be provided to small store owners and other businessmen who are not able to re-open their firms elsewhere. Herbert J. Gans, *op. cit.* p. 24.

can build up again." It will be recalled that the same idea was expressed by a shoemaker who had served the same neighborhood for thirty-five years. He stated that "the government should consider paying me for my job loss too."

Many of the establishments that did not survive the move following displacement report that, in forcing them to move, the government had deprived them of their livelihood. In their opinion the government had taken away everything but had not provided any compensation for their losses. This is exemplified by the owner of a variety store who had been in business for twenty-two years at the same location and served a neighborhood market. His reaction to the displacement was simply, "they took away my business." His bitterness was apparent in his comment that "one can spend the best part of your lifetime building up a business and have them tear it away by making you move." In his opinion the state had deprived him of his business since he was unable to relocate. He goes on to say, "I was paid only for the building – I did not receive anything for the value of the business."[9]

Still others who were dissatisfied with the price received reported that they could not replace the building for the amount received from the government. Approximately one-third of the non-survivors simply stated that their building was worth more than they had been given. It may be that the price offered by the government was fully equal to the "worth" of the building; however, at current costs at a different location, it may be that the building and site could not be replaced for the price received. Yet to continue in business, a comparable building would be needed. But such accommodations may be beyond the owners' ability to pay; consequently the establishments may be unable to afford the costs of relocation. This may well be the crux of the problem for many. At any rate, a majority of the non-survivors were dissatisfied with the financial aspects of the displacement.

9 Many have interpreted this aspect of public improvement programs as an involuntary subsidy and claim that this is what makes such programs financially possible. A report prepared by A. J. Panuch for the Mayor of New York City states: "The direct consequences of the exercise of the power of eminent domain on the commercial tenant is drastic and ruinous." Quoted in Jane Jacobs, *The Death and Life of Great American Cities,* p. 311.

SUMMARY

All types of business establishments are not affected equally by public improvement programs which cause them to be displaced from their established sites. One of the apparent consequences of these programs is that a substantial minority of the units affected go out of business. But, as these data show, the ones that do so differ significantly from those that successfully relocate. The non-survivors are made up disproportionately of food-related retail and service establishments. Among the non-survivors is found a disproportionate number of small businesses and those that serve predominately a small local market area and draw their customers from a specific ethnic or racial group. The non-survivors were largely marginal businesses at the original location with low sales but a low overhead which permitted the business to continue to operate even though the income to the owner was small. Many of these businesses were owned and operated by older persons, thus the business was a way of life as well as the source of limited income. Many of these owners did not have the financial resources needed in order to relocate. They felt that it would have been necessary to go into debt if they had moved to another site. This did not seem to be worth it at their age, thus they gave up their business and went into retirement.

A majority of the former owners, however, re-entered the labor force in other capacities. Of those who did so, nearly half hold manual-type jobs while slightly more than half have entered white collar positions. Many hold better jobs now than they had held prior to entering business originally; nonetheless, for a very large majority, their present income is less than what they were making from their business prior to displacement. This is found to hold regardless of their present type of work, but the decline is less among white collar workers than among those in manual occupations.

The non-survivors predominantly view displacement practices unfavorably. There is common agreement that they would be better off if they had been able to continue in business at their old location. To the extent that businesses have to be displaced, the non-survivors, in particular, feel that the government should pay for "the business" as well as the property involved. Since, in being displaced, the government "deprived" them of their livelihood, they should have been compensated for the value of their business. This is indeed a thorny problem.

Unquestionably, the non-survivors bore the full brunt of the public improvement programs which forced businesses to vacate their established sites, but those establishments which relocated may also have had problems, even though of a different sort. It is to this topic that we now turn.

CHAPTER 3

PROBLEMS OF RELOCATION

THIS chapter pertains only to those businesses that successfully relocated. The discussion is concerned with some of the kinds of problems encountered in finding a new site, and the changes in site characteristics that accompanied the move. Attention is also focused on some of the financial aspects of dislocation, particularly in reference to the cost of the move and changes in rents as well as sales.

Following displacement, more than half of the businesses that relocated (55 per cent) reported that they had encountered serious problems in finding a new site.[1] When asked what constituted the major problem in moving, the one that was most frequently mentioned concerned the high cost of alternate sites for rental properties or the cost of desirable buildings. This was reported by one business in five.

1 The problems of relocation have not gone unnoticed. The subcommittee on Housing of the House Committee on Banking and Currency held hearings in May, 1960. The Committee Report stated the problem thusly: "Once we have assured adequate funds for slum clearance grants to aid local communities in urban renewal operations, the most important obstacle to be solved is the problem of finding equitable ways to relocate the small businesses . . . . inevitably uprooted by urban renewal and other government assisted programs . . ."

PROBLEMS IN SITE SELECTION

It was generally thought by the displaced establishments that landlords "upped their prices," both for rentals and on buildings for sale, as a result of the increased demand from businesses that were being forced to move. This aspect of the problem is clearly demonstrated by the account of the owner of one of the larger establishments in the study. After several months of looking for a new site, he writes in his log that "the prices people are asking for property are terrifically high, as they feel that there will be a great demand as this freeway and the other freeways progress through the city."[2] This kind of appraisal, whether objectively the case or not, had serious implications, for it led to some apparently irrational decisions in selecting a site, or at least to what appear to be poor judgments. For example, an industrial supplies establishment owner who had rented the same quarters for nearly twenty years, claimed that "realtors, knowing that I had to move, raised rents." At the time of displacement, he was under the impression that he could avoid these "inflated" prices by moving to the suburbs. Consequently he focused his attention on the suburbs in looking for a new site. "By driving around" he noticed the present site was available so he rented it and moved in. Retrospectively he reports that he had not expected the move to affect his business. However, after more than a year at his present location, he is very dissatisfied with the progress he has made since the move. His rent is higher than at the old location, and he is doing less business. He also reports that he does not see any reason to expect business to increase as long as he stays at the present location. The owner of this establishment now expresses a marked dislike for the suburbs because "it is too far out of the city for this type of business." The old location was much preferred because it was centrally located and more accessible to his customers who came from the whole Providence area. These advantages of the original site were either not appreciated prior to dislocation, or were forgotten or ignored in the emotional reaction to the

2 A day-by-day account of his experiences in settling with the government and in finding a new location was carefully recorded by this man from the inception of the project which displaced his business. A copy of this log was made available to the writer.

problem of high rents in seeking a new site. At any rate, when asked about the main problem in finding a new location, this owner responds that "rents were too high – they were pushed up because businesses were forced to move." The lack of forethought that was given to the selection of a site by this respondent, other than the rent factor which was considered only in absolute terms and not in respect to the relative merits of the location, is further evident from his failure to try to estimate the amount of business he would do at the new location or even to estimate the costs of operation. In fact, he did not even consider any other possible location, so there was no real empirical basis for his belief that "rents were pushed up"; nonetheless he acted on this impression. As a result he made a very poor selection of a new site.[3]

A less dramatic, but related experience, where both the action and the results differed, is reported by the owner of a paint and wallpaper retail sales firm who had owned his building at the old location. This respondent also felt that prices were inflated, but he decided to pay the inflated price for the advantages of a specific location. Not only does he feel that he did not receive a fair price for his old building, which was a former private residence and a famous Providence landmark for 140 years, that had been converted to commercial use, but he reports that he was "gouged" in buying the present site for which he paid $52,000. This, he reports, represents an investment of $4,000 more than he received for his former site and an amount which is some $12,000 more than what the place is actually worth, in his opinion and according to what "others" have told him. He is of the opinion that he had to pay this additional amount "because of the local inflated prices due to the rush by displaced businesses for suitable commercial property." Nonetheless he bought the property, which is a large colonial-type house in an area zoned commercial, because "we wanted to come as close as possible to a place with a homey house appearance and atmosphere as we had at the old location." Also, he "did not want to get buried on a side street," and "this seemed like a good location since it can be seen a long way down the street, has big windows and is a clean, airy building," but "it

3 Perhaps in such cases, effective counseling from a government-sponsored relocation service would have avoided such an apparent mistake in the selection of a site.

just doesn't have the beautiful atmosphere of our old family building." His previous building "had been in the family for a century." He says that he "had been born there and that my father had practiced medicine there before we made it a commercial building." Thus, besides being a good location in that "everyone knew we were there and we didn't even need a sign outside," he had a strong emotional attachment to the building, even though it was in a very poor area.

Although he feels that he paid an unrealistic price for the present site, he nonetheless feels that he is better off here than at any other location because most of his business comes from "upper middle class and wealthy home owners" and "with all the restoration of very old homes in the area I am in a good location for this business." He elaborates further that "there is a real boom coming, and all the changes that are going on in Providence will make a lot of business for us." Apparently this owner resolved the inflated price problem more rationally than the industrial supplier firm above and seems to have made a much more satisfactory adjustment as a result.

It is worthy of note, however, that after nearly five years since the move, this owner still has moments of regret over the price he received for his building at the old location. This is evident from his remark that "each year that passes I know that I should have received more money (for my place)." And further, when he was asked if he would do anything differently if he had it to do over again he replied, "Yes, I would go to court to get a fairer price for my property."

Further evidence of the role of inflated prices in the selection of a site is found in the report of the owner of a commercial sign painting firm who, prior to displacement, had occupied the same location for more than a quarter century. In this instance, he reports that "the owners of industrial lots and buildings boosted prices when the movement started." This, coupled with the general shortage of industrial land in the city, prompted him to move his business to the suburbs where he could "get more room and where land is cheaper," even though it would place him a further distance from his customers. This businessman would have preferred to remain in the city so as to be nearer his customers, but he reports that "the land is far too expensive." Although he has made a very favorable adjustment at the new location financially, in a newer and bigger building, it does not have the convenience of his former site and he "has to work harder in order to make the same amount of money, and it costs more to operate from here." Even though he is quite satisfied with how he has done at his present site during the two years since the move, he still feels that "the city should build the industrial parks before they move you so you will have a place to go." This is a rather general opinion which is shared by many of the displaced establishments. This owner goes on to say, "the city should make sure that the real estate men don't get you over a barrel." And finally he sums up his reaction to the move thusly: "The inflated prices of land and buildings forced me to go to the suburbs."

The second most frequently mentioned problem in finding a new location was the inability of owners to find a building that was adequate for their needs. This was mentioned by one unit in six. For nearly one-tenth of the relocated businesses, zoning problems were the most serious obstacles faced.[4]

ZONING PROBLEMS

In some instances zoning problems were only an inconvenience, but in a few cases zoning restrictions worked a particular hardship on the displaced business. A rather extreme case is found in the experience of a small manufacturing concern which is owned by a fifty-six-year-old native of Providence who has only an eighth grade education. At the time of displacement, after sixteen years at the same location, he was given a full year in which to move. He claims, however, that he needed much more time to successfully relocate. At any rate, after three months of "looking around," he decided to move to a site which he had found where there was "ample parking and the right sized building." Even though the area was not properly zoned, he moved in his machin-

4 This problem is illustrated by the experience of a retail sales fish dealer who had decided on a new site and proceeded to prepare the building for occupancy. After investing $1,000 in alterations he learned that the home owners in the neighborhood were going to fight his request for a zoning change. He was convinced that this fight would prove to be a futile effort on his part and thus abandoned his plans. He reports that he lost his $1,000.

ery and proceeded to set up for production, on the assumption that he could get a zoning change. It could not be determined if he acted on misinformation, faulty advice, or on a lack of knowledge concerning zoning regulations, but he reports that after one month at this location, he found that he could not get a zoning change. Consequently, even before he got set up for production, he had to pack up again and move to another place. He spent another month "just looking around on my own" for a place and took his present site because "it was all I could get." He proceeded to set up his machinery for production. However, by this time he had lost many of his old customers who had found new suppliers while he was not in production.[5] He is currently doing much less business than while at the old location. As a result he is very dissatisfied and bitter about what has happened to him, as is evident from his remarks that he "was treated rotten," "they ruined me," and "zoning restrictions killed my business." It is obvious that many of his problems regarding zoning could have been avoided with proper forethought, or through an effective relocation service that would have properly advised him of the zoning problem at the first location. At any rate, zoning is perceived as the villain in this case. The business has declined, and he is much worse off now than before displacement. He sums up his views thusly, "the government should force zoning changes so a man can relocate."

A similar opinion is expressed by the young owner of a bakery firm who had also encountered problems of zoning in his attempt to relocate. This case is quite different, however, since after the move the business is much better off than before displacement. This owner has moved to a newer building in a better area that is growing and has experienced a sharp increase in the amount of business. Income has also increased. Nonetheless he feels that "in general, the zoning restrictions will have to be eased if they force you to move. Since they force you out, they should also force a change in zoning and let you locate in an area where you can do business." Comparable views were frequently expressed regarding licenses, particularly by junk yard dealers and the owners of liquor stores. It is generally felt by those affected that ex-

5 He manufactured pens and mechanical pencils largely for commercial firms who used them for advertising.

ceptions to the zoning and license regulations should be made in such cases.

Other problems in finding a new location which were reported, but less frequently, pertained to their inability to find a suitable site either in or near the old neighborhood where they wanted to remain or in an area that was considered suitable for their needs. However, more than one business in four reported that they encountered no single major problem in finding a new location. The ease with which many businesses did find a new location is clearly evident from the data on length of time required to find a new site. One-fifth of the businesses found a site in less than two weeks, and one-third did so within a two months period. However, a substantial number of the establishments did encounter difficulties, for we find that nearly two-fifths of the units required from three to twelve months and one unit in six was unable to find a suitable site within a one-year period. A point worthy of note, nonetheless, is that a substantial majority of the relocated businesses were able to successfully find a new site in less than six months.

METHODS USED TO FIND A NEW SITE

Most of the establishments report that they found the new site without any assistance from outside sources. In response to the question "How did you find this place?" a majority (54 per cent) report that they had found it themselves – and another 10 per cent report that they found it through friends. Only a slightly larger proportion (11.5 per cent) found their present site through real estate agents. It is particularly noteworthy that only about one business in twenty reports finding the present site through the government-sponsored relocation agency, which is the agency that is responsible for relocating both displaced residents and commercial establishments. However, 5 per cent of the units report that this agency had tried to help them by informing them of available property. This help largely took the form of providing the business units with lists of properties on file. However, a substantial majority of the businesses claimed that no one had tried to help them, but rather that relocation was predominantly an individual responsibility.

There is a striking similarity between these findings and those reported in an earlier study of residential displacements in one of the highway projects included in this study.[6] In that study it was found that 14.8 per cent of the displaced residents reported that the Family and Business Relocation Agency had tried to help them, but only 5.7 per cent of the respondents reported that their new residence was actually found through this agency. The comparable percentages for the displaced businesses in this study are 14.6 per cent and 5.3 per cent respectively.

Apparently the low proportion receiving effective help from the Relocation Agency is not peculiar to this area. In commenting on the Boston West End experiences, Gans points out that "previous relocation projects suggest that most people relocate themselves and only a small proportion are relocated by the agency."[7]

The actual role of the relocation service provided by the government is difficult to evaluate in that the assistance given by this agency has been largely limited to providing the displaced business units with a list of available comercial properties which have been registered with them. Thus, in moving to a site, some businessmen may feel that they found the new location on their own even though the particular address had been given to them on the list provided by the agency. Most of the businesses, however, view the addresses provided by the governmental relocation agency as of very limited value. This is evident from the quite typical remark made by the owner of a manufacturing firm that employed fifteen workers. In his opinion, "the Family and Business Relocation Agency only gets the kind of property the real estate people can't sell."

The owner of a bakery shop reports that the Agency tried to help him find a new location, and when asked what type of help they gave he said, "they gave me a list." However, he was not satisfied with the help received because he felt that they "did not take into consideration the needs of my business." A somewhat similar reaction was expressed by the owner of a jewelry firm with

6 Sidney Goldstein and Basil G. Zimmer, *Residential Displacement and Resettlement of the Aged,* Rhode Island Division on Aging, Providence, Rhode Island, 1960.

7 H. J. Gans, *op. cit.,* p. 23.

twenty employees who stated, "the Family and Business Relocation Agency gave us addresses but they didn't have anything that we could use." And a smaller jewelry manufacturer who reported that the state had tried to help them claimed that "they kept sending us lists which we found to be worthless."

Complaints concerning the help received were frequent and ranged from mild criticism to real cynicism. Thus we get the simple observation that "they should give more help in finding a new location" as expressed by a stationery store owner, and the remark of the owner of a service business who stated, "It's a very large and upsetting problem, but you are strictly on your own. There is little or no help to aid you." An auto parts dealer comments, "Relocation didn't do anything but tell me to come down and look at a list." There was also extreme criticism as expressed by a gas station owner who claimed that "the relocation part of the program was a joke." There is also evidence of bitterness, as is illustrated by the comments of the owner of a junk yard who states, "the relocation agency should really find businesses a replacement for their site and not just tell the newspapers how much they are helping businesses when they are not." And another junk dealer, who went out of business following displacement, says, "They (government) said they would find us a new location then forgot about us like a cloudburst and now I'm out of business and my money is gone."

It is abundantly clear that the general reaction to the relocation services provided by the government is distinctively negative; however, in rare instances, as already noted, the displaced businesses did use the relocation agency in finding a new location and in some instances the owners were very satisfied with the help received. This is illustrated by the reaction expressed by the owner of a firm that manufactured costume jewelry who had occupied the same location for nearly twenty years. This business took advantage of the move to go ahead with plans for expansion which could not have been done at the old location. The owner reports that they found their present site through the relocation service. He reports further that he "could have had many places but I wanted a place all on one floor." This site, which the relocation agency found for him, is "not too far from our original site and the building has the amount of space we wanted." Apparently, in his opinion, the agency did a thorough job in his case, for he reports that they "had all the figures for us on square footage, rent, etc." Further evidence of a positive reaction to the relocation service is found in the remarks of the owner of an elevator installation and maintenance firm, who had relocated in the suburbs in a site found through the agency. He reports that "they gave us lists, showed us pictures, and had figures for us." This type of reaction is, however, infrequently reported.

For the most part, little or no help was received from the government in respect to finding a new location. And even in the minority of cases where help was provided, not much positive recognition is accorded the relocation agency by the displaced businesses. Rather the reaction to the relocation service has been predominantly and frequently adamantly negative.

Finding a new location apparently was done quite informally by a majority of the businesses. Much was left to chance, and there seems to have been little rational choice in the selection of a site on the part of many establishments. A common method of locating a site was to "just drive around town" looking for vacant units. When asked how they found the present site, a frequent response was "saw a sign while driving by," "just happened to notice this place," "by riding around," "heard about it from friends or relatives who saw the sign in the window," and other such responses. It seems quite evident from our data that "finding a vacant unit" was a more important dimension in looking for a new location than specific site characteristics which would make the location a particularly advantageous one for the type of business involved.[8] It is also somewhat surprising that in relocation so much of the finding of a new site is through word-of-mouth contacts with friends, relatives or other businessmen.[9] Newspaper ads were reported in only a small minority of the cases.

Methods of finding a new location are somewhat different for

8 This is very similar to the method used in finding a site in which to start a business by a sample of new businesses. In that study, the authors report the largest single group found their locations by noticing a vacant store or building . . . several indicated that they noticed the vacancies while driving in their cars. K. B. Mayer and S. Goldstein, *op. cit.*, p. 45.

9 In establishing new businesses a similar large proportion were told about available vacancies by friends or relatives. *Ibid.*, p. 45.

businesses from renewal areas than for those displaced by the highway program. Businesses in renewal projects were more likely to find a new site informally through friends or other businessmen, whereas businesses in the highway projects were more likely to use the more formal and specialized services of a real estate agency. The greater dependence of renewal businesses on informal contacts probably represents the more primary type of relationships that have developed in these deteriorated areas over many years of business catering to the neighborhood. The differences are also likely due for the most part to the type and size of businesses involved.

There is abundant evidence that, in the displacement process, sufficient time is given for the businesses to move. In response to a question regarding this issue, 86 per cent of the units reported that they had been given ample time to move. Even though only 16 per cent took more than twelve months to find a new site, nearly half of the businesses reported that they had more than this amount of time to vacate the area. There seems to have been no real pressure on the units to move before they had an opportunity to find a suitable location. At any rate, we find very little evidence to suggest that more time is needed in such programs. Although there is opposition to being forced to move, we find few complaints about the amount of time that is given for the move. In response to the question, "How do you feel about the way you were handled?" less than four per cent said that they had not been given enough time.

IMPORTANCE OF SITE CHARACTERISTICS

The relative amount of importance attached to selected site characteristics in seeking a new location is shown in Table 1-3. The amount of space in the building was the site characteristic which was considered very important by the largest proportion of businesses. However, this was followed closely by the amount of emphasis which is placed on accessibility to customers and, to a lesser extent, parking accommodations. Less than one-fifth of the businesses rate any one of these characteristics as not being important in selecting a site. Type of neighborhood, however, is rated

TABLE 1-3

RELATIVE IMPORTANCE OF SELECTED SITE CHARACTERISTICS

Site Characteristics	Total	Very Imp.	Quite Imp.	Not Imp.	No Answer
Space in Building	100.0	54.7	36.2	8.4	.8
Accessibility to Customers	100.0	53.4	25.5	19.9	1.3
Parking Accommodations	100.0	46.7	33.1	19.0	1.3
Type of Neighborhood	100.0	39.2	25.6	34.4	.8
Type of Business in Area	100.0	21.2	26.9	50.7	1.3
Nearness to Bus Line	100.0	15.4	15.0	68.3	1.3

as unimportant by one-third of the businesses. However, two-fifths report that they consider this to be very important. For approximately one-half of the businesses that relocated, type of business in the area is not considered as an important factor in selecting a site. Although this is generally considered to be a significant site characteristic in the literature on location of business, only a minority (21 per cent) of the establishments rate this as very important in their consideration of a site. On the other hand, 51 per cent report it as unimportant. It seems quite evident that small businesses, as represented by these units, are unaware of the positive attractive features of having certain kinds of businesses in close proximity.[10] This is illustrated by the experience of the owner of a fish market whose selection of a site was primarily on the basis of the availability of a building. In looking for a new site he did not consider type of business in the area as an important factor. He feels differently about this now, however, since much of his business volume comes from people drawn in by the type of businesses in the area. He reports that, at the present location, he has more walk-in small sales business because of the advantages of the present site. His business has increased following displacement and even exceeds his expectations. Actually he says that he underestimated the foot traffic in the area because he "had not realized how many people the big mill outlet (across the street)

10 This may be due to the larger proportion of neighborhood businesses that expect only to attract customers from a very small area.

would bring into the area." Also there is a nearby supermarket which also attracts shoppers. Although he had not considered the positive effects of other businesses in the area at the time of his decision to move to the present site, he now appreciates the drawing power of these businesses. He called the interviewer's attention to "the large number of people in the area."

Of particular interest is the lack of importance of being near a bus line in selecting a new site. Nearly seven businesses out of ten report that this is not an important consideration in looking for a location. This, of course, shows the minor role of public transportation in the organizational structure of commercial activities. Clearly these businesses are built predominantly around the automobile as the mode of travel for their customers, if they are drawn from an area that is beyond walking distance, as well as their employees. Whether or not this is a valid assumption, we cannot determine from our data, but our findings make it abundantly clear that only a small minority of the businesses give any attention to bus transportation as an attractive feature of a business site. Rather, emphasis is placed on parking facilities. Although they are well aware of the need to be accessible to their customers and in some cases to be near a supply of labor, they apparently do not view nearness to public transportation as an important factor in this accessibility.

REASONS FOR SELECTING PRESENT SITE

The main reason for selecting the present site is quite different for the units that were displaced from renewal areas and for those displaced by the highway programs. Businesses from renewal areas placed more emphasis on the cost factor, but more particularly such businesses selected the present site because of the proximity to the old location, that is, it is in the same general neighborhood. This is the reason given by 34 per cent of the businesses from renewal areas, but by only 14 per cent of the units displaced by the highway program. No doubt this difference is due in large part to type of area from which the businesses draw their customers. Businesses in renewal areas were more likely to serve predominantly a neighborhood market and wanted to remain as close to the original area as possible. The merit of this judgment may be questionable, in that one also would expect local neighborhood markets to be precipitously reduced by the displacement of residential units. However, the judgment may well have been more rational than it would appear at first glance, for experience has shown that displaced populations tend to relocate in close proximity; thus to remain in the area is to remain close to, at least, a large part of the original neighborhood market.[1] At any rate, one-fifth of all of the displaced units selected the present site because of its proximity to the original location.

The single reason for selecting the present site which is given by the largest proportion of the units is the very general response that they thought "the location would be good for business." This is the reason offered by 24 per cent of the units, but this varies from only 16 per cent of the units in renewal areas to 28 per cent of those displaced by highways. The latter units are more likely to have selected their present site because it was the only thing available or they had already owned the building or land. This reason is given by 18 per cent of the units from highway projects, but by less than 10 per cent of the units from renewal projects. Altogether about half the reasons given for selecting the present site have nothing to do positively with the attractiveness of the location as a place to do business. Rather, the selection seems to have been based on a lack of choice or on some specific reason that had little or nothing to do with the site as a good business location. In short, there is very little evidence to suggest that sound business judgments, based on rational economic considerations, were made in the selection of a new location.[2]

SITE CHARACTERISTICS BEFORE AND AFTER MOVE

When selected site characteristics before and after the move are compared, we find that one-half or more of the businesses

1 The Family and Business Relocation Agency has mapped the displaced population after the move for several projects. These maps show a very high concentration in continguous areas.

2 Strikingly similar findings are reported for new business establishments in selecting a site. K. B. Mayer and S. Goldstein, *op. cit.*

show an improvement in each characteristic after relocation. The amount of space in the building is the particular site characteristic which has the largest proportion reporting an increase. Three units out of five have more space at present than while at the old location. Only a small minority of the businesses moved to smaller quarters, but this varied by type of project from which displaced. Less than one unit in five from renewal areas moved to less space, as compared with one in four displaced by highway projects. Approximately one-seventh of the establishments from both types of projects continue to occupy the same amount of space as prior to the move. A substantial majority of the businesses report that they have all of the space they need or want at the new location, while less than one-fifth of the units report that they do not have enough space.

While approximately half of the businesses moved to a newer building than the one from which they had been displaced, more than one-fourth moved to a building of the same age, and one-fifth moved to an older building. The latter, however, range from 18 per cent of the renewal units to 24 per cent of the highway establishments. An even smaller proportion moved to a building which is in worse condition than the one from which they had been displaced. As expected, the establishments least likely to move into a poorer building were those forced to move from urban renewal areas. A majority of the units moved to a better building than the one from which they had been displaced. The proportion is highest among the businesses displaced from renewal areas. Businesses from highway project areas were much more likely to move into another area of the same general quality as the one from which they had been displaced. One-third of the units report such a move, as compared with less than one-fourth of the renewal project businesses. But the most noteworthy observation, in comparing site characteristics before and after relocation, is the high proportion of businesses from renewal areas (48 per cent) that report moving into an area that is in about the same or worse condition than the one from which they had been displaced. Perhaps such moves reflect the very limited alternatives available or even poor judgment on the part of business owners; however, it may be that these businesses, which are likely quite marginal, depend predominantly on the type of population that lives in areas of decay and deterioration and on the relatively lower rent levels in such areas in order to survive. To the extent that this is the case, and such moves do occur for these reasons, each renewal project falls short of accomplishing its goal, for displacement merely redistributes many of the businesses to other areas of decline. As a result, it hastens the need for rebuilding additional areas. Consequently areas of blight may be extended in the very process of clearing selected areas. For the individual business establishment, such relocations provide only a temporary site which is readily subject to future displacement through expanded renewal activity. Such businesses may successively move to areas that are soon to be cleared, thus adding to the overall costs of renewal. This seems to be a likely consequence of moving into comparable areas. Yet this has been the direction of the move made by nearly half of the businesses from renewal areas. Nonetheless, relocation did improve the site characteristics for a majority of the units.

PARKING FACILITIES

The provision of adequate parking accommodations is one of the perennial problems faced by businesses in urban areas. This is particularly the case in the older densely settled sections of the city. Consequently in seeking a business location, it is not surprising that the parking problem is given high priority. This is one of the site characteristics which shows a marked improvement after relocation. At the old location, only 45 per cent of the businesses had off-street parking, but this increased to 66 per cent after the move. Parking conditions on the street also changed following relocation. While 32 per cent of the establishments reported that street parking, permitted at the old location, was metered, at the new site this decreased to 16 per cent. The proportion reporting non-metered parking increased to 66 per cent at the new location, whereas it had been 52 per cent prior to the move. At both locations, about one unit in six reported that no street parking was or is permitted.

Parking accommodations are evaluated quite differently at the new location than at the old site. When asked if parking facilities were adequate at the former location, only 39 per cent responded affirmatively, but the same query regarding the present site elicited an affirmative response from 71 per cent of the units. From this point of view, the typical new site apparently is a marked improvement over the original location. This is further evident from the responses comparing parking facilities before and after the move. Nearly two-thirds of the business units report that parking facilities are better at the present site. For one-sixth of the units, facilities at the new site are approximately the same as at the old location, and only a minority of the establishments moved to a site where parking accommodations are not at least equal to the facilities at the old location. Thus, in general, the move served to lessen the parking problem for a majority of the business establishments.

TYPE OF BUILDING OCCUPIED AFTER RELOCATION

Finding a suitable building was one of the major problems encountered by businesses in their efforts to relocate. This problem was resolved by nearly one-fourth of the businesses, as is shown in Table 2-3, by constructing their own buildings. New structures, on the average, were about double the size of the existing structures which were occupied. The median size of the buildings which

TABLE 2-3

SIZE OF STRUCTURE OCCUPIED BY NEW AND EXISTING STRUCTURES AND PROPORTION IN EACH SIZE CLASS THAT ARE NEW STRUCTURES

Size of Building (square feet)	New Construction	Existing Structures	New Construction		
			Yes	No	Total
Total	100.0	100.0	23.3	76.7	100.0
Under 500	5.7	21.2	8.3	91.7	100.0
500 – 999	7.5	19.2	11.8	88.2	100.0
1,000 – 4,999	52.9	38.5	31.8	68.2	100.0
5,000 and Over	34.0	21.1	35.3	64.7	100.0
Median	3,675	1,860			

are newly constructed is 3,675 square feet, as compared with only 1,860 square feet for the existing structures that are occupied by the relocated businesses.

The proportion having a building constructed increases markedly by size of building occupied. The major difference is found between buildings under and over 1,000 square feet. The proportion of buildings which were newly constructed range from only 8 per cent of the units with less than 500 square feet to 35 per cent of the units with 5,000 or more square feet. Stated conversely, more than 90 per cent of the businesses moving into very small structures occupied existing buildings, whereas only 65 per cent of those occupying 5,000 or more square feet moved into existing structures. Viewed differently, we find that only 6 per cent of the new structures were buildings that contained less than 500 square feet, but of the existing structures into which businesses relocated, 21 per cent were of this size. And while only 13 per cent of the new construction contained less than 1,000 square feet, more than 40 per cent of the existing structures which were occupied are of this size. At the other extreme, more than one-third of the new structures contain 5,000 square feet or more, as compared with only slightly more than one-fifth of the existing structures. There seems to have been a shortage of larger buildings needed to relocate a substantial proportion of the displaced businesses. But the size of building most in demand, whether new construction or existing structures, contained between 1,000 and 5,000 square feet. In this size class we find 53 per cent of the occupants of newly constructed buildings and 39 per cent of those that moved into existing structures.

Size of structure occupied after relocation varies markedly by type of area served, as is evident from the data presented in Table 3-3. The average size of structure into which the displaced businesses moved is 2,500 square feet, but the median ranges from less than 1,000 square feet for businesses that had served a predominantly neighborhood area to more than 5,000 square feet for those businesses that catered to a non-local market. The close relationship between size of building and area served is further evident from the proportion of establishments in different-sized buildings. Less than seven per cent of the neighborhood-type businesses occupy a structure with 5,000 square feet or more, but this increases to 25 per cent of the businesses that attracted customers from the whole community and to more than half of the units that served a non-local market. This, of course, is partly a function of needs varying by both size and type of business, which will be considered more fully below.

TABLE 3-3

SIZE OF BUILDING OCCUPIED BY TYPE OF AREA SERVED PRIOR TO DISPLACEMENT

Size of Building Occupied (square feet)	Area Served		
	Neighborhood	Community	Other
Total	100.0	100.0	100.0
Under 1,000	50.8	32.3	13.8
1,000 – 4,999	42.6	43.0	33.8
5,000 and Over	6.6	24.7	52.4
Median	982	2,435	5,441

KNOWLEDGE OF SITES

Among the business establishments that moved into an existing structure, nearly three-fourths moved into one that was vacant at the time it was found. It will be recalled that many of these were found in an informal way, largely by just driving or walking around. However, it is apparent that the businesses did seek at least a minimum amount of information on the previous use of the building, for we find that a majority knew how long the building had been vacant and the type of business that had previously occupied the structure. However, it is worthy of note that a substantial minority of the businesses had little or no knowledge of the previous occupancy of the building. More than two-fifths did not know how long the building had been vacant, and one-fourth did not know the type of business that had previously occupied the building. One-third of the owners did not know why the previous occupant had moved out. While one-fifth of the businesses knew that the previous occupant had "gone out of business," most of the units did not inquire to the point of finding out whether or not it was the specific site that contributed to the "failure." This lack of information may well be a crude index of the general lack of relative knowledge on which many small businesses operate.

Further evidence which suggests that many of the small businesses base their decision to relocate on limited knowledge is found in the general lack of consideration given alternate locations, as well as in the failure of most of the units to try to estimate the potential amount of business that the site would likely generate, and how much it would cost to operate their business at the site to be occupied. Two-thirds of the displaced units did not consider any other location than the one presently occupied. In making the decision to move, three-fourths of the businesses did not attempt to estimate the amount of business that they would do, and one-half of the units did not try to estimate operating costs. Yet both of these are obviously crucial if the business is to succeed.

Not all businesses, however, were as indifferent or irrational in selecting a site. Although only one-third of the establishments considered alternative locations before deciding to move to the building presently occupied, we find that the businesses that did so were also more likely to attempt to estimate the amount of business they would do and how much it would cost to operate the business at the present site. These data are shown in Table 4-3. Of

TABLE 4-3

ATTEMPTS TO ESTIMATE AMOUNT OF BUSINESS AND OPERATING COSTS BY CONSIDERATION OF ALTERNATE SITE

Considered Alternate Site	Tried to Estimate:		
	Total	Yes	No
		Amount of Business	
Yes	100.0	33.8	66.2
No	100.0	22.1	77.9
		Operating Costs	
Yes	100.0	65.0	35.0
No	100.0	42.3	57.7

those who considered alternate locations, one-third tried to estimate the amount of business they would do at the present site, and two-thirds estimated operating costs. Among the establishments that had not considered an alternate location, only slightly more than one-fifth tried to estimate amount of business and two-fifths estimated the cost of operations. The relationship between estimating amount of business and cost of operations at the present site is even more striking. Among those who tried to estimate the amount of business they would do at the new location, 92 per cent tried to estimate operating costs, and only 8 per cent did not do so. On the other hand, only one-third of those who did not attempt to estimate the amount of business estimated operating costs, whereas two units out of three did not do so.

DISTANCE MOVED TO NEW LOCATION[3]

The selection of a new site seems to have been influenced significantly by the place of residence of the owner, as is evident from the data presented in Table 5-3. Central city residents were much more likely to relocate in close proximity to the original site than those living in the suburbs. As the distance of the move increases, the proportion of owners living in the city decreases. The pattern is consistent and marked. Of the businesses relocating within a one-tenth-mile radius of the original location (Zone I) three-fourths of the owners live in the city as compared with less than one-fourth of the owners whose businesses moved more than one and one-half miles (Zone IV). That place of residence is a significant variable here is further evident from the changes in distance between home and business following relocation. As the distance of move increases, the proportion of business locations that are closer to place of residence before the move also increases. The change is substantial. Of the units that moved one

3 For purposes of analysis we have classified the moves into four distance zones. Distance moved was measured on a map by plotting the original location and the present location of each establishment and measuring the direct distance between the two points. In Zone I are those businesses that relocated within radius of one-tenth of a mile of the original location. Zone II ranges from one-tenth to one-half mile, while Zone III covers from one-half mile to one and one-half miles, and Zone IV includes all other distances moved. Nearly half of the establishments in the last zone moved more than three miles.

TABLE 5-3

DISTANCE OF MOVE BY PLACE OF RESIDENCE AND CHANGES IN HOME-WORK DISTANCE BEFORE AND AFTER MOVE

Place of Residence and Change in Distance	Distance Moved (Zones)			
	I	II	III	IV
Place of Residence				
Total Per Cent	100.0	100.0	100.0	100.0
Central City	72.5	54.1	37.6	23.8
Suburbs	27.5	45.9	62.4	76.2
Change in Distance				
Total Per Cent	100.0	100.0	100.0	100.0
Closer to Home	7.5	21.6	30.0	61.9
Same Distance	90.0	58.1	25.7	11.9
Further From Home	2.5	20.3	44.3	26.2

and one-half miles or more, the new location is closer to home for more than three-fifths of the owners, while it is further for only 26 per cent. Among the units that remained in close proximity to the original location, that is, within one-half mile, there is no apparent tendency to move in the direction of place of residence. We find that as many moved further from place of residence as moved closer to home. For a substantial majority however, the distance from place of business to place of residence remained unchanged. In general we find that the proportion moving further away from place of residence varies directly with distance moved up to a distance of one-and-one-half miles, but beyond this distance point the proportion moving further from home declines sharply. It seems safe to conclude that the longer moves result largely from a deliberate attempt to decrease the distance to work. The small proportion of moves in the more distant category, where the new site is further from home, is particularly worthy of note. The influence of place of residence in selecting a site will be considered more fully in the chapter on suburbanization.

The distance moved in relocation varies by size of market area served, as is shown in Table 6-3. Businesses that served predominantly a neighborhood market prior to displacement apparently made a deliberate effort to remain near to the old location.

TABLE 6-3

DISTANCE MOVED BY TYPE OF AREA SERVED PRIOR TO DISPLACEMENT

Type of Area Served	Total	Distance Zone				Median (miles)
		I	II	III	IV	
Total	100.0	17.6	32.6	30.8	19.0	0.50
Neighborhood	100.0	34.4	40.6	12.5	12.5	0.25
Community	100.0	14.7	36.4	30.2	18.7	0.49
Region – Other	100.0	6.0	19.4	49.3	25.4	1.00

Less than one-fifth of all the establishments relocated within a radius of one-tenth of a mile of the original location (Zone I), but the proportion doing so ranges from more than one-third of the neighborhood businesses to only 6 per cent of the establishments that served either a regional or larger market area. Three-fourths of the neighborhood-type businesses relocated within a one-half-mile radius (Zones I and II), but the proportion doing so decreases to one-half of the units that served the whole community and to only one-fourth of the businesses that served a more widespread market area. Only a small minority of units moved one and one-half miles or more (Zones III and IV). This ranges from one in eight of the neighborhood-type businesses to one in four of the establishments that served a non-local market. The close relationship between area served and distance moved is clearly evident from the median distance moved. For all establishments that relocated, the median move was .50 miles. However, neighborhood businesses moved only .25 miles, whereas those which attracted customers from the whole community moved .49 miles, and the median distance moved was exactly one mile for those businesses serving a non-local market.

Data on distance of move consistently show that the businesses which are primarily dependent on a small market area relocate close to the original site, that is, their effective choice of a new location is limited in that there is an apparent attempt to remain close to the original general area so as to continue to serve the same population. Part of this may also be due to the way such businessmen find a new site, that is by just driving around an area looking for a vacancy, a "For Rent" or "For Sale" sign or through some other informal means. Such contacts are likely to be highly localized and in an area with which they are familiar. Thus the selection of a specific site may be made with an unawareness of alternative locations. Apparently such businesses have very limited alternatives. However, businesses serving a non-local market seem to have much more freedom of choice since the specific location in relationship to customers is less important and restrictive. Consequently such businesses moved greater distances from the original location.

Small businesses, and particularly those serving a small geographical area, frequently attempted to minimize the consequences of the displacement by relocating in close proximity. However, this had serious repercussions in some cases, as is illustrated by the experience of the owner of a small cafe. When he was forced out of his old location, he moved his business only two blocks from the original site. His expressed reasons for doing so was to stay near his "good old steady beer and wine drinkers." Of his former site he says "that was a wonderful natural location." Things are much different at the new location, however, which seems to have come as a surprise to him. There is every indication that he overlooked what was happening to the area around him. He currently does less business even after five years than he had done prior to the move. This is a result of changes in the composition of the area. Displacements of jewelry firms and rooming houses in the area deprived him of his regular customers. He reports doing less business now because "my carefully built-up trade all moved away." He elaborates further, "there are no rooming houses left to supply me any customers around here anymore." At the old location he had catered almost exclusively to male customers from the surrounding rooming houses and workers in the jewelry plants in the area. However, now that the area has changed, he serves both men and women and no longer draws customers from a neighborhood area. And in place of the "good, dependable, heavy beer and wine drinkers" he served at the old location, he now classifies his customers as being made up predominantly of "lady chasers." In retrospect, he now knows that he was not realistic in his appraisal of this location as a business site. Not only is he doing less business than before, but his rent is higher and he sees no signs of any increase in business in the future. In short, he is very dissatisfied with how things have turned out. He claims the move nearly gave him ulcers. He now has a bad stomach and is about ready to give up and sell out if possible.

The greater the distance moved in relocation, the greater the improvement in the physical conditions of the site. When the present site is compared with the original location as is done in Table 7-3, we find that the proportion of businesses moving into a better area increases continuously by distance of move. Of the units that relocated in Zone I, only 10 per cent occupy sites where the

TABLE 7-3

SELECTED SITE CHARACTERISTICS BY DISTANCE MOVED

Site Characteristics Before and After	Distance Moved (Zones)			
	I	II	III	IV
Total Per Cent	100.0	100.0	100.0	100.0
Condition of Area				
Present Area Better	10.0	40.5	67.1	79.1
Both Areas Same	57.5	39.2	18.6	16.3
Present Area Worse	32.5	20.3	14.3	4.6
Age of Building				
Present Newer	45.0	35.6	60.0	65.1
Both Same Age	30.0	31.6	25.7	20.9
Present Older	25.0	32.8	14.3	13.9
Amount of Space				
More Space Here	55.0	55.4	64.3	74.4
Both Areas Same	17.5	16.2	15.7	11.6
Less Space Here	27.5	28.4	20.0	13.9

conditions of the area are better than at the old location; however, the proportion increases to nearly 80 per cent of the establishments that moved into Zone IV. A substantial majority of the businesses remaining in close proximity to the original site, that is, in Zone I, are in the same general type of area as the one from which they had been displaced, and for nearly one-third of the businesses the new location represents movement to a "worse" area. This decreases to less than 5 per cent among those moving to Zone IV. Those moving greater distances were also more likely to move into a newer and larger building than the one previously occupied. Although a majority of moves were to larger quarters, the proportion of units with more space after relocation ranges from 55 per cent of those remaining within Zone I to 74 per cent of those moving to Zone IV. Distance moved is also related to financial position of the business units. Those moving the greater distances report a higher income than those moving shorter distances. Of the units relocating in Zone I, more than 80 per cent report an income of less than $7,500 per year, but the proportion in this income category declines continuously by distance. In Zone IV, less than 30 per cent of the establishments are in this income category. These data are shown in Table 8-3. Nearly half (48 per

TABLE 8-3

DISTANCE MOVED BY PRESENT INCOME

Present Income	Distance Moved (Zones)			
	I	II	III	IV
Total Per Cent	100.0	100.0	100.0	100.0
Under $7,500	80.8	66.2	43.9	29.6
$ 7,500 – $9,999	7.7	12.3	31.6	22.2
$10,000 and Over	11.5	21.5	24.5	48.2

cent) of the units moving into Zone IV report an income of more than $10,000, as compared with only 12 per cent of those relocating within Zone I.

It is obvious from these data that the selection of a site for relocation was not a random choice. The present discussion suggests more rational decisions than our earlier data indicated. Specific market needs and ability to pay seem to have been major factors of influence. Low-income neighborhood-type businesses were most likely to remain near the original location. This may have been due to lack of knowledge of alternative sites, but it seems more likely to have been a deliberate choice. Longer moves were made by those with greater ability to pay and less dependence on a localized market. Thus the needs in relocation vary widely by the characteristics of the businesses involved, and the businesses, at least in part, respond accordingly.

COST OF THE MOVE

One of the important factors for the individual business unit in the displacement-relocation process is the cost of the move. The problem of concern is not only the absolute cost but the relative cost. Thus attention is focused on the cost of the move in relation to a number of selected sub-categories. The costs of the move as well as compensation by type of project are shown in Table 9-3.

The median cost of moving for all businesses was slightly more than $1,000.[4] The median cost varies only slightly by type of project. Businesses displaced by renewal projects paid approximately $100 more than those that had to relocate from highway project areas. However, in this case the median is somewhat deceptive as an average. An inspection of the distribution of costs shows that the businesses displaced by the highway have a much larger proportion in the highest cost category. Less than one-sixth of the urban renewal units report moving costs in excess of $3,000 as compared with one-third of the establishments from highway project areas. The modal cost for renewal projects is between $1,000 and $3,000 but is more than $3,000 for the businesses displaced by highway projects. These differences are due to differences in size and type of business. The costs of the move and the differentials by type of project take on added significance when it is re-

4 The average payment made for non-residential moves during the 1958-59 fiscal year in urban renewal projects throughout the country was $1,041.55. *Law and Contemporary Problems*, p. 24.

TABLE 9-3

COST OF MOVE AND COMPENSATION FOR COSTS BY TYPE OF PROJECT

Cost and Compensation	Total	Type of Project	
		Renewal	Highway
Cost of Move	100.0	100.0	100.0
Under $ 300	23.3	25.3	22.5
$ 300 – $ 999	20.7	16.9	22.5
$1,000 – $2,999	17.2	29.6	11.5
$3,000 and Over	27.3	15.5	32.6
No Data	11.5	12.7	10.9
Median Costs*	$1,026	$1,095	$985
Compensation for Costs	100.0	100.0	100.0
None	73.6	35.2	91.0
Some	10.6	15.5	8.3
All	14.5	46.5	.....
No Data	1.3	2.8	.7

*Based on more detailed breakdown.

called that in general no provisions have been made to cover the cost of moving from highway construction project areas. That this is important is clear when we note the proportion of costs covered by type of project.

In renewal projects, provisions for the cost of the move have been made, but frequently the amount paid by the government is insufficient to cover the full costs. At least this is suggested by our data. For nearly three-fourths of all of the relocated businesses, the cost of the move was the full responsibility of the individual establishment. This ranges, however, from only one-third of the businesses displaced by renewal projects to more than nine-tenths of the businesses in highway projects. On the other hand, nearly half of the businesses in renewal projects were fully compensated, whereas none of those in highway projects had all of the costs covered. It is obvious that a financial burden has been placed on many businesses in both types of projects, but the full impact of the burden was faced by those units displaced by the highway program.

That one-third of the businesses in renewal areas were not compensated, at least in part, for the cost of the move may seem high since such costs should have been covered under the provisions of the urban renewal program. However, compensation is not automatic; rather, it is only permissive. Accordingly, there are certain requirements which must be met in order to qualify for having the costs covered. Failure to receive compensation within the statutory limits may result from technically not meeting the requirements. For example, this could result from moving out of the area too soon.[5] If a business establishment leaves the area before the project has been officially condemned, the costs of the move are not covered. In respect to this, the timing and delays in carrying out projects, as well as poor communication between the redevelopment-relocation agency and the displaced businesses, may cause establishments not to qualify for reimbursement. We find, for example, that some businesses wanted to get out of an area that was to be torn down as soon as possible so that they could get settled at a new location and not have to try to do business in an area during the transition period when there are high vacancy rates. Accordingly many businesses flee the area as soon as they learn that it is to become a project area, so as not to be caught in the area during its rapid decline. This is a difficult problem since movement out in the early stages can hasten the decline of the area, to the detriment of the other businesses and owners of buildings that attempt to remain until the area has been formally condemned. This they must do not only to get the cost of the move covered in renewal areas, but the price received for the building is likely to be higher if it is occupied at the time of appraisal. Holding businesses in the area up to a given point can help to

5 Daniel Chill, "Business Relocation: A Moving Problem," Divisional paper, Yale Law School, New Haven, March, 1960. The paper cites examples for Providence where the firms have lost their claim eligibility by moving too soon or by filing relocation payment claims too late or not at all. This is further substantiated by a study in Hartford, Connecticut, reported in: William Kinnard and Zenon Malinowski, *The Impact of Dislocation from Urban Renewal Areas on Small Business,* University of Connecticut, Storrs, June, 1960.

maintain the original vitality of the area to the benefit of all businesses. Also it is likely to minimize the business declines of the units remaining in the area. In recognition of this, the urban renewal program will not cover the costs of the move unless the move is made after a specified stage in the project plan. The individual businessman, if he proceeds rationally, must choose between having the cost of the move covered, at least in part, and the advantages of moving early. It seems many businesses decide to move early and thus forfeit the right to payment for moving costs.

One advantage of moving early is that the number of available sites is likely to be greater than at a later date when the other displaced businesses are also competing for a new location. Moving early provides the further advantage of being able to find a new location before the pressure of other businesses seeking a site causes rents or sale prices to rise. A common complaint, as noted earlier, is that when an area is cleared and all of the units have to find new locations, landlords and building owners "push up their prices." Consequently there is fear that the higher prices placed on available sites due to this competition may more than absorb any compensation a business might receive for the cost of the move. Hence many establishments move early.

Businesses may not be compensated if they file for claims too late or if they do not file a claim at all. The latter could easily occur due to ignorance, confusion, or a lack of understanding of the proper procedure to follow. In some cases, businesses may not know that they have a right to be compensated for the cost of the move if they have not been effectively informed by one of the governmental agencies involved. Because of the large amount of condemnation that has been going on in the community for highway construction projects, where no compensation for the cost of the move is made, the displacees from nearby renewal areas may well think that the procedure is the same, and thus do not attempt to get compensation for the move on the assumption that none is available. In both types of projects, the same agency is responsible for relocation and in many instances renewal and highway projects have been in immediately contiguous areas. For example, in one area included in this study, one side of the street was part of a renewal project and the other side a highway project. One would expect a great deal of confusion among displacees because of the differences in procedures and policies of the urban renewal and the highway programs regarding relocation. To the business establishment involved, the primary concern is with displacement and how it is going to affect the business. It is likely in this highly emotional atmosphere that many businessmen are not fully aware of the "type of project" that causes them to be forced out of an area. And since neighboring businesses being displaced at the same time do not receive any compensation for the move, they may have little reason to even suspect that they would be treated any differently. Consequently they may not file a claim for reimbursement.

The cost of the move varies by both type and size of business. These data are shown in Table 10-3. The median costs range from less than $600 for service establishments to more than $2,700 for jewelry units. More than two-fifths of the jewelry firms and more than one-third of the manufacturing, construction, and wholesale establishments report spending more than $3,000 in moving. Non-food-related retail units also have a large proportion (30 per cent) in this cost category, whereas food-related retail and service establishments are disproportionately concentrated in the two lowest cost categories. Three businesses out of five among the food-related retail and service units report a cost of less than $1,000, but for all other business types, less than two-fifths of the establishments are at this cost level.

The relationship between cost of move and size of business is even more marked. The median costs range from less than $300 for units with no employees to more than $3,000 for units employing ten or more workers. The proportion of units that spent less than $300 for the move ranges from a high of 44 per cent among the businesses with no employees to a low of 6 per cent among those with ten or more workers. Expenditures of $3,000 or more are reported by only 3 per cent of the smallest units but by 55 per cent of the largest units. The modal costs for businesses with less than three employees were less than $300, but for establishments with ten or more workers the modal costs were $3,000 and over.

Median costs of the move vary directly by size. For businesses with no employees, the median moving costs are less than $300, but this increases to nearly $500 for establishments with one or

TABLE 10-3

COST OF MOVE BY TYPE AND SIZE OF BUSINESS

Cost of Move	Type of Business				
	Food – Related Retail	Other Retail	Jewelry	Service	Other
Total Per Cent	100.0	100.0	100.0	100.0	100.0
Under $ 300	28.2	19.3	16.3	34.2	22.7
$ 300 – $ 999	30.8	19.3	16.3	26.3	13.6
$1,000 – $2,999	25.6	15.8	14.3	13.2	18.2
$3,000 and Over	7.7	29.8	42.9	15.8	34.1
No Data	7.7	15.8	10.2	10.5	11.4
Median[a]	$ 708	$1,444	$2,714	$ 580	$1,875
	Size of Business				
	None	1-2	3-9	10 +	Total
Total Per Cent	100.0	100.0	100.0	100.0	100.0
Under $ 300	43.8	37.1	16.7	5.5	23.3
$ 300 – $ 999	25.0	29.0	17.9	12.7	20.7
$1,000 – $2,999	12.5	17.7	17.9	18.2	17.2
$3,000 and Over	3.1	6.5	34.6	54.5	27.3
No Data	15.6	9.7	12.8	9.1	11.5
Median[a]	$ 289	$ 494	$2,000	$4,428[b]	$1,026

[a]Computed by excluding no data category.

[b]More detailed data used than shown here.

two workers. Median costs increase to $2,000 for units employing from three to nine workers and to more than $3,000 for businesses with ten or more employees. That the actual cost of the move would increase by size of establishment is to be expected. But the question of concern is how the costs of the move vary by the ability of the units to absorb such costs. Thus attention is now focused on selected subgroups in an attempt to answer this question.

One rather crude index of the relative cost of the move is the per-employee costs. The relative costs for selected subgroups can be expressed by the ratio of the median costs of the move to median monthly sales prior to dislocation. These data are shown in Table 11-3 by type of business. It is readily apparent that service

TABLE 11-3

COST OF MOVE BY TYPE OF BUSINESS AND AREA SERVED

Type of Business	Median Cost of Move	Per Employee Costs	Ratio to Lowest Costs	Cost as % of Median Sales (Monthly) Old Loc.	Ratio to Lowest Per Cent
Food – Related Retail	$ 708	$295	151	29.8	216
Other Retail	1,444	253	130	13.8	100
Jewelry	2,714	377	193	43.4	314
Service	580	446	229	71.8	520
Other	1,875	195	100	14.3	104

units are faced with a much heavier burden than any other type of business, even though these units show the lowest actual median cost figures. The per-employee costs among service establishments represent a burden which is one-fifth larger than that reported by jewelry establishments. The latter rank second highest in per-employee costs and rank first in median costs per unit. The lowest per-employee costs are found among the businesses in the "other" category which is made up of manufacturing, wholesale, and construction units. Their per-employee costs are less than half the costs reported by service establishments.

When costs of the move are expressed as a per cent of monthly sales, service units and jewelry firms continue to show the largest relative burden. Service units exceed by more than five-fold the lowest cost ratio, which is reported by non-food-related retail units. Jewelry firms exceed the lowest ratio by more than three-fold. Thus, according to both indices, service units are faced with the biggest relative burden. They are in turn followed by jewelry establishments. On the other hand, the relative burden is least for non-food-related retail and manufacturing, wholesale, and construction establishments. The range of differences by type of business is larger when reported monthly sales data are used as a basis for computing relative costs than when per employee costs are used. At any rate, both indices indicate that the relative burden of the cost of the move varies significantly by type of business.

The relative cost of the move is also found to vary markedly by size of area served as well as size of business. These data are shown in Table 12-3. The cost of the move is found to be much more of a burden for neighborhood-type businesses and very small businesses than for the larger establishments and those businesses serving a larger market area. Even though the median cost of moving neighborhood businesses is only $625, this is equal to nearly one-third of the median monthly sales while at the old location and nearly half (47 per cent) of monthly sales at the new location. However, among businesses that served a more widespread market area, the ratio of the cost of move to monthly sales at both locations ranges between 21 per cent and 25 per cent. Thus when costs of the move are expressed as a ratio of monthly

TABLE 12-3

MEDIAN COST OF MOVE AS PER CENT OF MEDIAN MONTHLY SALES BY AREA SERVED AND SIZE OF BUSINESS

Area Served and Size of Business	Median Cost of Move	Cost as a Ratio of Median Monthly Sales	
		Before	After
Area Served			
Neighborhood	$ 625	31.3	46.9
Community	806	23.4	20.7
Other	3,167	22.5	24.6
Size of Business			
Small	300	34.8	40.6
Medium	965	20.8	20.9
Large	3,820	17.0	18.0

sales prior to displacement, neighborhood businesses are faced with a relative burden which exceeds that of other businesses by approximately 40 per cent. However, when costs are related to sales after the move, the burden faced by neighborhood businesses exceeds that of businesses serving larger areas by at least two-fold. This, of course, results from the sharp decline in sales following relocation among neighborhood-type businesses.

Similar marked and consistent differences are found by size of business. While the median cost of the move of the smallest establishment is only $300, this absorbs more than one-third of reported median monthly sales at the old location and two-fifths of the sales at the new site. Among medium-size establishments, the cost of the move is reported to be more than three times the cost of the smaller units, but it amounts to only 20 per cent of median sales reported by businesses in this size class at both locations. Thus the relative burden is only slightly more than half the burden placed on the smaller establishments. The largest units report a relative cost which is nearly 20 per cent less than that found for medium-sized units and less than half the burden placed on the smallest businesses. Thus while the absolute costs of relocation vary directly by size of business, the relative burden is inversely related to size. In short, it is the smaller establishments, service units, and those businesses that serve predominantly a neighborhood-type market that face the biggest burden as far as the cost of the move is concerned. Jewelry firms also carry a disproportionately heavy burden. This is due in large part to the heavy equipment used in this industry. For example, heavy dipping vats were costly to move. Some were so heavy that they had to be abandoned. In addition to this, there was a high loss rate due to cracking in the moving process.

It will be recalled that a substantial majority of the businesses did not receive any compensation for the cost of the move; thus attention is now focused on the reaction to the way they had been treated in the displacement-relocation process. When the relocated businesses were asked if they had been treated fairly by the government as far as the cost of the move was concerned, only two-fifths of the establishments answered affirmatively. Conversely, a majority of the businesses reported that they had not been treated fairly. However, the reaction to this question varies significantly and consistently by a number of sub-categories. Since we have already observed that compensation for the cost of the move varies by type of project, it is to be expected that the reaction to how they were treated would also differ by the type of project that caused the displacement. That this is the case is evident from the date presented in Table 13-3.

Two-thirds of the establishments from renewal projects report that they had been treated fairly, but the proportion declines to less than one-third among the businesses displaced by highway projects. This difference is unquestionably due to the different governmental policies that apply in the two types of projects regarding compensation for the costs of relocation. It will be recalled that only one-third of the units that moved from renewal areas were not compensated, in part at least, for the cost of the move, whereas this was the case with more than 90 per cent dis-

TABLE 13-3

TREATED FAIRLY BY GOVERNMENT BY TYPE OF PROJECT, COMPENSATION FOR COSTS OF MOVE AND COST OF MOVE

Selected Variables	Treated Fairly		
	Total	Yes	No
Total	100.0	42.9	57.1
Type of Project			
Renewal	100.0	65.7	34.3
Highway	100.0	32.3	67.7
Compensation for Costs			
None	100.0	32.5	67.5
Some	100.0	36.0	64.0
All	100.0	100.0	...
Cost of Move			
Under $ 200	100.0	73.7	26.3
$ 200 – $ 499	100.0	50.0	50.0
$ 500 – $2,999	100.0	39.4	60.6
$3,000 and Over	100.0	16.5	83.5

placed by highway projects. In the middle panel of Table 13-3, we find that less than one-third of the units that did not receive any compensation for the cost of the move report that they had been treated fairly, whereas all of those who had the costs fully covered respond thusly. A majority of the businesses that felt that they had not been treated fairly took the position, which seems reasonable, that since the government had forced them to vacate their site they should have been fully compensated for the cost of the move. Over and over again businessmen stated that "they forced me to move – they should pay the cost."

The proportion of businesses reporting that they had been treated fairly varies inversely with the absolute cost of the move. Thus among businesses where the cost of the move was less than $200, nearly three units out of four report that they had been treated fairly. However, in the next cost category only one-half of the units report fair treatment. The proportion continues to decline and reaches a low point in the highest cost category where more than four businesses out of five report that they had not been treated fairly. In a separate analysis, it was found that the businesses in this cost category had the largest proportion of units were none of the costs was covered. More than eight units out of ten in this cost category had to bear the full burden of the cost of the move. These businesses are predominantly jewelry manufacturing firms displaced by the highway program. Thus the unit costs of the move are high, and there are no provisions for covering moving costs.

That one-third of the businesses in highway projects should report that they had been treated fairly seems to be logically inconsistent, since there were no legal provisions for covering the costs of the move. Thus this leads us to ask under what conditions would owners of businesses report that they had been treated fairly as far as the cost of the move is concerned, when it is known that under the existing legislative provisions no compensation could have been received. A reading of the case materials suggests that the high proportion satisfied may be due in large part to owners who felt that the cost of the move had been covered indirectly through the price received for the building, even though this was not reported as covering the cost of the move as such. It seems to the writer that this is likely to be the case, particularly

TABLE 14-3

TREATED FAIRLY REGARDING COST OF MOVE BY TENURE AND SIZE OF BUSINESS PRIOR TO DISPLACEMENT

Tenure and Size of Business	Total	Treated Fairly	
		Yes	No
Own			
Less Than 3 Workers	100.0	55.0	45.0
3 to 9	100.0	52.6	47.4
10 and Over	100.0	38.9	61.1
Rent			
Less Than 3 Workers	100.0	51.2	48.8
3 to 9	100.0	36.2	63.8
10 and Over	100.0	21.7	78.3

among the larger units where the owners would be in a more favorable position to negotiate with the government for a better price.[6] The data presented in Table 14-3 provide considerable support for this interpretation. Among the establishments that employ three or more workers, there is a marked difference by tenure in the proportion who report that they had been treated fairly as far as the cost of the move is concerned. Among establishments with three to nine employees, more than half of the owners but only one-third of the renters respond thusly. There is a precipitous decline in the proportion of such responses among the larger units, but the tenure difference persists and is even larger. Among owners of businesses with ten or more employees and owning the building occupied, favorable or affirmative responses are given by two-fifths of the units, but among renters this declines

6 Larger units seemed to have had some advantage in settling on a price to be received for their building. At least larger establishments were more likely to report that they received a fair price. Among establishments with ten or more workers, 86 per cent in renewal areas and 73 per cent in highway project areas report that they received a fair price for their building. However, among smaller units the proportions decline to 62 per cent and 50 per cent respectively.

to only one-fifth. It is particularly noteworthy that, among the smaller establishments, a larger proportion report being treated fairly, but no differences are found by tenure status. Approximately half of the businesses in this size class in both tenure categories report that they had been treated fairly. Although the proportion declines by size and is particularly low among the larger units, the tenure difference among the larger units is worthy of note.

Further evidence that owners had a slight advantage in relocation is provided by the differences in compensation for the cost of the move in highway projects by tenure status. These data are shown in Table 15-3. Even though the law technically does not

TABLE 15-3

COMPENSATION FOR MOVE BY TYPE OF PROJECT BY TENURE PRIOR TO DISPLACEMENT

Compensation For Move	Renewal		Highway	
	Own	Rent	Own	Rent
Total	100.0	100.0	100.0	100.0
None	39.3	34.1	81.4	95.5
Some	7.1	22.0	18.6	4.5
All	53.6	43.9	.....	.....

make any provision for covering any part of the cost of the move, we find that nearly one-fifth of the owners report that they received some compensation, whereas among renters the proportion declines to less than 5 per cent. Thus owners were four times as likely as renters to report that they received at least some compensation for the cost of the move. However, in renewal areas, where provisions are made for covering the cost of the move, there is no such tenure difference in the proportion that did not receive any compensation. But it is to be noted that, even in renewal projects, owners were more likely to report full coverage of the cost by the government, and renters to report only partial coverage. How the owners gained this advantage in both types of proj-

TABLE 16-3

RECEIVED FAIR PRICE FOR BUILDING BY TREATED FAIRLY REGARDING COST OF MOVE BY TYPE OF PROJECT

Received Fair Price and Type of Project	Total	Treated Fairly	
		Yes	No
Renewal Project			
Received Fair Price			
Yes	100.0	78.9	21.1
No	100.0	50.0	50.0
Highway Project			
Received Fair Price			
Yes	100.0	45.8	54.2
No	100.0	20.0	80.0

ects is not clear, but these findings lead us to suspect that it may have been obtained through negotiations for the price to be received for the building, that is, owners may have received "a little extra" to help defray some of the cost of the move.[7] This we can test only indirectly and crudely by relating the responses to the question of whether the owners received a fair price for their building and whether they were treated fairly as far as the cost of the move is concerned. It is readily apparent from the data in Table 16-3 that those who report having received a fair price for their building are the owners most likely to report having been treated fairly as far as the cost of the move is concerned.

The same pattern of relationship is found within each type of project, but the variations are larger and more marked among businesses displaced by highway projects where no direct compensations were made for the costs of the move. It is the businesses from renewal areas that report having received a fair price

7 The lower proportion treated fairly among the larger renters is likely due in large part to the legislative upper limits that are established by the government in urban renewal projects. It is among these units that the cost of the move is likely to exceed the upper limits. Again it is suggested that owners may get around some of this through individual negotiations for the price to be received for their building, but no such opportunity is available to tenants.

for their building that have the highest proportion feeling that they have been treated fairly in regards to the cost of the move. There are perhaps two reasons for this. On the one hand, provisions are made in urban renewal projects to cover the costs of the move up to a maximum.[8] Many of the establishments would have been fully compensated within these limits. On the other hand, where moving costs exceeded this maximum, the owner of a building may have been able to recover part of this cost through the price received for his property. Perhaps this is part of the meaning of "fair price" as reported by the owners. At any rate, if the owner did not feel that he had received a fair price for his building, the proportion reporting fair treatment as far as the cost of the move is concerned declines to only 50 per cent as compared to 79 per cent among those who received a fair price for their building. The smallest proportion reporting fair treatment (20 per cent) is found among businesses in highway projects that did not receive what they perceived to be a fair price for their building. However, among the businesses displaced by the highway which received a fair price for their building, nearly half (46 per cent) report that they had been treated fairly. This is a particularly high proportion of favorable responses when there was no direct compensation to help defray the cost of the move. That nearly half of the businesses would report "fair treatment" when the whole burden technically had to be absorbed by the individual business suggests that some indirect help must have been received. Although the evidence is fragmentary at best, it seems to indicate that part of the cost of the move was covered through some adjustment in the price received for the building. Possible adjustments of this type would place the displaced property owners in a more fa-

8 The maximum paid has changed frequently during recent years. In 1956 Congress amended the Housing Act of 1949 to provide reimbursement in each case up to $2,000. In 1957 this was raised to $2,500 and two years later to $3,000. A new provision of the 1961 National Housing Act permitted the federal government to pay all moving costs incurred by a business in relocating from a redevelopment project area. However, a more recent change is outlined in Local Public Agency letter 246 issued August 9, 1962, which became effective October 2, 1962, and is the current practice. This provides for a maximum coverage of $25,000 for moving costs. Information provided by Melvin Feldman, Research Director, Providence Redevelopment Agency.

vorable position than renters.[9] Perhaps it would be difficult to argue with the intent of this practice in that it accomplishes through administration what should be done through legislation. However, it readily lends itself to abuses. Also it does not provide any method of compensation for renters. Consequently renters are likely to carry a disproportionate burden and thus, with justification, be less likely to feel that they have been treated fairly.

Some of the problems faced by owners and renters alike are illustrated by the comments of a jewelry manufacturer who owned the building occupied prior to displacement and sub-let to other occupants. In his own case, he reports that the move cost $24,000 of which only half was covered by the government.[10] In another context, he claims that "due to the move I lost $19,000 the first year I was here but I'm not kicking." The apparent reason for this is that, in his opinion, "the highways were the worst thing about the city," so he felt that there wasn't anything wrong with forcing businesses to move to make way for new highways, even though this placed a burden on the displaced businesses. However, he was very disturbed about how his former tenants had been treated when they were forced to move. He states that "at our old location we had good dependable tenants," but "some of our tenants were not treated as they should have been." In his opinion "the tenants should have been given more help." He comments further, "I hope the results of this survey go to the government people and they will realize how costly it was to the people who cooperated as we did."

Further evidence of general criticism regarding displacement is summed up in the remarks of the owner of one of the larger manufacturing concerns who had occupied rented quarters at the old location. He reports that "no one was treated fairly and everyone kicked about the lack of payment of moving costs," and he elab-

9 One owner claimed that he was offered $111,000 for his property; however, through threats of a court fight and proper contacts he was able to settle for $124,500 plus a full year of rent-free occupancy before he would have to vacate his site.

10 How this was done is not specified. Perhaps it was included as a "little extra" in the nearly $100,000 which he received for his building, which he considered to be a fair price.

orates thusly, "No one can understand the way business people were put out on the limb and forced to pay their relocation costs with no help from the government."

Another tenant, who owned a jewelry manufacturing firm that was displaced by a highway project, also reports that he was not treated fairly as far as the cost of the move was concerned. According to his figures, the move cost him $9,000 of which none was covered by the government. His reaction to this after five years at the new location is summed up thusly, "At the time I saw only my side of it; however, I've cooled down,[1] but it is still a mystery to me why the government couldn't pay our moving costs."

A used-car dealer was somewhat more critical in a general sense. The move had cost him $2,000, and due to lack of reserves he had to borrow funds to cover the costs. Things have gone very well at the new site, as is evident from his remark, "this corner has been a lucky break for me," but he still resents the way he was treated. Regarding this he states, "The government has plenty of money for foolish things like foreign aid, why can't they spend some on us Americans." A jewelry firm owner expressed a similar opinion thusly, "the government spends billions foolishly but can't help move heavy equipment."

A gas station owner reports that "they have a poor set-up for helping businesses relocate"; however, the only thing that he condemns is "the fact that we had to move and pay all the expenses out of our own pockets. This is not fair." In another context, this same respondent states, "the only kick most of us had was shouldering the whole cost of moving ourselves." In all other respects, "they treated us with kid gloves. They were wonderful to me." Further support to indicate the owners received preferential treatment is found in the experience reported by the owner of a manufacturing firm, displaced by a highway project, who claims that he was not compensated for the move which cost him $2,000. But he reports, "They said moving costs were figured into the price given for our building, but it wasn't enough." Although this owner was not satisfied with the settlement regarding the price for his build-

1 Perhaps the fact that his sales have nearly doubled at the new location has tempered his reaction to the move.

ing and the cost of the move, his company nonetheless accepted what was offered because, "we couldn't wait to fight them in court like we should have."

The owner of a smaller jewelry firm also reports that he had not been compensated for the cost of the move; however, he goes on to say, "but we were given a good price for our building." This same type of response is given by the owner of an electric appliance establishment who reports that the move cost him $5,000 and that none of this was covered by the state; however, he feels that "the price received for the building should about cover the cost of the move." Another owner of a jewelry manufacturing firm was, at first, satisfied with how he had been treated but, after hearing how other owners of property had made out, changed his mind. Because of the particular manufacturing process in which his firm was engaged, he was faced with unusual moving problems in that his heavy dipping vats were costly to move. Since some were too heavy, they had to be abandoned, in addition to the one-third loss due to cracking in the moving process. All in all the move cost the company approximately $5,000. None of this cost was covered since he was in a highway project area. Yet when asked about the cost of the move, this owner reports that he had been treated fairly. In commenting on this, he said, "They say it (the cost of the move) was contained in the price we received for our building." Later in the interview, however, it was apparent from his remarks that he was uncertain as to how he felt about the way he had been handled, for he says, "I now wonder when I hear how much better other building owners did than we did." He elaborates this point further by saying that if he had it to do over again he would "fight for a higher appraisal by the three men from the state." This owner complains that "favoritism has been shown to people with connections in the state house."

Evidence of dissatisfaction is also apparent in the reactions of the owner of a small manufacturing establishment who reports that the move cost his firm about $4,000. He feels that about one-fifth of this had been covered by the government. He explains this thusly, "we were paid in the built-in clause of a supposedly high price for our building but it was not enough." Consequently he feels, as many others do, that he should have gone to court for a more decent appraisal of his old property.

It is apparent from these selected, but not atypical, examples that owners were at least, in part, given some compensation to help cover the cost of the move through the price received for their buildings. However, in many cases this was not considered adequate since the owners were not satisfied with the price received. Owners, with few exceptions, were quite unaware that as a result of this practice they had advantages not enjoyed by tenants. The latter, however, claimed that property owners received preferential treatment. This is illustrated by the comments of a tenant owner of a machine tool sales firm who reports that he was treated fairly as far as the cost of the move was concerned. Although he was not fully compensated for the move, he sums up his reaction thusly, "As far as they could go, they went, but the law wasn't too generous." But his resentment regarding the advantages of owners is evident from his remark that "some owners were overpaid" and his further comment that "politics should be kept out of the appraising end of things."

The owner of a beer garden was much more emotional in his appraisal of the way renters were treated. He states, "Tenants get robbed. The owners of buildings get a much better deal but still it isn't very good." The owner of a firm that prints and sells business forms expresses a similar opinion. The move had cost him approximately $6,000, and none of the costs had been covered. He did not feel that he had been treated fairly. This is evident from his comment that "I feel the way all tenants in this thing feel; we got a rotten deal as far as moving costs go, and the government let us down." Although he does not explicitly state that the owners were treated differently, this is implied by his specific reference to tenants as a separate group. Further evidence of the way renters feel about how they were treated, as far as the cost of the move is concerned, is found in the comments of the owner of a machine shop who stated "they paid owners of land very well, we should have gotten the same as renters." This statement takes on added significance when it is noted that the owner of this business does not in any way regret the move. On the contrary, he wanted to move so that he could expand his business, which was not possible at the old location. This he was able to do successfully at the new site. He now carries a fuller line of products and has more customers than prior to displacement. Also, the number of employees has increased from two to four workers. Nonetheless, he feels that the renters were discriminated against in the relocation process. A jewelry manufacturer also comments, "The government should move us and give us the same considerations as building owners." A similar reaction is expressed by the owner of an industrial woodworking establishment who asks, "Why are the people who rent not treated the same as the owners of those old buildings?" His reaction to the whole process is succinctly stated, "It's brutal." He elaborates further, "The state or city should help us financially (the little guys who can't absorb this relocation shock)." A cabinet maker states the problem of the renter thusly, "all tenants should at least have moving expenses paid."

The view of the renters, as far as any compensation in the displacement process is concerned, is cynically summed up by the reaction expressed by a forty-six-year-old gas station operator who had occupied the same location for fifteen years. He says, "It's not right. Not only the landlords but the businessmen should be paid for his business. When you work eighteen years and have it taken away without getting paid for it – that's not right." He had rented at the old location but at the new site he reports that he owns the building. This change in tenure he explains thusly, "I bought this building so the next time I get moved I could make as much as the landlords did." The concern of renters, in particular, over the issue of the cost of the move is further evident from the responses to the general question asking for suggestions as to what the government should do when businesses are forced to move out of a condemned area. Nearly one-third of the renters (32 per cent) suggested that the government pay moving and set-up costs. However, this same response was given by only 7 per cent of the owners. Apparently this is a major issue only for the former.

CHANGES IN TENURE, RENTALS, AND SALES FOLLOWING RELOCATION

The proportion of businesses owning the building occupied increased slightly with the move. Prior to displacement, 32 per cent were owners but this increased to 38 per cent after relocation. Even though there were considerable changes in tenure as a result of the move, a substantial majority had the same tenure at both locations. Three businesses out of four continued either to own or rent as they had done prior to displacement. Of the total number of relocated businesses, about one in four owned both before and after the move, while slightly more than half of the establishments occupied rented quarters at both locations. Less than 10 per cent of the units moved from an owner-occupied structure to a rental, and for 15 per cent of the relocated units, tenure changed from rent to own. Thus approximately one-fourth of the businesses changed tenure status with the move. Viewed from a different perspective, we note that while 26 per cent of those who owned prior to displacement moved to rented quarters, the proportion of renters who moved to own was 21 per cent. However, the actual number of businesses that moved from own to rent (19 businesses) was less than two-thirds the number (33 businesses) that moved from rent to own. The net result was a small increase following the move in the proportion who owned the building they occupied.

Since displaced businesses were predominantly tenants both before and after relocation, an analysis of rentals at both locations will serve as a crude index of the relative costs of doing business for a majority of the establishments at the new site. Rentals before and after the move by type of project are shown in Table 17-3. It is abundantly evident that, in the aggregate, rentals were higher

TABLE 17-3

MONTHLY RENT BEFORE AND AFTER MOVE
BY TYPE OF PROJECT

Rental	Total		Renewal		Highway	
	Before	After	Before	After	Before	After
Total	100.0	100.0	100.0	100.0	100.0	100.0
Under $ 50	29.7	20.3	47.2	27.3	22.8	17.6
$ 50 – $ 99	25.8	30.5	30.6	39.4	23.9	27.1
$100 – $149	19.5	11.9	5.6	9.1	25.0	12.9
$150 – $299	14.8	16.9	11.1	21.3	16.3	15.3
$300 and Over	10.2	20.3	5.6	3.0	12.0	27.1
Median	$87.90	$97.15	$54.55	$78.85	$106.50	$122.50

after relocation than prior to displacement. For the total group the major shifts in the distribution of rents occurred at the extremes. The proportion paying less than $50 per month declined by one-third, that is, from 30 per cent to 20 per cent, and the proportion paying $300 or more doubled. The proportion in this rental category increased from 10 per cent to 20 per cent. The latter results in large part from a general increase in the rents paid, that is, following relocation, establishments tended to move up from the adjoining rental categories in which they were found prior to displacement.

Changes in rentals differ markedly by type of project. The increase in median rent for units displaced by highway projects is around $16, but for renewal projects the increase is $24. Thus the absolute increase in rent is 50 per cent higher among renewal units than among highway units. This difference takes on added significance when we note that rentals in highway project areas prior to displacement were nearly double those in renewal areas. Median monthly rentals were $106.50 and $54.55 respectively. Thus the per cent increase among units from renewal areas is approximately three times the proportionate increase among units displaced by the highway. Median rents among units displaced from renewal areas show an increase of 44.5 per cent as compared with only a 15 per cent increase among units relocated from highway project areas. But even after the move, establishments from renewal areas are paying less rent than was paid by those from highway projects prior to displacement.

Businesses relocated from renewal areas are predominantly overrepresented in the lower rental categories at both locations. However, at the new location, the proportion paying less than $50 per month is only 27 per cent, as compared with 47 per cent prior to displacement. It is evident that rentals were comparatively very low in the renewal areas and that the move resulted in increased rents for a large proportion of the units. Rent increases fell largely on those establishments from renewal areas that paid the lowest rentals at the original site. Thus it is quite likely that the increased costs were disproportionately placed on those businesses that could least afford an added burden. A comparable change is not found among businesses displaced by the highway projects. The latter show a marked decline in the proportion in the middle rental category, that is, $100 to $150, and a corresponding increase in the top rental group, that is, those paying more than $300 per month. The proportion of businesses in this rental category more than doubled following the move. The increase was from 12 per cent to 27 per cent. However, the proportion of rentals below $100 per month changed only slightly.

Among businesses from renewal projects, there is a substantial increase in the proportion in each rental category above $50 per month up to those paying less than $300. The proportion in these rental categories increased from 46 per cent to 70 per cent. The increase is largest in the top category. At this level, we find only 11 per cent before the move but 21 per cent at the new location. It is only in the extreme that we find a smaller proportion of the renewal businesses after the move. Apparently businesses from such areas had to move into higher rentals than they had occupied prior to displacement, but the higher rentals were in the middle category. Only a very small minority of the units moved into the top rental category, even fewer than was found at this rent level before the move. On the other hand, businesses displaced by the highway were nine times as likely as those in renewal areas to occupy a structure in the top rental category after the move, but were less than three times as likely to do so before the move. These differences by type of project are, of course, due to differences in the size and types of businesses displaced from the different areas. Areas needing renewal clearly were low rent-producing areas, but they served the function of providing space for marginal businesses, that is, those who could not afford higher rentals.

All of the evidence indicates that one of the consequences of displacement is that rental costs increase for a majority of the relocated businesses. This holds in both types of projects. When asked how rents at the present site compare with rents prior to the move, 57 per cent of the businesses report that present rents are higher, whereas 26 per cent report no change and the remaining 17 per cent report a decline.

Rent, of course, is but one dimension of the cost of doing business and it has meaning only in reference to ability to pay. One index of the latter is volume of sales. Thus in order to determine the relative position after the move as compared to the old location, ratios of rents to sales have been computed both before and after the move for a number of selected subgroups. These data are shown in Table 18-3. However, before discussing these ratios

TABLE 18-3

MEDIAN RENT AND SALES PER MONTH AND RENT AS PER CENT OF SALES BEFORE AND AFTER MOVE AND PER CENT CHANGE IN RATIO BY SELECTED CHARACTERISTICS

Selected Characteristics	Rent		Sales		Rent as Per Cent of Sales*		
	Before	After	Before	After	Before	After	Per Cent Change
Total	$ 88	$ 97	$ 5,902	$ 5,250	1.49	1.85	24.2
Type of Business							
Food – Related Retail	79	88	2,375	2,833	3.32	3.10	–6.6
Other Retail	138	212	10,500	9,975	1.31	2.12	61.8
Jewelry	80	94	6,273	5,000	1.27	1.88	48.0
Service	47	77	808	767	5.81	10.03	72.3
Other	171	150	13,125	11,591	1.30	1.29	....
Size of Business							
Small	41	57	861	738	4.73	7.68	62.4
Medium	102	111	4,647	4,606	2.19	2.41	10.0
Large	208	300+	22,500	21,250	.92	1.41+	54.3+
Area Served (Old Location)							
Neighborhood	64	79	2,000	1,367	3.20	5.77	80.3
Community	75	94	3,450	3,900	2.17	2.41	11.1
Region – Other	135	188	14,063	12,859	.95	1.46	53.6

*Median rents and median sales for each sub-group are used. At best this is only a rough approximation.

attention is focused on changes in median rents and sales for a number of selected sub-groups.

Median rentals at the new location are higher for all types of businesses except for those in the "other" category which includes manufacturing, wholesale, and construction establishments. The latter businesses report a slight decline. As will be shown later, this change is due largely to movement of such units to the suburbs. The most marked increase in rent is reported by service units where median rents increased by more than 60 per cent, and to a lesser extent by non-food-related retail establishments where rents at the new site are 54 per cent higher than at the old location. The smallest increase is reported by food-related retail units. Among these units, rents increased from $79 to $88 after the move. When rentals are computed by size of business, there is an increase after the move in each size class, but the relative increase is most marked among the larger businesses. Relative changes in rent also vary by type of area served. Neighborhood-type units show a larger increase in median rents following relocation than establishments serving the whole community, but less of an increase than businesses that reached a non-local market.

Median sales following relocation declined. This decline, however, is not randomly distributed among sub-groups. Rather, it is particularly marked for neighborhood-type businesses where sales declined by 32 per cent after the move. Disproportionately large declines are also reported by the small establishments, and among jewelry manufacturing firms.[2] The only type of business to show an increase in median sales at the new location is the food-related retail unit. This finding is contrary to expectation. It was thought that food-related retail units would be particularly sensitive to the move, since they tend to cater predominantly to a neighborhood market which would be disrupted by the forced move. Consequently such units were expected to experience a disproportionate decline in sales. This did not happen, due to a combination of atypical circumstances. That these units were able to increase their sales after relocation is attributed in large part to the heavy con-

2 It may be that much of this decline is unrelated to the move, in that the jewelry industry was in a slump at the time of this study. Owners claimed that the slump was due in large part to imports from Japan.

centration in this group of particular kinds of food-related businesses.

A more detailed analysis shows that more than one-third of the units came from a single renewal project where the units were predominantly Jewish-owned and were located in an old neighborhood which was made up in large part of first and second generation Jewish immigrants from Europe. Following displacement, the units remained in the area. They moved into a new cooperative shopping center which was built on the same site.[3] This was done through an organization formed by some of the businessmen in the area. Actually the displacement did not redistribute the businesses in the community, in that the new shopping center was constructed on cleared land immediately behind the original structures. The latter were continued in use until the new structures were ready for occupancy, then the old commercial buildings were razed. The area was cleared and converted into a spacious parking lot in front of the new shopping center buildings.

Thus the old dilapidated, crowded structures were replaced by new modern buildings surrounded by a large off-street parking lot. Consequently, following renewal, the structures occupied by these units were not only more attractive but, due to improvements in parking accommodations, were also more accessible.[4]

Other apparent inconsistencies are evident from these data. Prior to renewal in this area, these units had predominantly served a neighborhood market and had catered largely to a Jewish population; however, even though the businesses remained in the same area, the conditions of the market changed. Even prior to the renewal project, the population of this area was in transition, that is, the ethnic and racial composition of this area was undergoing change. At the time of this study the Jewish residents, in large numbers, had moved out of the area and the Negro population had moved in. While this change in composition had pro-

3 This is the Willard Center Project.

4 This and other aspects of this project will be covered in greater detail in subsequent chapters.

5 Only the commercial area was renewed. The residential section, although needing renewal, according to standards used in other neighborhoods in the city, was left unchanged.

found negative consequences for some businesses, it actually contributed to an increase in sales for the food-related retail units.[6] Because of the special appeal of the kosher food markets, facilitated by ample parking accommodations and a lack of effective competition from comparable units elsewhere in the community, these units were able to continue to serve the same population even though it had moved out of the area. Also, because of the location of the project and the improved parking accommodations following renewal, these businesses could more effectively reach the suburban Jewish population in two of the faster growing suburban areas contiguous to the city. The shopping center is located on a direct route between the central business district of the city and the suburbs.[7] Thus they have been able to retain their old customers and attract new suburban customers, while at the same time they increased their sales by catering to the local Negro residents. Because of the highly specialized products involved, the location remained a viable one for these units even though the population composition of the area changed.

These changes, however, had quite a different effect on other-type businesses in the area. This is illustrated by the experience of a disgruntled fifty-nine-year-old barber who had been in business at the same location for fifteen years. When displaced he also moved to another site in the same general area in close proximity to the new shopping center that had been built to accommodate many of the displaced businesses. He liked the neighborhood because "there was a good Jewish trade." By remaining in the area he had not expected the move to hurt his business. Since the renewal project involved only a small commercial area, and had not displaced many residential units, he had thought that the move would only be a temporary inconvenience. Over the years he had "built up a solid and dependable trade." The move, in fact, did not have any serious consequences. Business continued as usual for some time. However, shortly after the move, according to his account, the area started to feel the impact of residential displace-

6 See discussion on area served before and after displacement in chapter on Type of Business.

7 Actually a common practice is for the suburban housewife to phone in her order which is to be picked up by the husband on his way home from work in the central city.

ment from other areas. The composition of the area changed rapidly. The predominantly Jewish population moved out and the Negroes moved in. Thus, while he remained in the area, he lost his regular customers due to their out movement. At the time of the interview his trade had declined to one-fourth the regular volume. He feels that he has no choice but to leave the area. This he plans to do. He wants to move to the suburbs since "those areas are building up and better customers are out there"; however, he is concerned about the "higher rent" that he will have to pay in the suburbs. His bitterness regarding the changes that have taken place in his old neighborhood is readily apparent from such remarks as, "In the suburbs I wouldn't have to worry about Negroes," and, regarding displacement of businesses for public improvement programs, he says emphatically that "it is no good, you are driving too many goddam people out of here." It is obvious that what has happened to his business is quite independent of his own move. However, he sees his problem as a result of displacements in other parts of the city which have substantially altered the distribution of particular kinds of people within the area. What he does not realize is that the transition in his area was already underway at the time of displacement and merely reached advanced stages of development in recent years.

This case clearly typifies what can happen to the owner of a business who caters to a specialized group when that group moves away from his place of business. He is experiencing the full effects of migration even though his business remains in the same area.[8] As a result of the changing composition of the area, this business catered only to the few older Jewish residents who have remained in the area and to occasional "drop in" customers who are passing through the area to patronize the kosher markets.

When rents are computed as a per cent of sales for all businesses that relocated, both before and after the move, we find that the rent burden is larger at the new location. The average rent burden increased by approximately one-fourth. However, the changes

8 This aspect of migration, although totally neglected in the literature, also applies to personal relationships in an urban environment. That is, adjustments due to migration need be made not only by the migrants themselves but the non-migrants whose relationships are disrupted because of the move of others.

following the move are found to vary widely among subgroups. For the particular eleven selected subgroups shown in Table 18-3, the rent ratio decreased in only one category and remained the same in one other. But in the remaining nine subgroups, the rent ratio increased. The increases in the rent to sales ratio vary widely among sub-groups – but the increase is most marked among neighborhood-type businesses where the ratio increases from 3.2 to 5.8. Thus the ratio at the new location exceeds the ratio prior to the move by 80 per cent.

When attention is focused on type of business, we find that the rent ratio increases more among service establishments than for any other type of business. At both locations, the rent-to-sales ratio is disproportionately high for service units, but the difference is even more marked at the new location. The ratio following the move is increased by 72 per cent. The ratio at the new location is 10 as compared to 5.8 at the old location. Non-food-related retail establishments experienced a 62 per cent increase, while the jewelry firms added to their rent ratio by 48 per cent. While manufacturing, wholesale, and construction establishments experienced a decline in rent, they also report a corresponding drop in sales so that their relative position is unchanged. Food-related retail units pay more rent at the new site, but since sales increased proportionately more, the rent ratio is less at the new location. However, it is worthy of note that the absolute sales-rent ratio is higher for food-related retail units than for any other type of business except service establishments. The latter carry a rent-sales ratio at the new location which is from three to eight times higher than for other-type businesses, and much larger than the differences at the old location. Thus the rent burden among service units increased substantially with the move.

When rent-sales ratios are compared by size of business, it is the small establishments that show the largest increase following relocation. These establishments also have the highest absolute ratio both before and after the move. The ratio of rents to sales varies inversely by number of employees. The same pattern is observed at both locations, but the relative burden as well as the range increases following the move. Thus it is the smaller businesses in particular, that is, those with less than two employees, that have assumed the largest relative rent burden in moving their place of business. The rent ratio increased from 4.7 to 7.8 – a 62 per cent increase. Medium-sized units show the least change following the move. Large establishments show more than a 50 per cent increase in rent burden, even though the absolute rent is considerably reduced. Among the larger establishments, rents amount to less than 2 per cent of sales, as compared with nearly 8 per cent among the small establishments. The same relative differences are noted at both locations.

When businesses are classified according to type of area served prior to displacement, we find that neighborhood-type businesses show a larger rent burden than businesses serving either a community or non-local market. The latter have the lowest rent-sales ratio. Here also the same pattern is found both before and after the move. However, it is the neighborhood businesses that experience the most marked increase in this ratio following the move. Consequently these units are in an even less favorable position after relocation than prior to displacement. This is due to an increase in rent following relocation and a decline in sales. Thus while rents increased nearly 25 per cent, monthly sales declined by 46 per cent. Consequently there is a substantial increase in the rent burden. Businesses serving a non-local market also experienced a rent increase and a sales decline but the latter was less marked, so the relative position did not change as much as for neighborhood businesses. But even here the burden increased by more than 50 per cent. Businesses that serve a community market report an increase in sales but a larger relative increase in rents. It is these businesses that show the least relative change as a result of the move. In short, the increased rent burden following relocation fell disproportionately on small establishments, those serving a local neighborhood market, and businesses in the services.

SUMMARY

In looking for a new site, most of the units do so quite informally. There is considerable evidence that many owners selected new locations rather fortuitously, that is, the site was found by chance by "just driving around" or "happening to see" a vacant or for-sale sign. Little systematic effort was devoted to determine the merits of the site as a location for their particular type of business. However, sizable differences are found by type and size of business.

Most of the relocated businesses found their own sites. Little help was received from the government-sponsored relocation service. Actually a great deal of criticism is expressed in evaluating this aspect of the relocation program. There seems to be general agreement that one can get little if any help from the government. Consequently relocation has been essentially an individual responsibility. However, many of the businesses feel that the government should take a much more active part in helping establishments relocate and should also make exceptions to zoning and licensing regulations when these work a hardship in efforts to find a site.

For the most part, businesses are in a less favorable position financially after the move than prior to displacement. However, for many, particularly those from renewal areas, the physical environment is markedly improved. Parking accommodations also show a marked improvement after the move. Environmental improvements of this type vary directly by distance moved.

The cost of the move, which is largely covered in renewal projects but rarely covered in highway project areas, varies significantly by type and size of business. However, the relative burden, as far as ability to pay is concerned, seems to be larger for the smaller establishments and those serving a neighborhood market area. Owners seem to have some advantage in respect to the costs of the move, particularly in highway project areas where no formal provisions are made to compensate for this. Adjustments seem to be made in the price given for the building in order to help defray the cost of the move. However equitable this may be, it does administratively what legislation has chosen not to do.[9] But it discriminates against the tenant where no informal adjustment is possible. At any rate, owners are more likely than tenants to feel that they have been treated fairly as far as the cost of the move is concerned.

A majority of the units did not change tenure with the move; however, there was a slight increase in the proportion of owners after the move. Among tenants, rents increased substantially. The

9 More recent legislation provides that some of the costs of the move may be covered.

increases, however, were more marked among units from renewal areas than among those displaced by highway projects. This is due in part to the much lower rentals in renewal areas before displacement. Also, there are differences by type and size of business. The increased rent burden seems to fall disproportionately on small establishments, service units, and the businesses serving predominantly a neighborhood-type market area.

CHAPTER 4

SUBURBANIZATION

IN metropolitan areas in the United States during the last half century, there has been a marked and consistent trend in the changing distribution of population.[1] Suburban areas have been growing at a much more rapid rate than central cities.[2] This trend has accelerated during recent years.[3] The literature on this is abundant, thus there is no need for further documentation. The Providence area not only characterizes this national trend but exemplifies the advanced stages of the changing structure of the metropolitan community. Available data suggest that developments in this area have antedated the rest of the United States by

1 Donald J. Bogue, *The Structure of the Metropolitan Community: A Study of Dominance and Subdominance,* Ann Arbor, University of Michigan, 1949. A. H. Hawley, *The Changing Shape of Metropolitan America,* Glencoe, Illinois, The Free Press, 1955.

2 Donald J. Bogue, Components of Population Change 1940-1950, Oxford, Ohio, Scripps Foundation for Research in Population Problems and Population Research and Training Center, University of Chicago, 1957, pp. 30-31.

3 Philip M. Hauser, *Population Perspectives,* Rutgers University Press, New Brunswick, New Jersey, 1960.

several years.[4] During the past three decades, the central city of Providence has actually lost population, but the growth in suburban rings has been in excess of this loss. Consequently while the total area has continued to increase in size, albeit at a low rate, the central core has experienced a continual decline. The new widespread settlement pattern of the population will inevitably change the pattern of distribution of the community's institutions. This process has already been documented by a recent study based on a series of censuses of business and industry for the Providence metropolitan area. According to the last census of business, retail establishments and sales are increasing more rapidly in the suburban areas than in the central city.[5] Again it is noted that this is a general pattern of change that has been discerned in most metropolitan areas throughout the country.

Although systematic evidence is largely lacking, the limited data that are available indicate that the changing distribution of these functions is largely due to new businesses being established in the suburban areas rather than because of an exodus of businesses from the central city.[6] Thus the traditional pattern in the changing distribution has not been for the central city to suffer an actual loss in the number of establishments or in the amount of sales volume; but rather, its relative position declines due to a more rapid increase of these activities in the suburban areas than in the central city. Stated differently, even as sales in the total area increase, the trend has been for a high disproportionate volume of these sales to occur in the suburban areas. Consequently, while the absolute position of the central city remains constant or improves, the relative position has been one of decline. This pattern is par-

4 Kurt Mayer, *Economic Development and Population Growth in Rhode Island*, Providence, Brown University Press, 1953. Kurt Mayer and Sidney Goldstein, *Migration and Economic Development in Rhode Island*, Providence, Brown University Press, 1958. Myron K. Nalbandian, "Methods of Population Estimation for Small Areas With Particular Application to Rhode Island." Unpublished Ph.D. dissertation, Brown University, 1959.

5 Surinder K. Mehta, *Population Redistribution and Business Structure and Location, Rhode Island, 1929-1958*, Small Business Management Research Reports, Brown University, 1963.

6 Kalliope Mohring, "Mobility of Retail Establishments in Flint, Michigan," unpublished Social Science Research Project Report, University of Michigan, 1955.

ticularly marked in the metropolitan areas that have reached maturity. In the past, it has been largely a function of growth in the "natural" development of the community. But in more recent years and in the future, this trend may be accelerated by businesses leaving the city and moving to the suburbs when they have been displaced from their established locations in central cities, due to urban renewal or highway construction programs, because of the limited sites available in the city.

One of the significant questions concerning public improvement programs that displace commercial and industrial establishments is the extent to which such programs result in the loss of such units to the city. Losses can occur either through discontinuance of the business operation or through relocation beyond the corporate limits of the city. From the point of view of the theory of urban development, the question arises as to whether displacement programs will alter the present distribution of business establishments and culminate in a more widespread settlement pattern.

The present chapter is focused on the suburbanization of business as a result of displacement programs involving both urban renewal and highway construction projects. Attention is also focused on the extent to which this loss to the central city is selective. Our data show that movement out of the city is substantial. In the Providence area, approximately one out of every six business units that relocated after displacement did so in the suburban area. However, it is hypothesized that the significance of the loss to the city exceeds this proportion since the units moving out of the city differ markedly in many important respects from those that relocate within the city.

SELECTED CHARACTERISTICS OF THE SUBURBANIZATION MOVEMENT

The population shifts from the central city to suburban areas around Providence during the past decade have been made up disproportionately of younger persons and those high in education, as compared with the population remaining in the central city. This selectivity in the redistribution of population is typical of metropolitan areas in the United States.[7] The question of concern here is whether there is a comparable selectivity of business owners. Thus attention is first focused on whether the owners of businesses who moved to the suburbs after displacement differ in selected demographic characteristics from the owners who remained in the city. We would expect from the general movement within metropolitan areas that the owners moving their businesses to the suburbs would be younger and better educated than the owners of establishments that remain in the city. This is based on the assumption that the suburban areas will disproportionately attract those businesses owned by persons who are more similar to the dominant characteristics of the local population, whereas the city is expected to retain those businesses which are owned by persons who are more similar to the central city population. Among other reasons, the central city area is more likely to hold the older, less well-educated traditional businessmen who view the densely settled city as the "natural" environment for a business location. This view of the city is evident in the frequent remarks that "the city is where our type of business belongs," or "you can't go there (suburbs) with this kind of business." The younger, better educated businessmen are more likely to realize the greater potential of the growing suburbs. The latter are also more likely to be oriented to the suburbs because of place of residence in the metropolitan area, in that they have already disproportionately moved out of the city to find a home site. There is thus the added incentive, when established patterns are disrupted, to reduce the home-work distance. The latter would also be more aware of the site alternatives available in the suburbs because of their general familiarity with the area. In short, it is expected that the suburban areas will attract businesses selectively by type and size and that the problems of relocation and adjustment in the new site will differ by area of relocation.

SELECTED CHARACTERISTICS OF OWNERS

The age and educational composition of business owners who relocated in the city and in the suburbs differ. There is a tendency for the younger businessmen to seek a suburban location, whereas

7 P. M. Hauser, *op. cit.*

those in the older age groups are more likely to remain in the city. The age composition of those relocating their business in the suburban area shows the same selective differentials as does the suburbanization of population generally. The suburban area attracts firms whose owners are under forty-five years of age more so than does the city, and the latter retains a high disproportionate number of establishments the owners of which are over sixty-five years of age. However, the difference of particular interest is the higher proportion of owners moving to the suburbs that is found in the thirty-five to forty-four-year category. This selectivity comes closest to representing the typical young suburban population.

It is worthy of note that approximately three-fifths of the relocated businessmen in both areas are between forty-five years and sixty-four years of age. The concentration in these age categories is due largely to the fact that the median number of years the displaced businesses have been in operation is nearly seventeen years. Although the evidence of selectivity is not overwhelming, even small differences are thought to be significant, since the study is limited only to businesses that were sufficiently well established in a city location to withstand the disruptive effects of a forced move when at best only a few months notice was given. This afforded little time for the unit to build up a reserve to use in getting reestablished. Also the displaced units were central city businesses of long standing. Considerably less than one-tenth of the establishments had been in operation for five years or less, while two-fifths had been in business for twenty years or more.

The central city tends to retain business owners in the extreme educational levels, that is, those who have not completed high school and those who have had at least some college training. Nearly half (48 per cent) of the business owners relocating in the city have less than a high school education, as compared with approximately one-third of those who moved their business to the suburbs. A more detailed analysis showed that 28 per cent of the central city, but only 6 per cent of the suburban businessmen, have only a grade school education. At the other extreme, we find that 24 per cent of those remaining in the city, but only 16 per cent of those moving their business to the suburbs, have any college training. Of those who selected suburban sites following displacement, nearly half are high school graduates, as compared with only

TABLE 1-4

NUMBER OF EMPLOYEES, TENURE AND TYPE OF BUSINESS BY AREA OF RELOCATION

Selected Characteristics	Central City	Suburban
Number of Employees	100.0	100.0
None	18.5	13.4
1-2	28.0	16.3
3-9	32.8	35.1
10 and Over	20.6	35.1
Tenure in Building	100.0	100.0
Own	34.7	54.0
Rent	65.3	46.0
Type of Business	100.0	100.0
Food – Related Retail	18.9	8.1
Other Retail	23.7	32.4
Jewelry Manufacturing	24.7	5.4
Service	18.4	8.1
Other	14.2	45.9

one-fourth of those who remained in the city. The latter area apparently attracts and retains those with the least amount of formal training as well as those with the most education.[8] The median educational level of those remaining in the central city is slightly lower than the level of education of those moving to the suburbs. This difference is partly a function of age differences, but in this instance a median value is misleading because of the marked difference in educational composition of the owners in the two areas.

CHARACTERISTICS OF BUSINESSES

The central city retains a high disproportionate number of the smaller establishments, as is shown in Table 1-4. Of the units re-

8 The city apparently can accommodate more heterogeneity than can the suburban areas. It may be that the more homogeneous population in the suburbs will not support the variety of business activities that can survive in the city.

maining in the city, 18 per cent are owner-operated businesses with no employees, as compared with only 13 per cent of those moving to the suburbs. Similarly, business units employing one or two persons also disproportionately relocate within the city. These establishments account for 28 per cent of the central city units but only 16 per cent of those moving to the suburbs. It is the larger business establishments that are overrepresented in the movement to the suburban areas. More than one-third of those leaving the city following displacement currently employ ten or more workers, as compared with only one-fifth of those that relocated in the city.

Viewing these data from a different perspective, we find that the proportion of units moving to the suburbs increases as the size of the unit increases. Thus, of those units employing two persons or less, only 11 per cent relocated in the suburban area, as compared with an average of 16.3 per cent for all units. But among the larger units, that is, those employing ten or more, one-fourth moved out of the city The selectivity in the suburbanization of business units is also evident from a comparison of the average number of employees per establishment by area of relocation. The median size of the units remaining in the city is 3.8 employees, as compared with 7.2 employees among those who selected a site in the suburbs. Thus it is apparent that the city is retaining the smaller establishments but losing the larger units. This, of course, means that the suburbanization of "jobs," as a consequence of displacements, is more marked than the suburbanization of establishments. As noted elsewhere, the suburbanization of volume of business also exceeded the proportionate movement of establishments.

Business units moving to the suburbs are much more likely to occupy a building which they own than are the units that remain in the city. In the latter area, two-thirds are renters, but less than half of those that relocated in the suburbs occupy rented quarters. The higher ownership rate in the suburbs may be due in large part to the unavailability of rental sites in that area. Also, buildings in the suburbs are more likely to be single occupancy structures which would also encourage ownership, whereas in the city, particularly in the older areas, individual commercial establishments occupy only a portion of a large structure, which they are much less likely to own. The tenure of commercial establishments seems to follow the same pattern as residential tenure as between central city and suburban areas, and perhaps, in large part, due to many of the same reasons.

The central city tends to hold food-related retail functions, as well as jewelry and service establishments.[9] On the other hand, suburban areas tend to disproportionately attract non-food-related retail functions and more particularly the businesses classified as "other" which are made up of manufacturing (other than jewelry), wholesale, and construction establishments. The latter-type businesses account for nearly half (46 per cent) of the businesses that relocated in the suburbs but only 14 per cent of those that remained in the city.[10] Thus it is apparent that these businesses are more likely than any other type of business to seek a suburban location. This difference is likely a function of size and the greater need for space. Such sites are apparently more readily available in the suburbs at a lower cost.

In some cases, movement to the suburbs resulted in the business being in closer proximity to its customers than it would be in a central city location. This is illustrated by the experience of a roofing contractor who employed thirty-five workers at the time

9 Cuzzort found that suburbanization of population has considerable effect on some types of service trades, while it has very little effect on others. Raymond P. Cuzzort, *Suburbanization of Service Industries Within Standard Metropolitan Areas,* Studies in Population Distribution Number 10, Scripps Foundation for Research in Population Problems, Miami University, and Population Research and Training Center, University of Chicago, 1955. Mehta reports that, "Providence still holds the dominant position in the service trade structure of the state . . . that service establishments continue to prosper in the city despite the heavy losses in population . . . establishments in the city continue to be relatively more prosperous than those of the other communities of the state." Mehta, S. K., *op. cit.,* pp. 192-193.

10 The movement of wholesale activities to suburban areas is of recent origin. In a study of selected metropolitan areas it was noted that: "So dominant was the central city in this type of activity that, even as late 1929, the central cities in 13 metropolitan areas accounted for over 93 per cent of the wholesaling jobs in those areas. From that date on, however, there was a rapid decline in the relative importance of wholesaling jobs in all these cities . . . the forces which lie behind this shift can be traced in part to transportation changes and to the advanced state of obsolescence of the central city . . . Once the truck began to be used, the attraction of the central city as the preferred distribution point for wholesalers was weakened." Raymond Vernon, *The Changing Economic Function of the Central City,* Committee for Economic Development, New York, 1959, p. 47.

of the move. He moved to the suburbs because he needed space, that is "room enough for our trucks and supplies," and "land was cheaper here." His only reason for leaving the city was to be near his major business activity. He reports that he prefers the suburbs because "our home-owner customers are out here." He feels that business will be even better now that he is closer to his customers.

Service units account for nearly one-fifth of the relocated businesses in the central city but only 8 per cent of those that moved to the suburbs. Approximately nine out of ten of these units remained in the city. The reasons for the high concentration of service establishments in the city are illustrated by the comments of the owner of a shoe-shine and hat-blocking business who states, "this line wouldn't pay in the suburbs. This is a city business." For the most part, the displaced service establishments were predominantly neighborhood-type businesses and attempted to relocate in close proximity to the original area so as to continue to cater to the same or similar population.

Food-related retail units also account for nearly one-fifth of the businesses that remained in the city but less than 10 per cent of those that moved to the suburbs.[1] These units are even more likely than other types of business to predominantly serve a neighborhood market. The special advantages of the city are suggested by the restaurant owner whose business had been located in the jewelry manufacturing district of the city for the past eleven years. He preferred a city location because "I serve factory employees so I have to be here." Thus, in relocating, he wanted a site near to his old place so that he could continue to draw his trade from the jewelry establishments in the area. A move to the suburbs was not even considered since such a move would have resulted in the loss of his regular customers. Rather, he relocated in the same general area and continues to draw his customers from the same neighborhood, that is, employees of the jewelry firms in the area.

The owner of a liquor store reports that he wanted to remain in the city since he doesn't feel that there are enough people in the suburbs from whom to draw his customers, but his main rea-

1 Part of this may be due to licensing and zoning problems, particularly in the case of liquor establishments, since the license would not be valid outside of the city and, as frequently reported by the owners of such units, "licenses are difficult to obtain."

son for not moving to the suburbs was that his license would not be valid outside of the city. Even apart from this, however, he prefers the city because "there are more people here."

Businesses that cater predominantly to a particular type of group also favor a city location, as is evident from the remark of the owner of a kosher meat market who claims that in the suburbs there would be "no central trade" for his establishment. A very comparable reaction is expressed by the elderly owner of a specialty food store who had been in business for thirty years. In support of a city location he says that "a city location is easier for all customers in the area to get to." In his opinion there would be "a better class of customers" in the suburbs, but "there are not enough Jewish people out there" for his line of business. Prior to dislocation, more than two-thirds of his business volume came from Jewish customers. Consequently he looked for a new site only in the same general neighborhood.

It is quite evident in reading over the case materials that many businesses at the time of displacement did not realize the business potential of the outside area. This is illustrated by the experience reported by the owner of a sandwich shop who had been in business in the city for nearly twenty-five years. When this owner learned that the area in which he was located was going to be condemned and he would have to move, he was certain that, no matter where he relocated, his established business would suffer a decline. Nonetheless he attempted relocation. He found the present site within two weeks through his brother who knew the landlord. He selected this site since "it was easy to get and on a busy street in a nice area." There is no evidence to suggest that he actually made a rational decision to move to the suburbs, rather he heard about this place and it looked as though it was in a nice neighborhood, so he decided to try it. Prior to displacement, he had intended to remain at the old location indefinitely; however, his views have changed since the move. At the present location, his rent is less and sales are higher. Also his salary or monthly profit, after less than a year at the new location, is nearly 50 per cent more than at the old site. He likes his new location better, is doing more business than before, and expects business to increase even further next year because "more people are finding out that I'm here." He sums up his whole reaction to the move thusly, "I only wish that I had come out here at the beginning."

A somewhat similar reaction is expressed by a used-car dealer who had been "unhappy and worried" when he learned that he would have to move. He had been located for six years on one of the main arteries leading into the central city. This street has traditionally been considered one of the preferred locations for car dealers in the area. Consequently, in his opinion, a move was certain to hurt his business. However, after looking for a month, he decided on a suburban location which was available at a busy intersection. He did not have any particular reason for leaving the city, but after less than two years in the suburbs he reports that "things have worked out better here. This corner has been a happy break for me." Viewed retrospectively he now sees the relative disadvantages of the former location. On this point he states, "People are not hurrying on the road out here and will stop and come in to look. Also, people can take it easy shopping for a used car out here. On North Main Street, drivers rushed by in heavy traffic and hated to stop." He goes on to say, "North Main Street, car men now agree, has long been overrated as a used-car section." He now feels that "the suburbs are better than the old timers think."

The experience of a gas station operator is also worthy of note and further illustrates that many businesses did not fully realize the potential of the suburban area. After six years in business at the same location, the forced move was viewed with a great deal of apprehension. In his words, "The displacement news came as a big disappointment since I had a stable profitable business going, which would be very difficult to replace." At any rate, after six months of looking through a broker, even out of the state, he found his present site which he took because "it was the only place I could get at my price." Now, after two and one-half years at the new location, he likes it better than his previous site and, even though the amount of business is about the same as before, he feels that it has more potential than the former area and that business will continue to increase. His appraisal of what has happened to him is summed up in the following comment, "Probably in time the move will be the best thing that ever happened to me."

The displaced jewelry establishments, with rare exception, relocated in the city. These units constitute 25 per cent of the business establishments that relocated in the city but only 5 per cent of those that moved to the suburbs. Apparently this type of activity prefers a central location. The reasons for not moving to the suburbs are illustrated by the owner of a costume jewelry manufacturing firm, who in moving wanted more space and adequate parking which he felt he could have obtained more adequately in the suburbs than in the city; but he did not do so because, in his opinion, "jewelry should be in the city of Providence because it is the jewelry center of the world." The accessibility of a city location to buyers was apparently also an important consideration in his decision for he comments, "People who fly in here or come by train would not want to drive out to the suburbs."

This same theme is repeated frequently. For example, the owner of an electroplating firm who had been in business for twenty years in the same neighborhood selected his present location because "it was not far from my old place." In his opinion, there wouldn't be any advantages in having his business in the suburbs. Concerning this he elaborates thusly, "It would be senseless for this kind of outfit. People we do business with would wonder what we were doing out in the country." Another jewelry manufacturer commented that "the suburbs would have trees and pleasant surroundings but would be too far from the people we deal with." He shares the opinion expressed by many others that "buyers wouldn't be very happy to come out to the suburbs, in a lot of traffic, to see us." In short, "the city is the only place for us."

Many of the jewelry firms wanted to remain in the city so as to be near other firms with which they do business. This is clearly illustrated by the owner of an electroplating firm who, in essence, describes the jewelry industry in Providence as "a combination of a number of independently owned but interrelated and interdependent establishments." He has operated his business in the same area for sixteen years and feels strongly that he must remain in the same general area. This is evident from his remark, "I am an arm of the neighborhood manufacturing process and I must be close to the other firms." In his opinion, "Of all the businesses in Providence, this type is least likely to function properly in the suburbs." A very similar opinion is expressed by the owner of a firm engaged in the heat treating of metals who says of the suburbs as a business location, "never in this line. It would be a dead-end street. Few of my customers would care to take their small orders way out to the country." He goes on to point out that he could go out of Providence only if all of the other jewelry establishments also moved out to the same suburbs.

The interdependence of the jewelry firms is further evident from the comment of the owner of a jewelry manufacturing establishment who says, "I would be out in the suburbs right now but I like to be near my 'plater.'" He also feels that the suburbs would be "too far from our suppliers." The latter theme is frequently expressed. Thus, even though as one owner says, "all jewelry manufacturing in Providence seems to be in the worst sections of the city," relocated firms continue to concentrate in the same general areas because of the many location advantages. All of this is emphatically summed up by a 56-year-old jewelry manufacturer who states that "all of our jobbers are in the city," and he comments further that he prefers the city as a business location because "it is where our business belongs."

HOME-WORK RELATIONSHIPS

For two-thirds of the businessmen who relocated in the suburbs, the move decreased the distance between place of business and place of residence, as shown in Table 2-4. Relocation within the city had this effect in approximately one-fifth of the moves. For more than half of the relocations in the city, the distance between home and work remained unchanged after displacement, as com-

TABLE 2-4

PROXIMITY TO WORK BEFORE AND AFTER MOVE BY AREA OF RELOCATION

Proximity to Work	Central City	Suburban
Total	100.0	100.0
Moved Closer to Home	22.1	64.9
No Change in Distance	53.2	2.7
Moved Further From Home	24.7	32.4

pared with only 3 per cent of the moves to the suburbs. Movement to the latter area increased the home-work distance in one-third of the cases, whereas relocation in the city resulted in an increase for one-fourth of the business owners. But for a substantial majority, movement to the suburbs was a move closer to home. It may well be that part of the stimulus to move to the suburbs was to decrease the home-work distance.

The suburbanization of population may well portend changes in the metropolitan area which are far more significant than the changing distribution of residences. It may be that central city businessmen first change their residence to the suburbs and later move their place of business out of the central city also. The high proportion of those who moved to the suburbs and are now closer to home than prior to dislocation is worthy of note. Although the establishments in our study are not a representative sample of all businesses in the city, the relationship between place of residence and area of relocation is strong presumptive evidence that the selective aspects of the suburbanization of population may be such that they encourage also the flight of business from the city. This dimension is quite apart from the expected growth of businesses in the suburbs to service the local population.

Our data suggest that the place of residence of businessmen in the metropolitan area is an important factor influencing the selection of a new business site after displacement. This may be important only when circumstances make a change in location necessary, that is, place of residence may not lead to the movement of businesses to the suburbs in the absence of any other external conditions which would stimulate a move. In this case, the move was forced. The data presented in Table 3-4 show that suburban residents were more than five times as likely to relocate in the suburbs as central city residents. Among those living in the city, less than 5 per cent selected a site in the suburbs, but of those living in the latter area 27 per cent moved to a site outside of the city. Viewed from a different perspective, we find that of the businesses that relocated in the city, 47 per cent of the owners live in the suburbs, but of those who moved out of the city 87 per cent live in the outside area. For a substantial majority of the businesses, as noted above, the suburban location selected was much closer to their home than the original site.

TABLE 3-4

AREA OF RELOCATION BY PLACE OF RESIDENCE AND PRESENT PLACE OF BUSINESS BY PLACE OF RESIDENCE

Place of Residence and Present Business Location	Total	Central City	Suburbs
Place of Residence		Area of Relocation	
Central City	100.0	95.2	4.8
Suburban Area	100.0	73.3	26.7
Present Business Location		Place of Residence	
Central City	100.0	53.2	46.8
Suburban Area	100.0	13.5	86.5

FINDING A SITE

Businesses relocating in the city required less time to find their present location than those which moved to the suburbs. These data are shown in Table 4-4. More than half of the units relocating in the city found their new location within three months. Less than two-fifths of those in the suburbs found a new site within this time period. Of the businesses that moved to the suburbs, nearly two-fifths required six months or more to find their present site, whereas this amount of time was required by less than one-fifth of the units that relocated in the city. This suggests, in part, that movement to the suburbs may have been due to their inability to find an adequate site in the city. The longer time spent in finding a site and the way in which they found their present location suggest that those who moved to the suburbs had more difficulty in finding an adequate location than those which relocated within the city. It may well be that movement to the suburbs was done with a great deal of hesitancy. This is suggested by the owner of a firm that manufactures plastic parts. He spent a full year looking for a new site and finally settled on a suburban location because it was closer to where he lived and he had a chance to put up his own building which would be "suited to our needs." Nonetheless he

TABLE 4-4

TIME REQUIRED AND METHOD USED TO FIND NEW LOCATION BY AREA OF RELOCATION

Time and Method Used	Central City	Suburban
Length of Time to Find Present Site	100.0	100.0
Less Than Three Months	54.0	37.3
Three to Six Months	27.0	19.5
Six to Twelve Months	8.1	21.0
More Than Twelve Months	10.8	16.8
No Answer	.....	5.3
Method Used to Find Present Place	100.0	100.0
Located by Self	55.8	45.9
Through Friends	9.5	10.8
Landlord Contacted Me	5.8	.....
Real Estate Agent	7.4	32.4
Other Businessmen	5.3	.....
State or City Relocation Agency	5.8	2.7
Other	7.9	5.4
No Answer	2.6	2.7

was concerned about the location because "it was a bit far from the central city." Even after more than a year at the new site, he reports that this aspect of the location "occasionally bothers us." This hesitance seems to have been largely without justification, however, for business has improved since the move. His evaluation of the whole problem of relocation is optimistically summed up thusly, "all those businesses that moved will be better off than before – we are very happy here."

Those moving to the suburbs were much more dependent on real estate agents in finding a new site, whereas those remaining in the city found a location more informally, that is, they found their own site (just driving around – saw a sign of vacancy) or found it through other businessmen or through personal contact with the landlord. It is of special significance to note the very low proportion of displaced businesses which report that their new location was found for them by the City Family and Business Relocation Agency. In response to a question on how they found their present place, only 6 per cent of those in the city and 3 per cent of the units that moved to the suburbs reported that this agency found the site for them.[2] One-third of the suburban movers found their present site through real estate agents while only 7 per cent of the city units did so. However, in most cases in both areas, the owner found the new site on his own.

In looking for a location following displacement, the things looked for in a site were quite different for those remaining in the city and those moving to the suburbs. Of those who relocated in the city, nearly one in five looked for a site that was near to the old location or near to the downtown area. Those remaining in the city were apparently more cost-conscious in selecting a site than were those who moved to the suburbs. Only 3 per cent of the latter but 14 per cent of the former report that they had looked for a "low cost" site. Businesses moving to the suburbs report disproportionately that in the selection of a new site they had sought "more room," "proper zoning," and "parking facilities."

As noted in an earlier chapter, the problem of zoning, particularly for selected types of businesses, was a real obstacle in their efforts to relocate. Movement to the suburbs in some cases was a result of not being able to find a properly zoned area within the city, even though the business would have preferred such a location. This is clearly illustrated by the fifty-two-year-old auto parts dealer who had been at the same site on a main thoroughfare in the city for twenty-seven years. After displacement, he moved to the suburbs because "it was the only place where I could find the amount of space that was needed and I could get a license." He reports that the Family and Business Relocation Agency tried to help him get another location in the city but was unsuccessful. After fifteen months of looking he states, "I didn't have much choice at the end so I had to come out here." Although his physical facilities are better than at the old location in that he has more space, has a newer building, and is in a better area, his business has declined as well as his income, largely due to the loss of the transit business he enjoyed formerly because of the advantages of his location. He would prefer to be in the city because "there's more traffic."

2 For a fuller discussion of this, see Chapter III.

The problem of finding properly zoned sites is also illustrated by the experience of a small chemical (soap) manufacturing firm that had been in business in the City of Providence for more than thirty years and wanted to remain in the city. However, the owner's major problem in trying to relocate was that he could not find a building the right size in an area zoned industrial. He wanted to remain in the same general area from which he had been displaced since it was close to his home as well as to his regular customers; however, he could not get a zoning change for the site he wanted to occupy. All efforts to relocate in the city were unsuccessful. Since he could not find any land properly zoned in the city, he moved to the suburbs. When asked why he selected his present location he said that "it was all that I could get."

The importance attached to different site characteristics by businesses relocating in the central city and the suburban area is shown in Table 5-4. Businesses moving to the suburbs placed considerably more stress on space as a site characteristic.[3] Two-thirds report that the amount of space in the building was a very important site factor, as compared with approximately half of those remaining in the city. But a much larger difference between the businesses in the two areas is found in respect to the importance attached to the amount of land area. While less than one-fifth of those in the suburbs reported that land space in a site was not important, more than half of the city units did not attach importance to this characteristic. Businesses relocating in the city were much more concerned with the type of neighborhood and type of business in the area. Only 32 per cent of the city units did not consider type of neighborhood important, as compared with 46 per cent in the suburbs. The same pattern of difference is found in respect to type of business in the area. This was unimportant to 48 per cent of the businesses remaining in the city but to 70 per cent of the units that moved to the suburbs.

It is of particular interest to note that nearness to the bus line was considered unimportant by two-thirds of the units in the city and three-fourths of those moving to the suburbs. Apparently a

3 The same emphasis is placed on space for a home site by persons moving to the suburbs from central cities. See for example, B. G. Zimmer and A. H. Hawley, "Suburbanization and Some of Its Consequences," *Land Economics*, Vol. 32, No. 1, February, 1961, pp. 88-93.

TABLE 5-4

IMPORTANCE OF SELECTED SITE CHARACTERISTICS BY AREA OF RELOCATION IN CENTRAL CITY AND IN SUBURBAN AREAS

Importance	Space in Building	Land Space	Type of Neighborhood	Type of Business in Area	Nearness to Bus Line	Parking Space	Access to Customers
				Central City			
Total	100.0	100.0	100.0	100.0	100.0	100.0	100.0
Very Important	52.1	22.1	41.6	23.2	16.8	45.3	56.3
Quite Important	38.4	25.3	25.8	27.9	15.3	34.2	25.3
Not Important	8.9	51.0	32.1	47.9	66.8	19.5	17.4
No Answer	.5	1.6	.5	1.0	1.0	1.0	1.0
				Suburban Area			
Total	100.0	100.0	100.0	100.0	100.0	100.0	100.0
Very Important	67.6	51.3	27.0	10.8	8.1	54.0	37.8
Quite Important	24.3	27.0	24.3	16.2	13.5	27.0	27.0
Not Important	5.4	18.9	45.9	70.3	75.7	16.2	32.4
No Answer	2.7	2.7	2.7	2.7	2.7	2.7	2.7

majority of the businesses in both areas are oriented around individual modes of transportation. Further evidence of this is found in the emphasis placed on parking space. In both areas, this was listed as important by approximately four-fifths of the units. There is a tendency for the suburban businesses to place slightly more emphasis on the importance of parking space, but the difference is only one of degree of importance. Central city businesses placed more emphasis on accessibility to customers. Of this group, 56 per cent rated this as a very important site factor, while only 38 per cent of the suburban units did so. At the other extreme, we find that one-third of the latter report access to customers as not important as compared with 17 per cent of the city units. Generally the businesses that remained in the city placed more emphasis on type of neighborhood, type of business in area and accessibility to customers, while the units that moved to the suburbs placed more emphasis on space in building and land area, and to a lesser extent, parking space. In neither area was much importance attached to being close to a bus line.

The reasons given for selecting the present site also differ substantially by area of relocation, as is shown in Table 6-4. The modal reason in the city is the site's nearness to the old location

TABLE 6-4

GENERAL REASONS FOR SELECTING PRESENT SITE BY AREA OF RELOCATION

Reasons	Central City	Suburban
Total	100.0	100.0
Building Costs (rent or price)	11.6	13.5
Nearness to Old Location	24.2	.....
Only Thing Available	16.3	10.8
Accessibility of Location	20.5	40.5
Attractiveness of Building	10.0	21.6
Owned by Self or Family	2.6	2.7
Other	10.0	8.1
None	2.6	2.7
No Answer	2.1	.....

(24 per cent), but in the suburbs the most frequent reason is the accessibility of the location (41 per cent). The latter is also the reason given by one-fifth of the businesses in the city. The meaning of this response is not exactly clear, in that the point of reference is not the same for all respondents. It usually refers to accessibility for the customers, but in some instances it refers to the accessibility of the location for the workers or to the owner's home. Although the latter is not frequently given as the main reason for selecting a suburban site, it is frequently mentioned as a secondary or contributing reason. For example, the owner of a manufacturing plant with nearly 100 employees reported moving to the suburbs because he owned the land and also because "the present location is within easy distance for the people who work here." At the present location he has "a more dependable supply of workers."

Attractiveness of the building occupied accounts for 10 per cent of the reasons given for selecting the present site by establishments that relocated in the city, but for 22 per cent of the reasons given by businesses that moved to the suburbs. Building costs, that is, rental or purchase price, are cited as the main reason for selecting the present site by approximately one unit in eight in both areas. How cost is viewed by some of the units moving to the suburbs is illustrated by a firm that manufactures light fixtures for a national market. When the owner was forced to vacate his site in the city, he looked for "a building on a site where costs were not too high." He found that buildings which would meet his needs were more expensive in the city because of their central location. This firm moved to the suburbs, according to the owner, because "our business doesn't need to be downtown, so why pay for it?" However, it is clear in reviewing this case that one of the reasons for moving to the suburbs was to be nearer to his home. He reports that he likes doing business better here than at the old location because his present site is "nearer my home and it is easier for me to get to work."

EVALUATION OF NEW LOCATION

When the business owners were asked what they liked best about their present location, more than one-fifth of the units in the city and one-tenth in the suburban area expressed no particular likes. A much higher proportion of the suburban businesses report that their present location is in a better neighborhood than the former place of business, that is, 22 per cent as compared with only 3 per cent of the businesses in the city. The attractiveness of the present building is what is liked best by 27 per cent of the suburban units and by 36 per cent of those in the city. In no other respects do the things liked about the present site differ by area of relocation. "Parking accommodations" and the fact that the present site is a "good business location" account for approximately one-fourth of the things liked in both areas.

Suburban businesses are less likely than city businesses to report any dislikes concerning their present site. Of the former, 38 per cent do not report any dislikes as compared with 25 per cent of the city units. Things disliked by suburban units are largely the inaccessibility of the site to customers (19 per cent) and the unattractiveness of the building occupied (22 per cent). Comparable dislikes are each reported by only 11 per cent of the city units. Businesses that remained in the city are more likely to complain about parking problems and to be dissatisfied with the deterioration of the neighborhood in which they are located. Neither of these is mentioned as dislikes by the suburban businesses.

Regarding advantages of a suburban location, half of those in the city could see none, but less than one-fifth of those that had moved to the suburbs report that there are no advantages in such a location. While 39 per cent of the suburban units report "less congestion" and another 19 per cent claim "accessibility to customers" as advantages of the suburbs as a business site, these are mentioned by only 13 per cent of the units that remained in the city after displacement. Approximately one unit out of six in the city reports "better parking" and "a better class of customers" as advantages of the suburbs, but neither of these are mentioned as advantages by the units that relocated in the suburbs. These data are presented in Table 7-4.

Turning to perceived disadvantages of a suburban location, it is noted that only 6 per cent of the city units but 38 per cent of those in the suburbs could see none. The general inaccessibility of the suburbs to customers is reported by one-third of the city units, but among suburban units this disadvantage is mentioned by only one-

TABLE 7-4

ADVANTAGES AND DISADVANTAGES OF SUBURBS AS BUSINESS LOCATION BY AREA OF RELOCATION

Advantages and Disadvantages	Central City	Suburban
Advantages in Suburbs	100.0	100.0
None	50.0	18.9
Lower Costs	5.3	10.8
Less Congestion—Quiet	7.4	37.8
Accessibility to Customers	5.8	18.9
Better Class of Customers	4.2	.....
Better Parking	12.1	.....
Other	8.9	8.1
No Answer	6.3	5.4
Disadvantages in Suburbs	100.0	100.0
None	5.8	37.8
Inaccessible to Customers	33.2	21.6
Inaccessible	25.2	21.6
Everything	12.6	.....
Costs	6.8	.....
Other	8.4	16.2
No Answer	7.9	2.7

fifth of the businesses. City units are more likely to see other aspects of inaccessibility, such as to the downtown area, suppliers, accounts and other related types of activities as disadvantages also. These are, however, mentioned nearly as frequently by the suburban units. Of the units in the city, 13 per cent report that "everything" about a suburban location would be a disadvantage, and another 7 per cent perceive the cost of such a location as the main shortcoming, but neither of these is reported by the business units that have established a suburban location after being displaced from a city site. The point to be emphasized is that nearly three-fifths of the city units report some aspect of "inaccessibility" as the main disadvantage of having a business in the suburbs. This is consistent with our earlier observation that nearly half of the city units selected their present site because of its "accessibility" or "nearness to the old location." The concern over inaccessibility is the same type of attitude that is frequently expressed about the suburbs as a place of residence.[4]

The tax issue is a frequently mentioned reason for not moving to the suburbs by many of the businesses that relocated in the city. There seemed to be little uncertainty as to the relative future tax burden that will be faced in the outside area. This is evident in the remarks of an elderly gas station operator who says that he did not move to the suburbs because "taxes might zoom in the suburbs and I think they will." He goes on to say that he prefers a city location because "the city is old and wise in the ways of taxes and doesn't go overboard on some of these new expensive ideas the way a new place with growing pains does and will."

The elderly owner of a small manufacturing firm who had been in business in the same area for thirty years reported that he would not move his business to the suburbs because "I live in the suburbs and taxes are away out of line." The owner of a wholesale paint company also did not move to the suburbs because "suburban taxes will go up and will soon be higher than they are in the city." Still other businessmen were of the opinion that taxes in the suburbs would increase as more services were provided. In short, in terms of future taxes the suburbs did not seem to be a very attractive business location. On the other hand, taxes were expected to remain fairly stable in the central city.

The units that moved to the suburbs following displacement were further questioned along two lines of inquiry. In the one instance the question was an attempt to get at the "pull" factors of the suburbs, and a second question was aimed at the "push" factor that may have led the unit to leave the city. The responses to these questions do not show any clear-cut "pull" by the suburban area. In the majority of cases, the responses were largely unrelated to any attractive characteristic of the area. One-fourth of the units moved to the suburbs not because of any positive factor which the suburbs had to offer as a business site, but only because there were no alternative locations in the city.

4 Inaccessibility is also given as a disadvantage of living in the suburbs, see for example, A. H. Hawley and B. G. Zimmer, "Resistance to Unification in a Metropolitan Community," Chapter 4, in Morris Janowitz (ed.), *Community Political Systems,* The Free Press, 1961, p. 164.

Such is the case of the owner of a drug store who had occupied the same site for fifteen years and catered predominantly to a neighborhood market. He moved to the suburbs only because there was no place available in the city. However, now that he has been in the suburbs for more than four years, he views the location as a marked improvement over the old site. He reports that "this is a growing area and has most of the people with money. I'm in a nice new building and the other stores near here have a good reputation and pull customers." He likes doing business better here because he has "more room and serves a better class of people." The old area had been on the decline for several years, so he feels that he is better off now than if he had continued at the old location. Although he moved out of the city only because he could not find a suitable site, the suburban area is presently viewed very favorably as a business location.

For 11 per cent of the units, location didn't make any difference, so there was really no particular reason for selecting a suburban site over one in the city if one had been available in the latter area. Movement to the suburbs was of little significance for these units and it was not a matter of selective choice to gain any advantages. The site just happened to be available and they happened to find it rather by chance. Another equal proportion moved to the suburbs because they already owned land or a building in the area. Again it was not a matter of a pull by the suburbs because of any specific location advantage. Some of the establishments, approximately 10 per cent, moved to the suburbs in order for the business owner to be nearer his home.[5] However, one unit in six moved to the suburbs because of the cost factor; a suburban location was thought to be cheaper than one in the city.

It was generally believed that rents would be lower in the suburban areas. The evidence on this, however, is not conclusive. For example the owner of a business machine sales and repair shop reported moving to the suburbs because he couldn't find a suitable location at low rental in the city – yet he experienced a three-fold increase in rent following the move. However, facilities are much better at the new location. He now has ample parking facilities and has a nice new, clean, modern building in an attrac-

5 As noted above, however, this was much more frequently given as a secondary reason.

tive area. But the location is somewhat inaccessible since most of his customers are in the downtown area. In this case the perceived cost advantage apparently outweighed the convenience of a central location.

The general attractiveness of the area, its accessibility to customers, and the fact that the suburbs were growing were given as the reasons for moving to the suburbs by 16 per cent of the units. Thus only about one-third of the units that moved out of the city gave as the reason for moving to the suburbs some attractive characteristic of the suburban area as a business location.

When asked why they had moved out of the city, one-third of the units report that there was no particular reason for doing so. It is significant that the city should lose one-third of the units that moved out for no apparent reason other than that the city could not provide an attractive business site. This, of course, is strong supportive evidence for the need to develop through urban renewal activity, or other means, industrial and commercial sites within the city. All too often, however, such projects tend to be defended only on the grounds that new industry will be attracted to the area. Thus the index of success seems to be the number of new jobs that are added and the amount that is added to the tax base by the industries or commercial establishments that move into such areas. At the same time the opponents of such programs attempt to discredit their value by claiming that these developments do not bring in new industry, but rather that the new occupants tend predominantly to be businesses that have already been in the community. Accordingly the new industrial areas do not add to the tax base or increase the number of jobs in the community. And so the controversy continues. What is overlooked is that many of the establishments that move to these new industrial areas would have been lost to the city through movement to the suburbs if such sites had not been provided. In short, the gain that is realized is that a loss does not occur.

This problem is illustrated by the experience of the owner of a small manufacturing firm who wanted to remain in the city but could not do so because "there was no industrial land available in the city." The suburban location is inconvenient for him, in that it is a long drive from his home in the city and it is inaccessible for his customers. Movement to the suburbs apparently was not a result of any positive attraction of the outside area other than the availability of the site itself. Yet it is these conditions that accounted for one unit in three that moved to the suburban area. Regardless of the reason for the move, the exodus from the city has serious implications for the well-being of the city. If renewal and highway programs displace businesses in the city and these move to the suburbs, this hastens redistribution of business activity within the metropolitan area. And since local governments function within corporate limits, the movement of commercial and industrial units beyond the boundaries is to the long-range detriment of the tax base of the city. Programs that are designed to revitalize the central area are in fact realizing less than full potential through the loss of existing units to the outside area.

Only slightly more than one-third of the units that moved out of the city did so because of some shortcoming of the city, including such factors as the lack of good business locations, the higher costs in the city, license and/or zoning problems, or the congestion of the city, as well as the city government. Thus it is only in a minority of the cases that the move out of the city is an attempt to get away from the city for some specific reason that has to do with a "push" factor from the city.

An extreme example of a push from the city is found in the reaction of a machine shop owner who, prior to displacement, had occupied the same location for twenty-nine years in the city. Although his business was displaced by the state in a highway project area, he blames the city for what has happened to him, even though it is quite likely that his present status is independent of the move. Since the war, this business has generally been on the decline. During the war he had hired fourteen workers, but just prior to displacement the number had dropped to seven. At the present time he has only two family members working for him, that is, his wife and a brother. This case illustrates the distorted view that some businessmen have of what has happened to them. In this case the government serves as a convenient scapegoat. It would seem that a specific location within a community would be of limited value to this type of business since it reached a worldwide market. Yet the owner feels that the move ruined his business. (It seems to the writer that the business was about to fail prior to displacement). He views his present location in the suburbs very unfavorably. According to him, "It is a junky place – I am not making any money and I can't do any business from this location." Business has apparently dropped since the move and is expected to decline further in the future. Consequently he plans to close down and sell out. Yet he feels that if he had not been forced to move and could have continued at the old location, he would not have been ruined. The degree of his negative feeling (as well as his immaturity) is evident from his stated plans for the future. In his own words: "I plan to sell out and leave Rhode Island. I hope to go to the Orient or out of the United States at least." In another context he says, "I'm fed up with Providence people and Providence government." He is fifty-five years of age and has lived here all of his life. And he goes on to say: "In this area you can't protect what you've worked all your life to build." When he was asked how he felt about the way he had been handled in the whole process of displacement, he commented, "like I was dirt they treated me." His final comment was that "the law that lets them take away your business is wrong. They should pay you for the business they destroy."

The attractive features of the suburbs for the relocation of displaced businesses seem to be its growth rate, lower costs, and the more lenient regulations pertaining to licenses and zoning for particular types of businesses. Apparently the latter are less restrictive in the suburbs than in the city. But even these apply to only a minority of those moving to the suburbs. The push factor from the city seems to be largely related to the general lack of attractive sites. But it is evident that for many the move out was fortuitous, for the owners could not cite any particular reason for relocating in the suburban area.[6] But regardless of the motivation for the move, each such relocation is a cost to the city.

SELECTED SITE CHARACTERISTICS

Since cities are generally older than suburban areas, it would seem that the outside areas would offer more attractive sites in

6 Businesses moving to the suburbs seem to have been less deliberate, perhaps less rational, in their choice of a site than those which relocated in the city. Partial evidence for this is found in the lower proportion which considered an alternate location. While 38 per cent of those relocating in the city considered other locations, only 14 per cent of those moving to the suburbs did so. Part of this difference, however, may be due to the prior ownership of land in the suburban area.

terms of physical features. Our data clearly support this contention. In moving to the suburbs, 78 per cent of the units selected a site where the general condition of the area is better than the one occupied prior to dislocation, while only 45 per cent of the units in the city moved to a better area. More than one-third of the city units, but less than one-fifth of the suburban units, moved to a location which they judged to be qualitatively nearly the same as the one previously occupied. For 21 per cent of the city units, but only 3 per cent of the suburban units, the old area is viewed as being in better condition than the one presently occupied. Thus while only about one-fifth of the suburban units moved to an area which is in about the same or in worse condition than the old location, more than half of the units remaining in the city have done so. For these units displacement and relocation did not improve the general quality of the area in which their business operates. This takes on added significance when it is noted that a large proportion of the displacements took place in deteriorated areas.

Suburban units tended also to move into newer structures than the units that remained in the city. Among the latter, 48 per cent moved to a newer building, as compared with 62 per cent of the establishments that moved to the suburbs. Thus nearly half of the businesses in the city and two-thirds of those in the suburbs occupy a newer building after relocation. A slightly higher proportion gained more space. This too is in favor of the businesses that moved to the suburbs, but the difference is not large. Of the latter, 70 per cent have more space after the move as compared with 60 per cent of those relocating in the city. One-fourth of the units that relocated in the city moved to less space than previously occupied, but less than one-sixth of those who moved to the suburbs moved to a smaller building. However, our data indicate that space is not a problem of major concern in either area, for 81 per cent of the city units and 89 per cent of the suburban units report that they presently have enough space to meet their needs or wants. While lack of space is more likely to be reported by city units than by those that moved to the suburbs, such obtains for only a small proportion of the establishments.

In Table 8-4 is shown the proportion of units occupying buildings by size categories and by area of location. It is evident that the buildings occupied by those who moved to the suburbs are substantially larger than those occupied by businesses in the city.

The median size of structure in the suburbs is 4,500 square feet, as compared with less than 2,500 square feet in the city. Differences in size are evident particularly in respect to the extremes. Whereas nearly one-fifth of the establishments remaining in the city have less than 500 square feet of floor space, less than 3 per cent of those in the suburbs occupy buildings in this size category. However, at the other extreme, we find that only 25 per cent of the city units but 44 per cent of the suburban units have more than 5,000 square feet of space. A more detailed breakdown by size shows that more than one-fifth of the establishments in the suburbs but only one-tenth of those in the city occupy more than 10,000 square feet of floor space. Land area differences are even more marked. Thus it seems clear that in moving to the suburbs the businesses are obtaining the advantages of space both in building and land area. These data indicate that the city is disproportionately losing the kinds of units that need larger buildings; thus the actual losses to the city are likely greater than the number of units lost would imply.

TABLE 8-4

SIZE OF BUILDING OCCUPIED AND PROPORTION MOVING INTO NEW STRUCTURES BY PRESENT LOCATION

Structures Occupied	Central City	Suburban
Size of Building (square feet)		
Total	100.0	100.0
Under 500	19.1	2.8
500 – 999	16.9	8.3
1,000 – 4,999	39.3	44.4
5,000 and Over	24.6	44.4
Median	2,440	4,500
Have Building Constructed		
Total	100.0	100.0
Yes	19.5	43.2
No	80.5	56.8

As already noted, the businesses moving to the suburbs are more likely than those that remain in the city to own the building they occupy, and are more than twice as likely to move into a new building which was specifically constructed for their occupancy. Among the businesses in the suburbs, more than two-fifths (43 per cent) report that they moved into a new building which they had constructed, whereas only one-fifth of those in the city did so. Thus one of the apparent consequences of moving to the suburbs is that it afforded the business an opportunity to move into a newly constructed building. Many owners reported that it was less costly to operate their business in such a building. Land sites for new buildings are, of course, more readily available in the suburban areas.

Space differences by area of relocation also show up in improvements and adequacy of parking facilities. Improvements in parking facilities are reported by a majority of establishments relocating in both areas; however, the changes are more marked in the suburban areas. Among units that remained in the city, 57 per cent have better parking facilities after the move than prior to displacement, but a comparable change is reported by 96 per cent of the units that moved to the suburbs. A point worthy of note is that while none of the businesses that moved to the suburbs have poorer parking facilities at the new location than at the old site, one-fourth of the establishments in the city report that they had better parking accommodations at the old location. Thus, with few exceptions, one of the gains in moving to the suburbs was the improvement in parking facilities.

A further inspection of Table 9-4 indicates that the gains in parking accommodations were substantially greater in the suburban areas than in the city. Also, those moving to the suburbs were the units that had the largest proportion of inadequate facilities at the old location, which may in part account for the greater emphasis placed on space as a site characteristic. More than two-fifths of the units that relocated within the city had adequate parking at the previous location, but this increased to two-thirds of the units after the move. This represents slightly more than a 50 per cent increase following the move in the proportion of establishments that have adequate parking accommodations. However, among the businesses that moved to the suburbs, there was more than a four-

TABLE 9-4

CHANGES IN PARKING FACILITIES AND PARKING ADEQUACY BEFORE AND AFTER THE MOVE BY AREA OF RELOCATION

Change in Facilities and Adequacy of Parking	Central City	Suburban
Change in Parking Facilities:	100.0	100.0
Better After Move	56.9	95.5
Same in Both Areas	18.2	4.5
Better Before Move	24.8	.....
Parking Adequacy:		
Before Move	100.0	100.0
Yes	41.6	22.7
No	58.4	77.3
After Move	100.0	100.0
Yes	66.4	100.0
No	33.6	.....

fold increase. Prior to displacement, more than three units out of four reported parking to be inadequate, but after the move none of the units did so. Thus all of the units that moved to the suburbs have adequate parking accommodations at the new site, whereas one-third of the establishments that relocated in the city report parking facilities to be inadequate for their needs.

AREA SERVED

Following displacement, the units which drew their customers predominantly from local neighborhood areas were more likely to relocate in the city than to move to the suburban area. Of the units remaining in the city, as shown in Table 10-4, nearly one-third had drawn their customers largely from the immediate neighborhood while at the old location, as compared with only one-tenth of the units that moved to the suburbs. Units moving out of the city were more likely to have drawn customers from an area more extensive than a regional market. Such business units account for one-fifth of the businesses moving to the suburbs, but only one-tenth of those remaining in the city. Suburban movers also tended to draw customers from the whole Greater Providence area while at the old location, more so than the units that remained in the city. Thus, in general, the more limited the area served, the more likely that a unit will relocate in the city. But if the area served is more dispersed, the business unit is more likely to select a site in the suburbs. Such units are less dependent on being immediately accessible to their customers; thus their range of choice of a site is much less limited than for other-type businesses.

Movement to the suburbs, however, was more likely to result in a change in area served than movement to another location within the city, even though in the latter instance the new area was more restrictive in size. Among the city units, 55 per cent continue to serve the same area as before displacement, as compared with 46 per cent of the units that moved to the suburbs. Among the latter units 49 per cent now draw customers, in whole or part, from a different area than that served prior to the move. The cor-

TABLE 10-4

PROXIMITY OF CUSTOMERS BY AREA OF RELOCATION

Proximity to Customers	Central City	Suburban
Previous Location	100.0	100.0
Immediate Neighborhood	31.6	10.8
Same Side of Town	7.9	13.5
Greater Providence Area	32.6	37.8
Other New England	17.9	16.2
Other	10.0	21.6
Present Versus Old Location	100.0	100.0
Same Areas as Before	55.3	45.9
Different Areas	26.8	29.7
Both Same and Different	10.5	18.9
No Particular Place	7.4	5.4

responding changes in area served involve only 37 per cent of the city units. Thus, movement out did affect the business-customer relationship more so than relocation in the city, but the differences are not particularly marked.

BUSINESS CONDITIONS

Movement to the suburbs appears to have been a movement away from competition. At any rate, our data show that the businesses remaining in the city are in closer proximity spatially to their competition than the units in the suburbs. More than two-fifths of the city units have competitive establishments within two blocks of their site, as compared with only one-fifth of the suburban units. Conversely, 78 per cent of the suburban units, but 58 per cent of the city units, are separated from their competition by two blocks or more. At their present location, 11 per cent of the city units report they have more competition than while at the old location, but only 5 per cent of the suburban establishments have experienced increased competition following the move. On the other hand, more than one-fourth of the suburban units, as compared with less than one-sixth of the city units, report less competition at their present location. But for a majority of the businesses in both central city and suburban areas, the level of competition did not change with the move.

Movement to the suburbs seems to have resulted in an improvement in business for the establishments, more so than relocation within the city. When the units are compared on a number of selected variables before and after the move, the suburban units appear to be in a more favorable position relative to before the move than the units that remained in the city. These data are presented in Table 11-4. For one-third of the businesses in both locations, the move had little effect on their volume of business. However, the businesses that remained in the city have a larger proportion that report a decline. More than one-third of the city businesses report a decline, as compared with only one-fourth of the businesses that moved to the suburbs. The latter units are more likely to report that their business increased in value following relocation. Only two-fifths of the city units, but more than half

TABLE 11-4

CHANGES IN SELECTED ECONOMIC CHARACTERISTICS FOLLOWING RELOCATION BY AREA OF RELOCATION

Direction of Change	Selected Characteristics				
	Volume of Business	Value of Business	Investment in Insurance	Number of Employees	Income from Business
			Central City		
Total	100.0	100.0	100.0	100.0	100.0
Increased	32.9	41.9	42.8	21.7	21.0
No Change	31.3	38.2	50.3	54.5	33.2
Decreased	35.7	19.9	6.9	23.8	45.8
			Suburban Area		
Total	100.0	100.0	100.0	100.0	100.0
Increased	36.1	51.3	55.6	35.1	33.3
No Change	38.9	37.8	36.0	45.9	36.1
Decreased	25.0	10.8	8.3	18.9	30.5

of the suburban units, report their business to be more valuable at present than while at the old location. On the other hand, for 20 per cent of the city units, the business decreased in value following the move, whereas only 10 per cent of the suburban units changed in this direction. For slightly less than two-fifths of the units in both areas, the value of business did not change after relocation. In both areas the proportion reporting a decrease in value is substantially less than the proportion reporting a decline in volume of business. Thus, the changes in value would seem to be due largely to the site and not to improvement in business.

The improved position of those in the suburbs is further indicated by changes in the amount invested in insurance. Of the suburban units 54 per cent increased the amount of insurance after relocation, but only 42 per cent of the city units did so. Approximately one-third of the units in the suburbs have the same investment in insurance as prior to the move, as compared with half of the business units that remained in the city. Apparently units remaining in the city had nearly the same insurance needs after the move as in the old location, but such needs apparently increased among the units moving to the suburbs, due to the increase in value. It may be, however, that, in part, the suburban units increased their insurance coverage because of the greater risks involved, due to a lower level of community services, such as fire and police protection. This may be one of the hidden costs of a suburban location.

A further indication of the differential development of units according to the area of relocation is found in the changes in the number of employees following displacement. The number of workers remained the same for 54 per cent of the city units and 45 per cent of the suburban units. But more than one-third of the units in the latter area report an increase in the number of workers, while only one-fifth of the units that remained in the city have more employees now than prior to displacement. On the other hand, the city has a larger proportion of units that report fewer employees at the new location. Apparently the units that moved to the suburbs have made a more favorable adjustment following relocation than the units that remained in the city. It may be that those moving to the suburbs took advantage of displacement as an opportunity to expand their business. Some evidence of this was noted earlier when we observed that one-fifth of the suburban movers looked for "more room" in selecting a new location. Also, these units placed much more emphasis on "space" in building, land area, and parking as site characteristics than did the units that remained in the city. Further, suburban units have a larger proportion that moved to a better area, a new building, and to a larger building than had been occupied prior to displacement.

In some instances the forced move provided the business with an opportunity to expand its operations, which it had planned to do anyway. Displacement in such cases is viewed favorably, as is illustrated by the roofing firm that had occupied the same location for thirty-seven years. Ownership had passed from father to son in recent years. After the son took over the business, he wanted to expand, but as the place he occupied was too small, he was thinking about moving. Displacement provided the opportunity. He selected the present site partly because the family already owned the land, but more importantly "it had room for parking and is on a good highway with a lot of traffic but no congestion." He did not feel that his type of business "needed to be in the crowded city center." In his opinion, the old location was too congested and was not a good place to run a roofing business. When asked how he felt about being forced to move, he stated that "we were glad because it permitted us to expand our business. We knew we would be better off at a different location." He sums up his reaction to the forced move thusly, "it was a good thing it happened to us. We are doing much better here than at the old location."

A jewelry manufacturing firm that had occupied the same location in the city for twelve years reports a similar experience. The owner states that "we had outgrown that location." That the move was viewed favorably is evident from the comment, "we were glad to get the chance to move." However, here too it was the site, and not a desire to escape the city, that attracted this establishment to the suburbs. This was the only available site the owner could find with a building that would suit the needs of his firm and provide the room needed for expansion. Although this firm gained by the move, the relocation was a loss to the city. This was one of the larger firms displaced. With the expansion permitted in a more spacious site, the firm employs sixty workers. From a tax point of view, this is a revenue loss to the city, but according to the owner, the firm had little choice but to move out since it could not find an adequate site in the city. The owner of this business expresses a commonly shared opinion that the government should "try to provide places in the city so businesses can stay there if they want to."

That suburban units were more successful following the relocation is also evident from the changes in income at the new location as compared with changes experienced by the establishments that remained in the city. While only one-fifth of the latter reports an increase in income after the move, nearly one-third of the units in both areas remains unchanged, but nearly half of the units in the city experienced a decline in income after relocation, whereas only 30 per cent of the suburban units experienced a decrease.

REACTION TO NEW LOCATION

Business establishments that moved to the suburbs appear to be more satisfied with the progress they have made following displacement and relocation than the units that remained in the city. Among the latter, only two-fifths of the businesses express a high level of satisfaction with the progress made since moving into their present site, but among the suburban movers seven out of ten units express this level of satisfaction. But while only one-tenth of the suburban units express dissatisfaction with the progress they have made at their present location, one-fourth of those that remained in the city do so. These differences are consistent with the more favorable economic adjustment that has been made by the suburban units.

Viewed from a different perspective, the owners of businesses that relocated in the city are more likely to feel that their business would have done better if they had continued at the old location. Approximately 25 per cent more of the city units than suburban units report that they would have done better if they had not moved. The proportion responding thusly was 37 per cent and 30 per cent respectively. On the other hand, more than half of the suburban units as compared with two-fifths of the city units report that they would not have been any better off even if they had not moved. As far as these units are concerned, displacement did not work an economic hardship. It is worthy of note that approximately one unit in five in both areas seems to be uncertain as to whether or not it would have done better if no change had taken place. At any rate, only a minority of the establishments report that business would have been better for them if they had not been forced to move.

A substantial majority (64 per cent) of the suburban units like doing business at their present location better than in the old area, but among city units, less than half (47 per cent) prefer their present site. On the other hand, one unit in three in the city expresses a distinct preference for the former area, but among suburban units this response declines to only one in five. Clearly the suburban business owners seem to be more satisfied with their present site than are the units that relocated in the city. It is noteworthy that the most frequent responses in both areas are favorable regarding the new location.

A larger proportion of suburban movers also report that they have done better following relocation than they had expected. Among the establishments that remained in the city, only 16 per cent are doing better than expected, as compared with 24 per cent of the suburban units. On the other hand, more than one-fourth of the former are doing less business than expected, but among suburban units the amount of business falls short of expectations in less than one-sixth of the cases. The main explanation for the decline offered by the owners in both areas is that their regular customers lost track of them after they moved. However, as noted earlier, the city retained the kinds of units that would be most affected by a move, that is, those that were disproportionately dependent on a specific market area. Accordingly the move proved to be more disruptive.

RENTALS AND SALES

A significant index of the relative financial position of the relocated businesses before and after the move is the rent-to-sales ratio at both locations. These changes, however, pertain only to those businesses occupying rented quarters. The experiences of

TABLE 12-4

RENTALS AND SALES AND RENT AS PER CENT OF SALES BEFORE AND AFTER MOVE BY AREA OF RELOCATION

Rentals and Sales	Present Location	
	City	Suburbs
Median Rent		
Before Move	$ 80	$ 204
After Move	95	200
Per Cent Change	+18.8	−2.0
Median Sales		
Before Move	$5,382	$ 8,250
After Move	4,303	10,179
Per Cent Change	−20.0	+23.4
Rent as Per Cent of Sales		
Before Move	1.48	2.47
After Move	2.20	1.96
Per Cent Change	+48.6	−20.6

such businesses may be quite different from those which occupy their own building.[7] However, as noted earlier, renters do account for nearly half of the suburban businesses and two-thirds of the units in the city. Thus such an analysis at least applies to a substantial number of businesses in both areas. But these data are not representative of all of the displaced businesses. Rather, this analysis pertains disproportionately to those businesses in the lower income categories, for we find that only 35 per cent of the renters, as compared with 61 per cent of the owners, report an income of $7,500 or more at the new location. However, focusing only on the renters, we find that marked changes occurred in the rent-sales ratio by area of relocation. This is abundantly evident from the data presented in Table 12-4.

7 Data available are insufficient to permit the development of a comparable index for owners.

Among establishments that relocated in the city, the rent-sales ratio increased nearly 50 per cent following the move, whereas a decline of more than 20 per cent was experienced by the businesses that moved to the suburbs. Businesses that relocated in the city, on the average, experienced a rent increase and a sales decline, while the units that moved to the suburbs paid approximately the same in rent as prior to displacement but experienced a substantial increase in sales.

Median rentals in the city increased by nearly one-fifth while median sales declined by approximately the same proportion. Among the firms that moved to the suburbs, median rents declined by 2 per cent while median sales increased by nearly one-fourth. As a result of these changes, the businesses that moved to the suburbs are in a much more favorable position economically, relative to the old location, than the businesses that relocated in the city.

The businesses that moved to the suburbs differ significantly from those that remained in the city in terms of rents and sales at both locations. These differences are consistent with our earlier findings regarding the type and size of business that moved to the suburbs as compared with those that remained in the city. Prior to displacement, the firms that moved to the suburbs paid more than two and one-half times the rent paid by the establishments that remained in the city. After the move, this gap narrowed, but the businesses that moved to the suburbs paid more than double the rent paid by the establishments that remained in the city. At the same time, the gap in sales increased after the move. Prior to displacement, the businesses that moved to the suburbs had median monthly sales which were 50 per cent larger than the sales reported by businesses that remained in the city, but after the moves suburban sales exceeded central city sales by some 140 per cent. Thus movement to the suburbs seems to have offered certain advantages.

While at the old location, the businesses that relocated in the suburbs had a less favorable rent-to-sales ratio than did the business that remained in the city. Among the latter, rents were 1.5 per cent of sales, but for the former the ratio was 2.5 per cent. The reverse is found at the new location. Rents, as a per cent of sales, are higher in the city than among the suburban units. Thus it appears as though the suburban area attracted disproportionately the high-rent-paying establishments and it was able to do so with no increase in rent. At the same time, the suburban area apparently was able to offer a more favorable market, as is reflected in the sharp increase in sales.

For the central city in metropolitan areas, these experiences may well portend some of the negative consequences of displacement programs. As cities build future highways or engage in wide-scale urban renewal programs, the city may suffer a loss in commercial employment as well as in sales, and thus in tax revenues. The latter is of more significance than can be judged by merely counting the relative number of businesses that move from the city.[8]

SUMMARY

Displacements due to public improvement programs in the central city seem to have an accelerating influence on the suburbanization of commercial and other non-residential units. The full impact on the city is more extensive than is indicated by the relative number of displaced establishments that move out of the city, since the suburban movement is selective particularly of the larger establishments. Thus the loss of employment and the loss of taxable property is disproportionately larger than the relative number of units that are lost to the city.

Movement to the suburbs occurs predominantly among the owners who already live in the suburban areas. Consequently the new site is much closer to their home than the original location. This suggests that the suburbanization of population is of more significance than the loss of numbers to the city, since such movement may well portend the movement of businesses.

The businesses most likely to move to the suburbs are the non-food-related retail units and those in the manufacturing, wholesale, and construction category. Conversely the city tends to hold food-related retail, jewelry, and service establishments.

8 In a recent analysis of the census of business for the 1929 to 1958 period it was found that the suburbs experienced very large gains in the share of retail establishments, with even larger gains in their share of retail sales. Mehta, S. K., *op. cit.*, p. 148.

A majority of the businesses that moved to the suburbs own the building they occupy, whereas in the city a substantial majority are tenants. The buildings occupied in the suburbs are much larger than those in the city and are much more likely to have been newly constructed for their present occupants. In general, businesses moving to the suburbs show more of an improvement in site characteristics than do the units that remained in the city.

Jewelry manufacturing units, in particular, attempted to remain in the same general area from which they were displaced, because of the marked advantages that obtain by being in or at least near to the jewelry district, even though this was located in an old section of the city. Rarely did we find such units moving to the suburbs.

As compared with the establishments that relocated in the city, the businesses that moved to the suburbs seem to have made a more favorable economic adjustment after the move and respond much more favorably in evaluating their new location as compared with the original site. Thus the displacement of these businesses resulted in a distinct loss to the central city, but from the point of view of the businesses moving to the suburbs, displacement appears to have provided them with an opportunity to establish themselves in a more favorable site.

CHAPTER 5

TYPE OF BUSINESS

THE ability to survive displacement has already been shown to vary by type of business. In an earlier chapter, we observed that the non-survival rates were highest for those units in food-related retail businesses and among service establishments. These are the kinds of businesses that are primarily dependent on a regular and recurrent relationship with a limited number of customers living in close proximity. Consequently, displacement effectively disrupts an established relationship on which the units are largely dependent. To be forced to vacate their site and relocate in a different area, for these businesses in particular, may be tantamount to starting all over again. It logically follows from this that the problems of site selection, and the adjustment of those that survived displacement, would also be expected to vary by type of business. This is the problem of concern in the present chapter. Specifically, the discussion will focus on the relocation problems faced by different kinds of business establishments. Before doing so, however, let us examine the social and cultural characteristics of the owners of different types of businesses, as well as their background and preparation for a business career.

SELECTED CHARACTERISTICS

Retail trades tend to be composed of younger businessmen than other-type businesses. The modal age, as shown in Table 1-5, for each type of business is between forty-five years and fifty-four years, and the median age is less than fifty years for both types of retail units, but exceeds fifty years in the other three business types. A close inspection of the age composition shows that approximately one-third of the businessmen in retail trades are under forty-five years of age, as compared with only one-fifth of those in services and in the "other" category, which is made up of manufacturing, wholesale, and construction activities. Nearly half of the businessmen in the "services" and in the "other" category are over fifty-five years of age, as compared with only slightly more than one-fourth in the retail trades and the jewelry industry. The owners in the jewelry industry tend to be younger than those in the services and the "other" category, but older than those in the two retail categories.

The educational composition varies markedly by type of business. The owners with the lowest educational attainment are found among the food-related retail, jewelry, and service establishments. Three-fifths of the owners of service units and food-related retail establishments have eleven years or less formal training. Of even more significance is that more than two-fifths of those in the services and one-third of those in food-related retail are found in the eight years or less educational category. In the jewelry industry, more than half of the owners have not completed high school. However, only one-fourth of the owners of non-food-related retail establishments and less than two-fifths of the owners of manufacturing, wholesale and construction businesses did not complete high school. At the high end of the educational scale, we find that more than one-third of the owners in the latter businesses have at least some college training, as compared with one-fifth of those in jewelry and 10 per cent or less of the owners of food-related retail and service establishments. The median level of education is highest (12.6) for those in non-food-related retail and lowest (9.2) for those in the service category. These differences are partly a function of age differences. Older owners are disproportionately concentrated at the low end of the educational scale.

TABLE 1-5

SELECTED CHARACTERISTICS OF BUSINESS OWNER BY TYPE OF BUSINESS

Characteristics	Food – Related Retail	Other Retail	Jewelry Mfg.	Service	Other*
Age					
Total Per Cent	100.0	100.0	100.0	100.0	100.0
Under 35 Years	12.8	12.3	4.1	5.2	9.1
35 - 44	20.5	24.6	24.5	15.8	11.4
45 - 54	38.5	36.8	42.9	31.6	31.8
55 - 64	23.1	19.3	22.4	23.7	29.5
65 Years and Over	5.1	7.0	6.1	23.7	18.2
Median	49.3	48.6	52.3	54.5	54.2
Education					
Total Per Cent	100.0	100.0	100.0	100.0	100.0
8th Grade or Less	33.3	12.3	28.6	42.1	22.7
9 - 11	28.2	14.0	24.5	15.8	15.9
12	28.2	36.8	24.5	28.9	27.3
College	10.3	36.8	20.4	7.9	34.1
No Answer	.....	.....	2.0	5.3	.....
Median	10.8	12.6	11.6	9.2	12.4
Cultural and Ethnic Origin					
Total Per Cent	100.0	100.0	100.0	100.0	100.0
Southeast European	41.0	22.8	65.3	44.7	20.4
Italian	(35.9)	(17.5)	(57.1)	(34.2)	(15.9)
Northwest European	15.4	42.1	20.4	13.2	40.9
Jewish**	38.5	24.6	10.2	26.3	29.5
Negro	.....	1.8	.....	10.5	.....
Other	5.1	8.7	4.1	5.3	9.2

*Includes manufacturing, wholesale, and construction establishments.

**This group is reported separately since many persons responded "Jewish" to the ethnic background question; therefore it was decided to combine this question and the one on religion so that these could be placed in a single category. Consequently these categories are in part ethnic and in part religion. Thus the first three categories are not mutually exclusive.

The variation in level of education is closely related to the cultural and ethnic origins of the businessmen in different-type businesses. The three business types with the lowest educational level are made up predominantly of Italians and others of southeast European origin, whereas the two business types with the highest level of education are composed disproportionately of persons whose ethnic origins are countries in northwest Europe. The latter make up two-fifths of those in non-food-related retail and in the "other" category, but account for less than one-fifth of those in the other three business types. On the other hand, persons of southeast European origin account for two-thirds of those in jewelry and more than two-fifths of those in the service category. In both types of businesses, Italians constitute a large majority – accounting for 57 per cent of those in the jewelry business and 34 per cent of those in the services. Persons of this ethnic origin account for one-third of the food-related retail units also, but less than one-fifth of those in non-food-related retail and of those in the "other" category. The latter businesses are made up largely of persons of northwest European origin. The Jewish group accounts for one-fourth to nearly two-fifths of all businesses except for those in jewelry. In the latter only one person in ten is from the Jewish group.

In short, persons of southeastern European origin, who are predominantly Italian, are disproportionately overrepresented among food-related retail, jewelry, and service establishments, whereas persons of northwest European origin are overrepresented in the non-food-related retail and "other" businesses. The Jewish group has the largest proportion in food-related retail, and the smallest proportion in the jewelry business. It is noted, however, that the jewelry businesses included in this study are manufacturing units.

The high proportion of Jews in the food-related businesses is due largely to the displacements from only one renewal project. A more detailed breakdown shows that 80 per cent of the food-related units in this project (Willard Center) were Jewish-owned establishments (kosher markets) as compared with only 13 per cent of all other displaced food-related businesses included in this study. There are two aspects of the predominantly Jewish-owned establishments that make them atypical of the experiences of food-related businesses in general. First of all, these are kosher establishments and thus are not subject to the typical competitive market, because they are less dependent upon customers in close proximity. Thus they can effectively draw customers from a distance that would not be possible for other food-related units, and (secondly) they relocated on the same site but in a new shopping center that is cooperatively owned. Thus in effect they did not move, but marked changes were wrought in the physical environment.

While the food-related units in this one project are predominantly Jewish-owned establishments, a majority of all other displaced food-related businesses are owned by Italians. However, the latter businesses come from a number of different renewal projects and highway clearance areas, and relocation sites are distributed throughout the community; that is, they differ from the above in that they are not concentrated in any single area. Because of the marked differences within the food-related category, these businesses will be sub-divided in our subsequent analysis so that the predominantly Jewish-owned markets, which were displaced from the one urban renewal project area and relocated in the shopping center, can be distinguished from all of the other food-related retail establishments.

Before proceeding with our discussion of problems of relocation by type of business, attention is first focused on the training background of these businessmen prior to entering business. Our data indicate that a very large proportion of the businessmen displaced during the period covered by this study had no special training to run the particular type of business in which they are engaged.[1] Only 13 per cent of the owners report any special training, but marked variations are observed by type of business. None of those in food-related retail and only 6 per cent of those in jewelry manufacturing report any special training, but this increases to 30 per cent of those in non-food-related retail businesses.

The major method of learning how to operate a business was by "picking it up" on one's own. This is the method reported by more than two-fifths of the units. The largest proportion is found among jewelry manufacturing firms where more than half learned

1 For more recent but similar experiences see: "Who Opens a Small Business" in Kurt B. Mayer and Sidney Goldstein, *The First Two Years,* Small Business Research Series No 2, Small Business Administration, Washington, D.C., 1961.

the business in this way.[2] Another frequently used method was to learn the business from other family members. Nearly one-fourth of the units report having done so. This is particularly high among food-related retail units, which is due largely to the predominantly Jewish-owned establishments where 60 per cent report learning the business through the family. The point to be emphasized here is that two-thirds or more among each type of business learned how to run the business either by "picking it up on their own" or they learned it "from other family members." Thus it is readily apparent that a substantial majority of the owners entered business without any special preparation. That is, what they knew about operating a business they had learned informally. Much of this, however, may pertain to the trade or type of business rather than to ownership as such. Nonetheless, over the years they had made a successful operation out of their businesses and even succeeded in moving following displacement.[3] However, the move to a new location, as already observed in Chapter III, was not without problems. It is to this topic that we now turn with attention being focused on type of business.

SITE SELECTION

When asked the major problem in trying to find a new location, food-related retail units have the largest proportion reporting "none." But it becomes evident in a more detailed breakdown that this high proportion is due mainly to those Jewish-owned units that were displaced from the one project which was largely converted into a cooperatively owned shopping center. Among these units, two out of three report that they had no problem in finding a new location, but among all other food-related retail units the proportion responding thusly declines to only 20 per cent. This is

2 The responses to this question may be misleading in that they may refer to how the respondent learned the trade or occupation rather than refer to the technical aspects of business ownership. See for example: *Ibid.*, p. 34. The same weakness applies to all of the responses given to this question. Future studies should carefully differentiate between preparation for business ownership as such and preparation for engaging in "this line of work."

3 The median number of years in business was approximately 17 years.

lower than that found among any other type of business except those in manufacturing, wholesale, and construction activities.

The kinds of problems encountered in trying to find a new site differ by type of business. The major problem among the businesses in the "other" category centered around building needs. More than one in four report that they could not find a suitable building. While this particular problem was faced by less than 10 per cent of the food-related retail and service establishments, it was quite frequently mentioned as a major problem by non-food-related retail establishments and by those in the jewelry industry. Owners of jewelry manufacturing and of service units tend to report the "high rentals" of the new sites as a major problem more frequently than do other-type businesses. Part of this may have been due to their attempts to relocate in the same general area from which they had been displaced. And such sites may have been very limited because of the clearance that had taken place in the area. Thus rents may have been increased accordingly. Jewelry firms wanted to remain in the jewelry district since they can apparently operate more effectively and economically if in close proximity to other interrelated firms. Not only are there advantages in the manufacturing process, in that there is a great deal of sub-contract work done in the area, but gains are also to be realized in respect to marketing.[4]

For food-related retail units, zoning and license problems are mentioned by more units than any other single problem. This is an especially acute problem when a liquor license is involved. The zoning problem is also likely encountered more frequently by these kinds of businesses than other-type units because of the need to establish such businesses in, or at least in close proximity to, residential areas so as to be close to their customers. Such areas are not usually zoned for business use. Food-related retail and serv-

4 This finds support in the following statement: "In general, the proximity of dealers in the same line is desirable where the market to be served is regional or national, where shopping, comparison, and selection are important steps in the buying process . . . Another advantage of the proximity of competitors is the opportunity such location affords for filling out orders when shortages occur in certain items." Quoted from: Richard U. Ratcliff, "Demand for Non-Residential Space," reprinted from *Urban Land Economics* in *Readings in Urban Geography*, ed. Harold M. Mayer and Clyde F. Kohn, The University of Chicago Press, 1959, p. 409.

ice units have the largest proportion that report that their major problem was trying to stay in the old area, but this was rarely mentioned by other-type businesses. Thus the major problem faced in their attempt to find a new site differed by type of business; however, for a substantial minority no major problem was encountered.

The length of time required to find a new site varies by type of business, but the differences are not particularly marked. The major difference is found within the food-related retail units, that is, between those establishments that relocated in the shopping center and those that selected a site on the open market. The latter have the smallest proportion (one in eight) that found a site within a two-week period, whereas more than half of the former did so. Non-food-related retail units and service establishments required the least amount of time to find a new site. More than two-fifths of these units had found a new site in less than three months, whereas only about one-third of the other business types, including food-related retail units, except those that moved into the shopping center, were able to do so. At the opposite extreme we find that nearly two-fifths of the jewelry businesses and nearly half of the manufacturing, wholesale, and construction establishments required six months or more to find a new location. However, this amount of time was needed by only one-third of the service units and one-fourth of the non-food-related retail establishments. The longer time required by jewelry and "other"-type business is likely due to the special building needs of these businesses. At least this is a frequently cited problem of these units.

The length of time required to find a new location does not appear to be closely related to the distance moved, although distance moved does vary by type of business. Of particular significance is the high proportion of food-related retail units that remained very close to the original site. Nearly half of these units moved within a distance of one-tenth of a mile, and more than 70 per cent relocated within a one-half-mile radius of the original location. Again we find marked differences within the food-related group. The high concentration in the first distance zone is due in large part to those units that moved into a new shopping center on the same site from which they had been displaced. However, even when the analysis is limited only to the other food-related businesses, we find shorter moves than among other business types. Nearly three-fifths of the latter establishments remained within a half mile of the original location. A comparable concentration within the one-half-mile zone is found among jewelry firms. Service units also tended to relocate close to the original site. Only one-fifth moved within the one-tenth-mile zone but more than two-thirds moved one-half mile or less. The proportion selecting a new site in such close proximity declines to only two-fifths of the non-food retail units and one-fifth of those in the "other" category.

Service and jewelry units both have a very low proportion of units that moved more than one and one-half miles from their displaced sites. The jewelry units likely remained close to the old site because of the lack of alternative locations and, as already noted, these units wanted to remain in the jewelry industry area. Service units and food-related retail units apparently attempted to remain close to the old location so as to be near to their regular customers. The latter establishments were largely neighborhood-type businesses, and they tried to remain in a familiar area because of their need to be in close contact with their customers. This is considered more fully below. A point worthy of note here is the relatively high proportion (20 per cent) of the food-related retail units that moved more than one and one-half miles. While, as already noted, such units disproportionately attempted to remain in close proximity to the original location, a substantial number broke clearly with the past and attempted to establish themselves in a new area. Many of these moved to the suburbs to take advantage of the growth that was occurring in the outside areas.

It is among the manufacturing, wholesale, and construction establishments that we find the more distant moves. Rarely did these businesses relocate within one-tenth of a mile. The new site is within a one-half-mile radius for less than one unit in five. But at the other extreme, we find that more than one-third of the units moved beyond one and one-half miles, whereas less than one-fifth of all of the relocated units did so. Non-food-related retail units were also more likely to move greater distances than other-type businesses.

When viewing the median distance moved, the variation by type of business is marked. The median distance moved ranges from a low of only .12 miles for food-related retail units to a high of 1.15 miles for manufacturing, wholesale, and construction establishments. The median distance moved by service units was only .35 miles, while jewelry firms moved .43 miles and non-food-related retail moved .78 miles. The median for all units was one-half mile.

HOW THEY FOUND NEW LOCATION

In a majority of cases, as is shown in Table 2-5, the displaced business units report that they found their new location through their own efforts and initiative. This proportion varies, however, from 45 per cent of the non-food-related retail units to 60 per cent of the service establishments. From slightly more than one-tenth to nearly one-third of the businesses found their new location informally through friends, other businessmen, or landlords. Food-related retail units had the highest proportion which found their new location in this way. However, within this group, marked differences are observed. Among the units that relocated in the shopping center, nearly three out of ten report that they found their present site through other businessmen. This is to be expected in that the center was a cooperative venture by the businessmen in the area. That is, the businessmen in the area got together and decided to collectively solve the relocation problem in this way. Among the other food-related units, only 4 per cent report that they found their present site through other businessmen, but nearly one-fifth of the units found their site through friends. The greater emphasis on friends among the latter units is likely due to the large concentration of Italian owners who catered to an ethnic market and who belong to a close-knit ethnic community.

Real estate agents found the new site for 21 per cent of the non-food-related retail units and 16 per cent of the "other" type businesses, but for only 8 per cent of the jewelry firms, and even less frequently for the other two business types. It is particularly worthy of note that only a very low proportion of all businesses reports that they found their new location through the government-sponsored relocation agency. While only 5 per cent of the units report they found their new site through this agency, the proportion ranges from a low of 2 per cent among those in the "other" cate-

TABLE 2-5

METHOD USED TO FIND SITE BY TYPE OF BUSINESS

Method Used to Find Site	Food – Related Retail			Other Retail	Jewelry Mfg.	Service	Other
	Total	W. C.*	Other				
Total Per Cent	100.0	(100.0)	(100.0)	100.0	100.0	100.0	100.0
Located by Self	53.8	(46.7)	(58.3)	45.6	59.2	60.5	54.5
Through Friends	12.8	(6.7)	(16.7)	10.5	8.2	10.5	6.8
Landlord	5.1	......	(8.3)	5.3	6.1	5.3	2.3
Other Businessmen	12.8	(26.7)	(4.2)	.....	4.1	5.3	2.3
Real Estate Agent	5.1	......	(8.3)	21.0	8.2	2.6	15.9
Relocation Agency	2.6	(6.7)	......	8.8	8.2	2.6	2.3
Other	5.1	(6.6)	(4.2)	8.8	4.1	10.5	9.1
No Answer	2.6	(6.6)	......	.....	2.0	2.6	6.8

*Willard Center.

gory to a high of 9 per cent among non-food-related retail establishments. This agency was apparently most helpful to non-food retail units and to jewelry firms, but rarely of help to the other business types. This does not mean that help was not offered,[5] but it does mean that the relocated businesses do not view this agency as providing a major source of aid in finding a new site. The reaction of an auto parts owner is not atypical. He evaluates this service thusly, "relocation didn't do anything but tell me to come down and look at a list" (of addresses).[6]

THINGS LOOKED FOR IN A SITE

In looking for a new location, jewelry firms and service establishments both stressed cost factors more so than did other-type businesses. Among these businesses, nearly one unit in five mentions cost factors as the main things looked for in a new site, as compared with only 10 per cent or less of the other business types. Jewelry firms and, to an even greater extent, manufacturing, wholesale, and construction businesses, stressed "more room" as a feature looked for in a site, but this was mentioned infrequently by retail and service establishments. Both food-related retail units and service establishments disproportionately report that they wanted to be "accessible to customers." These were the things looked for by at least half of the food-related retail businesses in both sub-categories and two-fifths of the service units. Only a very small proportion of the other businesses wanted a place in the old area or stressed accessibility to customers. The only exception to this is found among the non-food-related retail units. "Access to customers" was stressed by nearly one-fourth of these units.

While food-related units looked for a site that was in the old area and accessible to customers, non-food retail establishments were mainly concerned with accessibility to customers. Few wanted to remain in the old area. Jewelry firms were about equally distributed in the proportion which looked for "low rent or costs,"

5 In response to the question "Who tried to help you?", the relocation agency was mentioned by 15 per cent of the units.

6 For a further discussion of this, see Chapter III.

"more room," and an "attractive building" in a new site. Other specific things looked for in a site were reported by only a small minority of the establishments. Service units predominantly stressed "costs," "place in old area," and "access to customers" as the things looked for in a new site. And those businesses in the "other" category more frequently report that they looked for "more room" and an "attractive building." It is of special interest to note that "parking" was rarely mentioned by any of the business types. It may well be that this does not constitute a major site characteristic, but it may become a prime consideration only after other requirements have been satisfied. Further evidence of this is presented later in our discussion.

A further inquiry into site selection included a question on the relative importance attached to selected characteristics.[7] Our analysis of these responses shows marked differences among the business types. Food-related retail units in particular seem to place a great deal of emphasis on the type of neighborhood and on accessibility to customers. Three units out of four report both of these characteristics as being very important. The proportion is even higher for the food-related units that are distributed throughout the community than for those that largely relocated in the shopping center. Of the latter, only 60 per cent emphasized accessibility to customers, and 67 per cent emphasized type of neighborhood as very important site characteristics, while among the former the proportions are 79 per cent and 88 per cent respectively. These differences are likely due largely to differences in type of customer served. The units that relocated in the shopping center catered to a special group, that is, Jewish customers, but it is not necessary for them to be located in the same neighborhood, nor even to be readily accessible, because a large proportion of their customers would come to them regardless of their location. This is due to a lack of an alternative for the specialized products involved. Thus they can effectively draw their customers from a larger area than can other-type food-related units. The dependence on a larger market area is suggested by the greater emphasis these units place on parking accommodations and land

7 The site characteristics listed in the question were: Space in Building, Space in Land, Type of Neighborhood, Type of Business in Area, Parking Accommodations, Accessibility to Customers, and Nearness to Bus Line.

space as site characteristics. We find that 40 per cent felt that land space was very important, and 67 per cent report parking accommodation as also important. However, among all other food-related retail units, the proportion responding thusly is only 13 per cent and 42 per cent respectively. Establishments in the shopping center also place more emphasis on being near to a bus line. Of these units, 27 per cent consider nearness to a bus line as very important, whereas only 8 per cent of all other food-related retail units do so. If we look at the proportion that reports this characteristic as not important, we find that only half of those in the shopping center rate it thusly, as compared to 8 out of 10 of the other units. Thus the food-related retail units that do not have the unusual advantage of a "captured" trade are much more sensitive to type of neighborhood, type of business in area and access to customers than are any other types of business. Service units tend also to place a disproportionate amount of emphasis on type of neighborhood and accessibility to customers. The similarity between service units and food-related establishments is likely due to the frequency of recurrence of their customer relations. Such units are dependent upon a close relationship with their customers.

Service establishments are least likely to emphasize the importance of type of business in the area. Apparently these units do not perceive any advantage to be gained by locating in proximity to any other particular type of business which might serve to attract customers to the area. Also they are less likely than other-type businesses to see any merit in being near to a bus line. These units consider the amount of space in the building as very important, but little attention is given to land space, and only a minority report parking accommodations as a very important site characteristic.

Non-food-related retail establishments also place emphasis on amount of space in the building to be occupied and its accessibility to customers. In respect to these characteristics, they are quite similar to both service units and food-related retail establishments. However, they differ from the service establishments in the importance attached to parking accommodations, and they differ from both types of businesses in the importance placed on type of neighborhood. While this characteristic is emphasized particularly by the food-related units, it is rated as very important by only one-third of the non-food-related retail businesses. Type of business in the area is also rated as very important by only a small minority of the non-food-related units. Only one-fifth consider it as very important, while nearly half of the units rated it as not important. Little attention is given to nearness to the bus line.

Jewelry manufacturing and other manufacturing, wholesale, and construction businesses are quite similar in their rating of selected site characteristics. These businesses place particular emphasis on space in the building and to a lesser extent on parking accommodations. However, they place less stress on parking facilities than do retail businesses. This is to be expected, since customer relationships differ both in respect to type and frequency of contact. For those businesses that need to be accessible to their customers, parking facilities help to provide this accessibility. However for manufacturing and related establishments, parking accommodations are more likely needed for their workers than for customers; thus the needs would be viewed differently.

There are two important differences between the jewelry manufacturing firms and those units in the "other" category. These differences pertain to the relative importance placed on type of businesses in the area and nearness to the bus line as site characteristics. Jewelry manufacturing firms place more emphasis on nearness to the bus line than do any other businesses. Such units are also likely to stress the importance of type of businesses in the area. In this instance, however, it is to gain the advantage of being close to other jewelry firms. Consequently, when seeking a new site, these businesses tended to relocate in the jewelry industry area near the center of the city, even though it was generally in poor repair. The apparent shortcomings of the area in terms of its deterioration were compensated for by the advantage of remaining in the district.

The disproportionate emphasis of the jewelry manufacturing establishments on nearness to the bus line is probably for the benefit of their employees and not because of their customers. Such establishments tend to employ married women who are predominantly secondary family workers and are thus likely to be dependent on public transportation as a means of getting to work. At any rate, one unit out of four rated this as a very important site characteristic. This is not much less than the proportion that emphasized accessibility to customers. While type of neighborhood is important to food-related retail and service units, little attention is given this characteristic by the jewelry units or those in the "other" category. Similarly, the latter two types of business are less likely to place importance on being accessible to their customers.[8]

It is of particular interest to note that a substantial majority of all business types reports that nearness to the bus line is not considered important. At the other extreme, only a small minority of the units rate this as being very important. These responses range from a low of only 8 per cent of the service units to 25 per cent of the jewelry firms. These findings clearly indicate the degree to which business establishments are now oriented toward individual modes of travel. The meaning of the question is somewhat confusing, however, in that it is not clear as to whether the response is given in terms of customer relations or in terms of their employees. It is possible that the frame of reference may even have varied by type of business. In the case of jewelry firms, which have the lowest proportion reporting that this is unimportant and the largest proportion reporting it as "very important," the response, as already noted, is probably largely in terms of convenience for employees. To a lesser extent, this may also be the case with non-food-related retail units. At any rate, more than two-thirds of all units, except jewelry firms, report that nearness to the bus line is not an important consideration in the selection of a site.

These data clearly show that the type of characteristics stressed in selecting a site for relocation varies by type of business. The differences that are expressed seem to be largely a function of variations in the type of customer-business relationship that exists. Those units, such as food-related retail units, that have frequent and recurrent contacts with their customers place particular emphasis on type of neighborhood, type of business in the area, and accessibility to customers. However, these characteristics are of little importance to those units that are dependent upon a different customer relationship. While there are marked differences among types of business, there seems to be a rather substantial agree-

8 The latter observation should be viewed with caution, particularly for the jewelry units, for we have already observed that many did not move to the suburbs because it would be too inaccessible for their buyers when they came to town.

ment within each type of business as to the importance that should or should not be attached to selected site characteristics.

REASONS FOR SELECTING PRESENT LOCATION

The specific reason for selecting a site may be quite different from the characteristics thought to be important in rating sites in general, or even different from the things specifically looked for in trying to find a new location. Thus we now turn our attention to the reasons given for selecting the present site. Again we find that there are marked variations by type of business. While nearly half of the food-related retail establishments selected the present site because of its close physical proximity to the original location, the proportion declines to less than 10 per cent among jewelry manufacturing firms and among those in the "other" category.[9]

When attention is focused on the variations within the food-related group, we find that the same tendency is observed within each subgroup, but it is apparent that the high proportion selecting the site because it was near to the old location is due largely to the units that relocated in the shopping area on the same site. Four-fifths of these units report selecting the present site for this reason. But even apart from these units, a high disproportionate number of the food-related establishments give proximity to the original location as the reason for selecting the present site. Service units also have a high proportion that respond thusly. However, this reason is rarely mentioned by any of the other businesses. Thus it is the units that serve a limited market area and the businesses that provide frequently used products that try to minimize the negative consequences of the move by remaining close to the original area.

In many cases, there was no definite reason for selecting the present site. Approximately one unit in six or seven selected the present site only because of the lack of alternative locations, that

9 Earlier we observed that nearly half of the jewelry firms relocated within one-fifth of a mile of the original site. The purpose, however, was not stated in terms of wanting to remain in the old area, but rather they selected the site so as to be close to other jewelry units with which they were functionally interrelated.

is, the present site was the only thing available at the time. It was not selected because of any positive features. On the other hand, nearly one-third of the non-food-related retail and one-fourth of the jewelry and "other" businesses decided on the present site for the very generalized reason that they thought it would be a good business location. However, the characteristics of the site which, in their opinion, made it a good location, were not specified.

The general attractiveness of the building was the determining factor in site selection for 25 per cent of the "other" businesses and for 16 per cent of the non-food-related retail units. This, however, was not an important consideration for either food-related retail or service establishments. In a small minority of cases in each type of business, the selection of the present site was due to the prior ownership of property by the individual or by his family, but this occurred infrequently and does not vary by type of business.

There seems to be less uniformity or consensus in the reasons given by jewelry and service units than by other types of business, for 20 per cent and 26 per cent respectively give reasons for selecting the present site which were so varied that they were necessarily grouped in the "other" category. Such reasons tend to be highly individualistic and particularistic.[10]

The point we wish to emphasize from these data is the strong tendency for food-related units to select a site because of its nearness to the original location. It will be recalled that such businesses reported this feature as a very important site characteristic. Apparently these units thought they could minimize the disruptive effects of the forced displacement by remaining in or near the original area. Service units did also, but to a much lesser extent. To the remaining-type units the specific geographical location was of less importance, which is due in large part to differences in the type and frequency of the customer-business relationship. The manufacturing, wholesale, and construction establishments have the largest proportion that report selecting the present site because of the attractiveness of the building. These businesses, as already noted, were also more likely than other-type businesses to report space in the building as being very important as a site char-

10 Among jewelry firms this includes "wanting to be near other jewelry establishments"; however, this did not justify the creation of such a category in the coded data, since it did not apply to the other businesses.

acteristic. Perhaps it was the amount of space that made the building attractive. At any rate, they placed more emphasis on the building than did the other businesses. It is noteworthy also that a substantial minority of all businesses selected the present site because it was the only one available at the time.

THINGS LIKED AND DISLIKED: NEW AND OLD LOCATIONS

In an attempt to get at some of the consequences of relocation, questions were asked pertaining to the likes and dislikes about both the present and the former site. Attention is focused first on the positive aspects of each location. Since in most instances displacements occurred in old deteriorated areas, it is a little surprising that such a small proportion of all businesses should report that what they like best about their new location is that it is in a better neighborhood. This response varies little by type of business. Also it is of particular interest that the proportion responding thusly is as high or even higher for food-related retail units than for the other business types, even though nearly half of the former units selected the present site because of its proximity to the old area. However, even though the general condition of the new area is reported by a substantial number to be better than at the old location, as already noted, this improvement is rarely selected as the feature liked best about the new site. Our data show that more than one-fourth of the food-related retail units (one-third of those not in the Willard Center area) and two-fifths of the service units do not find anything to their liking in the new area. The proportion responding thusly among other business types is substantially lower, however.

The attractiveness of the building is mentioned as the thing liked best about the new location by nearly half of the jewelry firms and the businesses grouped together in the "other" category, even though this was given as the reason for selecting the site by a much smaller proportion. Among the other-type businesses, approximately one-fourth of the establishments report this as the feature of the new site that they like. This is the only feature liked about the new location that is reported by at least a substantial minority among each type of business. Although parking accommodations improved markedly with the move, only a small minority reports this as the feature they like about the present site. The highest proportion responding thusly is found among jewelry manufacturing firms, but even here this feature is reported by less than one-sixth of the units. Service establishments have the lowest proportion in this response category.

When the food-related retail firms are divided into sub-groups, it is found that parking accommodations are emphasized by those units where a majority relocated in the new shopping center. Among these units, one in three mentions parking as the feature liked about the present location, whereas none of the other food-related units do so. The change among the Willard Center units following the move is particularly marked, for none of these units mention this regarding the old location. Even though parking accommodations are mentioned by only a small minority of all units at the new location, the proportion doing so is much higher than for the old location. The increase is particularly marked among non-food-related units (3.5 per cent to 12.3 per cent) and among manufacturing, wholesale, and construction establishments (2.3 per cent to 11.4 per cent), where there is a five-fold increase.

In recalling the things liked about the old site, prior to the move, the characteristics mentioned most frequently pertain to very general advantages of the location. Thus the most frequent responses are to the effect that prior to displacement they had "a good trade established" or that it was "a good location and accessible." Food-related retail units in particular emphasize that, at the old location, they had a good trade established. This response is highest among the food-related units from areas other than the Willard Center project. Service units also have a large disproportionate number that respond thusly. Apparently it is the business volume, the security of an established trade at an established location, that is evaluated highly and not the physical characteristics of the site.

Food-related businesses from the Willard Center were more likely to emphasize the low costs of the old location. This is to be expected since these units occupied deteriorated slum buildings in a congested area, but due to the specialized nature of these businesses (kosher markets) they were able to maintain a good trade, even though the buildings and area were unattractive. It is noted that, while none of these units mentioned parking accommodations as something that they liked at the old locations, one-third gave this as an attractive feature of the new site. This, of course, is consistent with the changes that actually occurred. Prior to clearance these units had a very real parking problem, but the new shopping center provided ample off-street parking adjacent to the store fronts.

Non-food-related retail units and, to a lesser extent, service establishments, disproportionately report that the old site was a good location and accessible; however, regarding the new location the feature that is reported most frequently is the attractiveness of the building occupied. It is particularly noteworthy that only 5 per cent of the service units report no likes for the old site, but 40 per cent do so in reference to the new location. A similar but less marked difference between present and former location is observed among food-related retail units also. The proportion reporting no likes for the area nearly doubles following relocation. But among the businesses in the "other" category, change occurs in the opposite direction. Thus, while nearly one-third report that there was nothing that they liked about the original site, this declines to nearly one-tenth of the establishments at the new location. Among these units, less than 10 per cent liked the attractiveness of the building in the former area, whereas nearly half of the units report this as the feature that they like about their present site. A similar change is found among jewelry manufacturing firms. Non-food-related retail establishments emphasize the accessibility of the former location more so than any other characteristic. They report this more frequently than any of the other businesses, but to a lesser extent this characteristic is also emphasized by service establishments.

There seems to be little consensus among jewelry firms as to things liked about the old location, for no single feature is mentioned by even one-fifth of the establishments. Rather, their responses seem to be distributed throughout the whole range of likes reported by other businesses. However, following relocation, nearly half of the units report that the feature they like is the attractiveness of the building occupied. Parking accommodations are also frequently reported as an attractive feature of the new site. These responses are very similar to those reported by manufacturing, wholesale, and construction units.

In short, service units have the largest proportion reporting that there is nothing that they like about the new site, whereas these units are the least likely to respond thusly regarding the original location. The food-related retail units also have a disproportionately large number of establishments that report no likes for the new area. Jewelry firms emphasize the attractiveness of the building occupied at the new location, but there seems to be little agreement on what they liked prior to the move. A similar high proportion of the manufacturing, wholesale, and construction units emphasize the attractiveness of the building occupied at the new site, but these units, more so than any other businesses, report no likes for the original location. It is only the service establishments, and to a lesser extent the food-related units, that have a large number who find nothing to their liking at the new location.

Turning now to the responses regarding things disliked about the old and present site, we find that food-related retail and service establishments have the largest proportion reporting no dislikes in appraising the original location, but they have the lowest proportion responding thusly in respect to the new area. More than half of the service establishments report no dislikes concerning their original site, but the proportion of such responses declines to only 13 per cent in evaluating the new location. For food-related retail units, the proportion of comparable responses declines from 39 per cent to 21 per cent. However, among the latter, substantial differences are found between the businesses from the Willard Center area and those from all other projects. Half of the latter, but only one-fifth of the former, report no dislikes for the original location. The pattern of difference is the same after the move, but the proportion reporting no dislikes declines.

It is the businesses in the manufacturing, wholesale, and construction category that are least likely to report no dislikes in evaluating the old area, but these establishments have the largest proportion reporting no dislikes in the new area. Apparently these units have found the new location more satisfactory than their original site. However, as already noted, this was not the case for food-related retail and service establishments. But for non-food-related retail and jewelry firms, the proportion reporting no dislikes remains substantially the same after the move.

It will be recalled that a large proportion (48 per cent) of the food-related retail units gave as their reason for selecting the present site its proximity to the old location; however, when asked what they disliked about their new site, the most frequent criticism is that they are in a "poor area in transition." This criticism of the new location is rarely mentioned by any of the other businesses. But, apart from jewelry firms, approximately one-fifth of each type of business criticized their former sites because of the "poor neighborhood" in which they were located. Complaints concerning the condition of the area around the present site come largely from those units that were displaced from the Willard Center project and that moved into the new shopping center at the same location. While 60 per cent of the units in this sub-group complain that the present site is in a poor area in transition, only 4 per cent of all other food-related units respond thusly.[1] The latter either report no dislikes for the present site or report that they dislike the "poor business" they are doing at the new location. The condition of the area is a frequent complaint regarding the old location, but is rarely mentioned as a dislike after the move.

Among jewelry firms, 45 per cent report that they disliked the unattractiveness of the building occupied in the former area, but only 18 per cent mention this as a shortcoming of the present site. The latter, however, exceeds the proportion reported by any other type of business. The high proportion after the move is due in part to the tendency for these units to remain in the old jewelry area for the advantages of such a location. The unattractiveness of the building is mentioned among the "other" businesses by 27 per cent of the establishments before the move, but by only 11 per cent in the new area. It is the businesses in this category that are least likely to report any dislikes for the present site. For all businesses, except services, there is a decline following the move in the proportion reporting that what they dislike about their site is the unattractiveness of the building occupied. This is rarely mentioned regarding the new location.

Poor parking is frequently reported as a dislike concerning the area formerly occupied, but is rarely mentioned as a dislike fol-

1 The Willard Center area is undergoing a rapid change in the composition of the population. Longtime Jewish residents are moving out and Negroes are moving in. The significance of this change is explored below.

lowing the move, except among the jewelry firms and service units where the proportions are about the same for both areas. In general most businesses are more critical of the new location and are more specific in their dislikes than they are when asked to evaluate the original site. Perhaps this is as much due to nostalgia for the "good old days" as to anything else. Being somewhat displeased with having to leave an established site, as indicated by their reported likes of the old area, they tend to find things as shortcomings in the new area which they may not even have noticed at the old site. At any rate, the businesses which are primarily dependent on a market that is recurrent on almost a daily basis, such as food-related retail and service establishments, seem to have had fewer dislikes at the old location but are more likely to report dislikes for the present site. These reactions are probably due more to changes in volume of business than to changes in the physical features of the site.

CHANGES IN SELECTED SITE CHARACTERISTICS

It seems quite clear from the data presented in Table 3-5 that for a substantial majority of all business types the move improved the general physical condition of their business location. For nearly two-thirds of the units within each type of business, except jewelry manufacturing, the move was to a larger building. Businesses in the "other" category have the largest proportion that moved to a building that provided more space than occupied prior to displacement. This was the experience of seven units out of ten. Less than one unit in five moved into a smaller structure. A similar proportion of service units also moved into smaller quarters, while slightly more than one-fourth of the retail and jewelry establishments moved to a building with less space. Jewelry firms were less likely than other-type units to increase their space following the move, but were more likely to move into another structure with the same amount of space. Service units also tended disproportionately to move to a site with the same amount of space as the building previously occupied.

Considerably more variation by type of business is found in respect to the relative age of the building occupied at the new loca-

TABLE 3-5

SELECTED CHARACTERISTICS OF SITE BEFORE AND AFTER MOVE BY TYPE OF BUSINESS

Characteristic	Food – Related Retail			Other Retail	Jewelry Mfg.	Service	Other
	Total	W. C.	Other				
Amount of Space							
Total Per Cent	100.0	(100.0)	(100.0)	100.0	100.0	100.0	100.0
More Here	66.7	(66.7)	(66.7)	63.2	49.0	60.5	70.4
Same	10.3	(13.3)	(8.3)	10.5	26.5	18.4	11.4
Less Here	23.0	(20.0)	(25.0)	26.3	24.5	21.1	18.2
Age of Building							
Total Per Cent	100.0	(100.0)	(100.0)	100.0	100.0	100.0	100.0
Present One Newer	60.5	(73.3)	(52.2)	54.4	36.7	42.1	59.1
About Same Age	18.5	(26.7)	(13.0)	28.1	36.7	23.7	27.3
Present One Older	21.0	......	(34.8)	17.5	26.5	34.2	13.6
Condition of Building							
Total Per Cent	100.0	(100.0)	(100.0)	100.0	100.0	100.0	100.0
This One Better	64.1	(80.0)	(54.2)	56.1	53.1	42.1	68.2
About Same	23.1	(20.0)	(25.0)	28.1	28.6	21.1	15.9
This One Worse	12.8	......	(20.8)	15.8	18.3	36.8	15.9
General Condition of Area							
Total Per Cent	100.0	(100.0)	(100.0)	100.0	100.0	100.0	100.0
This Is Better	46.2	(13.3)	(66.7)	59.7	40.8	34.2	68.2
Same	25.6	(40.0)	(16.7)	26.3	51.0	36.8	18.2
This Is Worse	28.2	(46.7)	(16.7)	14.0	8.2	28.9	13.6

tion. With the exception of jewelry firms and service establishments, a majority of the businesses moved into newer buildings than they had occupied prior to displacement. It is the manufacturing, wholesale, and construction units, and to a lesser extent non-food-related retail units, that have the largest proportion moving into a new building. Part of this difference is due to a higher rate of suburbanization among these units, since businesses moving to the suburbs, as already noted, are much more likely to occupy new structures than those that remained in the city. Jewelry firms and service establishments tended to remain close to the original location; consequently they either moved to another structure which was older or about the same age as the one from which they had been displaced. While only a small minority of all businesses moved to an older structure, more than one-fourth of the service units and one-third of the jewelry establishments did so. The reasons for this are probably quite different, however. In the case of jewelry manufacturing, the move was to an old building in order to remain in the jewelry industry district. For service units the move, in part, was to another structure in close proximity, but it should also be noted that these units would have less choice in selecting a site because of their small size and limited ability to pay, as is suggested by their sales volume. Nearly half of the units do not have any employees.

Marked differences are found within the food-related units. Nearly three-fourths of the establishments from the Willard Center area moved into a newer building. Most of these units moved into the new shopping center. However, only one-half of all the other food-related businesses moved into a newer building, while more than one-third moved into older structures. Similar differences within the food-related group are found in respect to the relative condition of the building occupied and the condition of the area after relocation, as compared with prior to the move. While 80 per cent of those from the Willard Center project report the present building to be in better condition, only 13 per cent report an improvement in the general condition of the area. This is to be expected since most of the units remained in the same area. Among the other food-related businesses, only 54 per cent report an improvement in the building, but 67 per cent report that the present area is better than the one from which they had been displaced. On the other hand, only 33 per cent report the condition of the area to be the same or worse, as compared with 87 per cent of those from the Willard project. Those from the latter area show more of an improvement in building than the establishments from all other areas; however, the latter have a much larger proportion reporting that their present site is in a better area. Thus those that moved into the new shopping center at the same location show more of an improvement in the quality of the building occupied than other-type food-related retail units, but this was at the expense of remaining in a deteriorated area, that is, they remained at the same location. However, these units rate the area as being "worse" than before. This is due to the changes that are occurring in the contiguous area. The buildings are old and rapidly progressing in disrepair, and the population is in the process of changing from a largely Jewish concentration to a Negro neighborhood. Although these businesses in the past catered predominantly to a Jewish market, the change in composition of the area seems to have been to the advantage of these businesses. In short, they have been able to retain the former Jewish trade, even though it moved away, since these are kosher markets, and they also serve a neighborhood market which consists of Negro customers. Consequently their volume of business has increased.

This, of course, is an atypical experience and thus is not representative of the consequences of displacement and relocation of food-related retail units. Rather, it is the other food-related units that are more representative. For a majority of the latter establishments, the move was to an improved site. Not only did they move to a newer building and one that is in better condition than the one previously occupied, but they also moved to a better area. Thus the physical environment was substantially improved. However, a substantial minority moved to less space and to an older building in worse condition than the one from which they had been displaced. A small minority moved to a less attractive area.

Non-food-related retail establishments and those in the manufacturing, wholesale, and construction category tended more than any other types of business to improve the general quality of their sites after relocation. Not only did a substantial majority move to newer and better buildings but also to areas which they rated as superior to the one from which they had been displaced. Only a very small minority moved to a site which they considered to be inferior in quality to the one previously occupied.

It is among the jewelry firms that the least amount of change is found because of their marked tendency to remain in the jewelry district. Consequently the move for these units was largely an inconvenience and had little effect on the physical aspects of their site, even though the displacement was from a deteriorated area. However, even among these units, more than half moved to a better building, although it was neither newer nor in a better area. Service units, in particular, did not improve their site characteristics. Although a minority did move to a newer, better building in a better area, a nearly equal number moved to a site the characteristics of which they rated lower than the one from which they had been displaced. Thus we find that one-third or more moved to an older structure and one in worse condition than the one from which they had moved. Also, more than one unit in four moved to an area which they rated as worse than the one previously occupied. For a majority of the service units, the move was not to an improved site even though, as observed elsewhere, they experienced a sharp increase in rents – an increase that exceeded that of any other type of business. Concurrently they experienced a substantial decline in business activity.[2] Apparently for this type of business, displacement is much more than an inconvenience. Not only do they have a relatively high non-survival rate, but those that successfully relocate must on the average pay substantially more for little or no improvement in the physical characteristics of their site.

In general, there is an upgrading in site characteristics following relocation, but for a substantial number of the units there is no improvement in the overall quality of the site. The businesses with the largest proportion improving their relative site characteristics are the non-food-related retail units and those in the manufacturing, wholesale, and construction category. The latter units, in particular, have a substantial majority which moved to a newer, larger, better building in a better area than the one occupied prior to displacement. A substantial minority of the service units, how-

2 Some of the economic aspects of relocation were considered in Chapter III.

ever, moved to an older building in worse condition and in a worse area than the one from which they had been displaced. The new location does have more space, a site characteristic that was considered important in selecting a new location.

NEW CONSTRUCTION AND SIZE OF BUILDINGS

Most of the displaced businesses moved into existing structures. However, nearly one-fourth of the units moved into a new building. The proportion doing so ranged from a low of only 10 per cent to the service units to a high of 39 per cent of the food-related retail establishments. These data are shown in Table 4-5. The high proportion of new construction among the latter units is due largely to the establishments from only one of the renewal projects, that is, Willard Center where many of the businesses moved into a new shopping center. Among these units, nearly three out of four had a new building constructed, as compared with less than one in five of all the other displaced units of the same type. Thus, under ordinary circumstances according to these data, we would expect a large majority of the food-related units to move into existing structures. Also a majority of these units require little space. Of those that moved into existing structures, more than half occupied less than 1,000 square feet.

The businesses in the manufacturing, wholesale, and construction category also have a high disproportionate number of units that moved into a new building, while nearly all of the jewelry firms and service units moved into existing structures. One reason for this is that jewelry firms tended to remain in the jewelry district which is in an old built-up area near the center of the city. In this area, the cost of new construction would be prohibitive, and sites for new construction are not available. Also their needs could best be met in the older structures where they could get a large amount of space at comparatively low rents.[3] The latter would also apply particularly to service establishments. However, as noted earlier, even under these conditions rents increased substantially following the move.

3 For an interesting discussion of the need for aged buildings in cities see: Jane Jacobs, *The Death and Life of Great American Cities*, Ch. 10, Random House, 1961.

TABLE 4-5

SIZE OF BUILDING OCCUPIED AND PROPORTION HAVING BUILDING CONSTRUCTED BY TYPE OF BUSINESS

Have Building Constructed and Size of Building	Food – Related Retail			Other Retail	Jewelry Mfg.	Service	Other
	Total	W. C.	Other				
Size of Building Occupied							
Total Per Cent	100.0	(100.0)	(100.0)	100.0	100.0	100.0	100.0
Under 1,000	44.7	(26.7)	(56.5)	27.3	27.0	64.7	6.8
1,000 – 4,999	47.4	(60.0)	(39.1)	36.3	50.0	26.5	38.6
5,000 and Over	7.9	(13.3)	(4.3)	36.4	23.0	8.8	54.5
Median	1,267			2,923	3,267	750	5,309
Have Building Constructed							
Total Per Cent	100.0	(100.0)	(100.0)	100.0	100.0	100.0	100.0
Yes	38.5	(73.3)	(16.7)	17.9	12.2	10.5	36.4
No	61.5	(26.7)	(83.3)	82.1	87.8	89.5	63.6

In response to the question on why they had decided to put up a new building, we find that 30 per cent of the establishments did so in order "to be able to get a specific location which they wanted" or "to be able to stay in the same neighborhood." More than one-third of the reasons given for putting up a new building included "needed special-type building," or "no other suitable building was available." Nearly one-sixth of the new buildings were put up because the owners "wanted a new plant," largely because it was considered cleaner, more efficient, and cheaper. The emphasis placed on specific building needs probably accounts for the high disproportionate number of new buildings constructed for businesses engaged in manufacturing, wholesale, and construction activities. Also, this was facilitated by the high rate of movement to the suburbs where businesses were more likely to move into a new building. The specific reasons given for moving into new structures would less likely apply to jewelry and service establishments. Also the latter disproportionately relocated in the city where the availability of sites for new buildings is much more limited. The lower rentals in the older buildings are also an important factor.

The non-food related retail units have a larger proportion moving into new structures than is found among jewelry and service establishments, but a lower proportion than is found among the "other"-type businesses. It may be that there is less need for new construction for these establishments since their specific space needs, as suggested by the median-size buildings occupied, is approximately equal to the average size of building occupied by all of the relocated units. Since their apparent space needs were rather typical of the spaces available, they could more readily find a site among existing structures. On the other hand, among the units with a high proportion moving into new structures, we find that the average size of structure occupied exceeds 5,000 square feet and only a very small proportion (7 per cent) of the units moved into a building with less than 1,000 square feet.

Building needs for relocation apparently vary significantly by type of business. It is the manufacturing, construction, and wholesale establishments that occupy the largest buildings. The median size is slightly more than 5,300 square feet. While more than half of the establishments have more than 5,000 square feet of space, less than 7 per cent report that they occupy less than 1,000 square feet. Jewelry firms occupy less space than the manufacturing, construction, and wholesale establishments, but the median-size structure exceeds that of any of the other business types. Jewelry establishments on the average occupy approximately 3,300 square feet. There is, however, considerable range in size of building occupied. Thus while less than one-fourth of the jewelry units have 5,000 or more square feet, we find a slightly larger proportion occupying less than 1,000 square feet. The latter are probably smaller firms which do subcontract work for the larger establishments in the district. A majority of the units are found in the middle-size group.

Service establishments in particular occupy very small structures. The median size is only 750 square feet. Two-thirds of these units occupy less than 1,000 square feet, while less than 9 per cent report occupying a structure with more than 5,000 square feet. The latter is very similar to the proportion of food-related retail units occupying the larger structures, but the average space of these retail units is nearly double the space reported by service establishments. Food-related retail units are more concentrated in the middle-sized category, that is, buildings with from 1,000 to 5,000 square feet. It is noted, however, that it is the markets in the Willard shopping area that account for most of this. A majority of all other food-related retail units have less than 1,000 square feet. Other-type retail units report approximately two and one-half times as much space as the food-related retail establishments. Such businesses are much more likely to occupy structures in the largest category, and less likely to occupy structures in the smallest category.

It is readily apparent that space needs in relocation vary markedly by type of business. Service units require the least amount of space, while manufacturing, wholesale, and construction units require more space than any other type of business. Also, service units and jewelry firms tend disproportionately to relocate in existing structures, which is likely due to their peculiar location needs as well as cost needs. Manufacturing, wholesale, and construction units also disproportionately occupy new structures. This is probably due in part to their tendency to move to the suburbs. Also they may have used displacement as an opportunity not only to get the space that they wanted but also to provide the type of building needed.

PARKING ACCOMMODATIONS

In urban areas, as already noted, businesses are perennially faced with the problem of providing adequate parking accommodations. Thus a question of concern is the extent to which there is a change in parking adequacy following relocation. Accordingly businesses were asked if parking facilities were adequate at the former location and at the present site. The responses to these questions by type of business are shown in Table 5-5. At both locations there is considerable variation by type of business in the proportion reporting adequate parking. It is readily apparent, however, that within each business type the proportion reporting adequate parking increases substantially following the move. At the new location a majority of all business types reports that parking facilities are adequate.

The most marked change is found among the food-related retail units, where the proportion reporting adequate parking increases from 37 per cent to 71 per cent. However, this change is largely due to changes in the one sub-category, that is, among the businesses displaced in the Willard Center project. Among the latter, only 21 per cent report adequate facilities at the old location, whereas 93 per cent do so regarding the present site. This is to be expected, however, in that most of these units moved into a new shopping center which provided ample off-street parking. It is among the other food-related retail units and service establishments that the least improvement in parking is found. Even though both show an increase in parking adequacy, the proportionate increase is less than is found among the other types of business.

At the new location, jewelry firms have the largest proportion that report parking to be inadequate, and this in turn is followed by service establishments. This is, of course, due to the type of areas into which these businesses moved, that is, they continued in the old built-up areas of the central city. On the other hand, the businesses that disproportionately moved to the

TABLE 5-5

PARKING ADEQUACY AT FORMER AND PRESENT LOCATION BY TYPE OF BUSINESS

Adequate Parking	Food – Related Retail			Other Retail	Jewelry Mfg.	Service	Other
	Total	W. C.	Other				
				Former Location			
Total Per Cent	100.0	(100.0)	(100.0)	100.0	100.0	100.0	100.0
Yes	37.1	(21.4)	(47.6)	56.8	43.8	55.2	52.6
No	62.9	(78.6)	(52.4)	43.2	56.2	44.8	47.4
				Present Location			
Total Per Cent	100.0	(100.0)	(100.0)	100.0	100.0	100.0	100.0
Yes	71.4	(92.8)	(57.1)	81.8	59.4	65.5	73.7
No	28.6	(7.1)	(42.9)	18.2	40.6	34.5	26.3

suburbs have the largest proportion reporting adequate parking at their present site. This is particularly high among the non-food-related retail units. Among these units, the proportion reporting adequate parking increases from 57 per cent prior to displacement to 82 per cent after relocation. Thus one of the apparent positive consequences of the move is the marked improvement in parking accommodations. This is shared by all types of business but not to the same extent.

AREA SERVED

The size of the area served varies significantly by type of business. This is clearly evident from the data presented in Table 6-5 for both the old and the new location. However, for some types of businesses, the move did have an appreciable effect on the size of the area served. In a majority of cases, the modal area from which customers were drawn did not change with the move; nonetheless important changes did occur. The most marked changes are found among food-related retail units and service establishments.

At the old location, food-related retail units had the smallest market area. Nearly three-fourths of the establishments drew their customers primarily from the immediate neighborhood, and more than 90 per cent drew their customers from the same side of town in which they were located. Thus their customers came predominantly from a rather limited geographical area. The move, however, changed this rather dramatically, for the proportion servicing an immediate neighborhood area dropped to only 44 per cent, and the proportion drawing customers from the same side of town decreased to approximately two-thirds. Thus the size of the area served after relocation was still more limited than for any other type of business, but there was a sharp increase in the proportion of customers who did not come from the neighborhood or even the same side of the city in which the business was located. The proportion of customers coming from the larger community increased nearly four-fold, from less than 8 per cent before displacement to more than 30 per cent following the move.

Once again we find that the changes observed among the food-

TABLE 6-5

AREA SERVED BEFORE AND AFTER RELOCATION BY TYPE OF BUSINESS

Area Served	Food – Related Retail			Other Retail	Jewelry Mfg.	Service	Other
	Total	W. C.	Other				
Former Location							
Total Per Cent	100.0	(100.0)	(100.0)	100.0	100.0	100.0	100.0
Neighborhood	71.8	(66.7)	(75.0)	12.7	14.3	52.6	2.3
Same Side of Town	20.5	(13.3)	(25.0)	6.3	8.2	5.3	4.5
Larger Community	7.7	(20.0)	......	31.7	38.7	36.8	45.5
Region – Other	.....	......	......	49.2	38.8	5.3	47.7
Present Location							
Total Per Cent	100.0	(100.0)	(100.0)	100.0	100.0	100.0	100.0
Neighborhood	43.9	(33.3)	(50.0)	10.5	8.2	34.2	.....
Same Side of Town	25.6	(33.3)	(20.8)	10.5	12.2	13.2	6.8
Larger Community	25.4	(33.3)	(20.8)	36.8	40.8	44.7	43.2
Region – Other	5.1	......	(8.4)	42.1	38.8	7.9	50.0

related retail units are due in large part to the establishments from the Willard Center project, which are made up disproportionately of kosher markets. When attention is focused on these units as compared with all other displaced food-related retail establishments, we find that the experiences of the two groups are quite different. Even before the move, the Willard Center units were less dependent on a neighborhood market. Two-thirds served such an area as compared with three-fourths of all the other comparable units. After the move, the proportion dependent only on a neighborhood market declined within both subgroups, but the proportionate decrease was substantially larger for the unit from the Willard Center project. Following relocation, even though most of the establishments remained in the same area but in a new shopping center, the proportion drawing their customers only from the immediate neighborhood declined to only one-third. Among other food-related units, the decline was only to 50 per cent.

The larger decline among the Willard Center project establishments is due to a combination of factors. For one thing, they greatly improved their parking facilities and thus could better accommodate non-local customers, that is, those that would be traveling by car. Consequently they could continue to effectively reach the former residents of the area who had moved either to a different section of the city or to the suburbs. That this was accomplished is suggested by the larger market area served after the move. Since these units catered predominantly to a Jewish population and this population moved out of the neighborhood in which the businesses were located, but continued to purchase its food from these same establishments, the size of the market area changed. This type of change would occur only when a highly specialized product was involved and competition from other areas was limited. The experiences of these units, however, are in no way typical or at all representative of the consequences of relocation for other-type food-related retail units. Our data show that the other food-related units continued to serve a more circumscribed market area, even though the proportion serving a non-neighborhood area increased following relocation. But even at the new location, these units were more likely than any other type of business to serve only a neighborhood market.

Service units also experienced a change in type of area served, but the magnitude of the difference is considerably less. But even here the change is marked and shows the same pattern. More than half of the service units had served an immediate neighborhood market prior to displacement, but this dropped to only one-third of the units after relocation. This was partially compensated for by the increase in the proportion of customers who came from the same side of town. This proportion more than doubled. The increase was from only 5 per cent at the old location to 13 per cent after the move. No doubt these were largely the same customers served at the old location. These units moved only a short distance.

For all of the other business types, no really marked change in area served accompanied the move. This is not surprising in that the other units generally attracted customers from a broader area prior to displacement. Of their customers, only a very small minority came from within the neighborhood or even from the same section of the city in which they were located. Thus such businesses would be much less sensitive to a specific change in location, since the move would not be as disruptive to their customer relationships as in the case of food-related retail and, to a lesser extent, service establishments. The latter-type businesses, however, since their customers came disproportionately from a small geographical area, would more likely feel the full brunt of displacement. Even if they relocated in close proximity, which some attempted to do, they were unable to retain their established customer relationships, since many customers had also been displaced and were thus no longer living in the area. Nonetheless it is evident that one of the reasons for food-related retail units, in particular, wanting to relocate close to the old area, as noted earlier, was to retain their neighborhood market. However, for a substantial number, as is readily evident, this was not effective, for the market area changed following the move. They lost their neighborhood market. For a substantial majority of these units (nearly three units out of four), the area served after the move was different from the area served prior to displacement. Thus it is evident that they had to depend at least in part on establishing relationships with new customers after the move. This was the case for service units also, but to a lesser extent. Among the latter units, more than half served a different area following relocation.

CHANGES IN VOLUME AND VALUE OF BUSINESS

One of the crucial questions related to displacement and relocation pertains to the relative economic position of the businesses after the move, as compared with conditions while at the original site. In effect, the question of concern here is just what are some of the economic consequences of displacement for those units that succeed in moving to a new site? Thus the relocated business owners were asked to evaluate the changes that had occurred in the volume, as well as the value, of their business at their present site, as compared with the old location. Responses to these questions show that changes vary substantially by type of business. However, within each type of business, there is considerable variation in how the move has affected both the volume and value of the business.

One-third of the establishments report an increase in volume of business after the move; however, the proportion ranges from a low of one-fifth of the service units to a high of nearly half of the food-related retail establishments.[4] At the other extreme, half of the service establishments report a decline in volume of business following relocation. By way of comparison, one-third of all of the relocated businesses report a decline. It is evident that service units are much more sensitive to the effects of the move than are any other business type. This is likely due to their greater dependency on a localized market. Also their relationships to their customers are more recurrent than for many other types of businesses. Thus a specific location and accessibility to customers take on added importance. Service establishments are also more likely to report a decline in value at the new location than are any other business types, and are least likely to report an increase.

The types of units with the smallest proportion reporting a decline in volume of business following the move are those in the "other" category, that is the manufacturing, wholesale, and con-

4 This would not have been expected in terms of the ordinary relationship food-related retail units have with their customers; however, this proportion is unduly influenced by types of units that are less dependent on being in close proximity to their customers, that is, those in the Willard Center.

struction units. For a majority of these establishments, the move did not have any effect on their volume of business, for it is reported to be the same at both locations. These units also have the smallest proportion reporting their business to be worth less at the new location and the largest proportion reporting an increase in value.

Of particular interest are the findings pertaining to food-related retail establishments. A disproportionately large number seem to have relocated successfully, at least as far as volume of business is concerned. Nearly half of the units report doing more business at the new site than prior to the move. Also nearly half of the units report their business to be worth more now than formerly. However, for a substantial minority, there was a decline in volume after the move. While more than one-third report a decline in volume of business, less than one-fifth report their business to have declined in value.

The rather favorable outcome for the food-related retail units is due in part to the units from the Willard Center project area. Both in respect to the amount of business and value of business a majority of these units report an increase. However, among the other food-related units, as many report business declines as report an increase. The only other businesses with a larger proportion reporting a decline are the service units. The more favorable economic adjustment by the units from the Willard Center project is due to the type of market served. As noted earlier, these units, because of the type of products involved, were able to retain their Jewish trade, even though this population no longer lived in the same neighborhood. Thus these units were not only able to retain their usual customers but also added the incoming Negroes as new customers. Consequently they experienced a rise in volume of business. The value of their businesses increased not only because volume increased but because they occupied new structures in a shopping area with adequate parking facilities. Again it is noted that this group is quite atypical. Rather, it is to the other food-related units that one should look to determine the consequences of displacement. Among the latter units, two out of five experienced a decline in volume and one in five a decline in value. Only service units have a larger proportion reporting a decline.

Among non-food related retail units, two out of five experienced an increase in business after the move, while nearly one-third report no change. However, nearly three units out of ten experienced a decline at the new location. The value of these businesses did not decline accordingly. Nearly half of the establishments report an increase in value, and more than one-third report no change. Only 13 per cent report their business to be worth less now than prior to displacement. Thus for these units the financial losses resulting from the move are limited. The only other businesses to experience less of a decline in volume of business, as well as of value, are those in the manufacturing, wholesale, and construction category. Of the latter, only 19 per cent report less business, and 11 per cent report a decline in value.

Jewelry manufacturing firms have a high disproportionate number that experienced a decline in volume of business following the move. This was the experience of more than two units out of five. However, a much smaller proportion reports a decline in value. Nearly half of the units report no change and more than one-third report an increase; thus it is only a small minority that experience a decrease in value at the new location. These findings must be viewed, however, with a great deal of caution, for more is involved here than the consequences of displacement and relocation. It is evident from the comments of the owners of these businesses that most of the decline is quite independent of the move. Rather, it is attributed to recent changes in market conditions due to foreign imports into this country, particularly of costume jewelry from Japan. There is general agreement that a decline would have occurred even if they had not been forced to move. Displacement did occur, however, at an inopportune time when the businesses were faced with financial problems because of general economic conditions in this industry.

Every type of business has a much larger proportion reporting a decline in volume of business than reports that the value of the business declined following the move. This difference is particularly large among jewelry firms and service units, but the difference is also marked among both types of retail establishments. For example, 41 per cent of the jewelry units report less business, but only 16 per cent report that their business is worth less now than prior to displacement. Similarly, among service units, nearly half report a drop in business, but a much smaller proportion reports their businesses have declined in value. Similar but smaller differences are also found among the other business types. It is evident that a substantial number of the establishments suffered a loss in business after displacement, but this could well be viewed as a temporary phenomenon. At least it must be so perceived by the owners, for only a small minority report their business to be worth less now than prior to the move.

Viewed differently, we find that businesses are more likely to experience an increase in value, rather than in volume, of business. This pattern of difference is observed within each type of business, but the difference is particularly marked among those units in the manufacturing, wholesale, and construction category. Only one-fourth of these units report an increase in volume, but more than half of the units report that their business is worth more now than prior to displacement. It is probable that the value of business is expressed in large part not in terms of volume but rather in respect to the worth of the building occupied and the business potential of the area. That is, value is being expressed in terms of future expectations as to the amount of business that will be generated at the new location. Also these businesses disproportionately improved their buildings as well as other aspects of the physical environment.

In short, it seems as though it is the units that are predominantly dependent on a localized market that are most likely to experience a decline particularly in volume of business following the move. Such businesses also have a larger proportion reporting a decline in value, but the differences are less marked. Service units seem to be particularly sensitive to the disruptive effects of the move. Half of the relocated units report an actual decline in business, and three out of ten establishments also report their business to have declined in value. Food-related retail units that are dependent largely on a neighborhood market are also particularly sensitive to the move. The consequences of displacement are quite different for the non-food-related retail units and those in the manufacturing, wholesale, and construction category.

REACTION TO NEW LOCATION

Many of the businesses are doing better at the new location than they had expected, but the proportion doing so varies markedly by type of business. This is shown in Table 7-5. Service units in particular have a very low proportion who report that business at the new location is better than they had expected it to be. There is no way to determine how systematic or realistic they were, or even the basis for their expectations, but at any rate, among service establishments in only 5 per cent of the cases did the amount of business exceed expectations, whereas for one-third, business fell short of expectations. Among food-related retail units, the proportion that fell short of expectations is even higher. More than two-fifths of the units are doing less business than they had expected to do at the new location. This is the highest proportion reported by any type of business. It is only in a small minority of cases among both non-food retail and "other" businesses that the volume of business falls short of expectations; however, in both instances business is better than expected for nearly one-fourth of the units. This is not exceeded by any other type of business.

With the exception of food-related retail units, a majority of business units reports the amount of business they are doing is about what they had expected at the new site. While nearly one-third of the jewelry firms report doing less business than expected, the major reason for this does not seem to be related to the disruptive effects of displacement and relocation. Rather, it is largely attributed to a general slump in the jewelry industry. This was viewed in part as a temporary phenomenon, but it was frequently reported that this was also a continuation of a long-term decline that had been plaguing the jewelry industry in Rhode Island for several years. The current year had apparently witnessed an above-average dip, but most of the owners reported that conditions would improve in the near future.

No such interpretation would, however, apply to the large proportion who did less than expected among the food-related retail and service establishments. In the latter instances, perhaps the expectations were unrealistic or based on incomplete information, or they may have been retrospectively established. At any rate, it clearly indicates an inability on the part of these businesses to prop-

TABLE 7-5

REACTION TO NEW LOCATION BY TYPE OF BUSINESS

Selected Reaction	Food – Related Retail			Other Retail	Jewelry Mfg.	Service	Other
	Total	W. C.	Other				
Volume of Business Compared With Expectation							
Total Per Cent	100.0	(100.0)	(100.0)	100.0	100.0	100.0	100.0
Better Than Expected	15.4	(6.7)	(20.8)	22.8	18.4	5.3	22.7
About What Expected	41.0	(53.3)	(33.3)	66.7	51.0	60.5	63.7
Less Than Expected	43.6	(40.0)	(45.8)	10.5	30.6	34.2	13.6
Satisfaction With Progress at New Location							
Total Per Cent	100.0	(100.0)	(100.0)	100.0	100.0	100.0	100.0
Very and Quite Satisfied	33.3	(20.0)	(41.7)	61.4	32.6	31.6	59.1
Satisfied	35.9	(60.0)	(20.8)	26.3	40.8	28.9	29.6
Very and Quite Dissatisfied	30.8	(20.0)	(37.5)	12.3	26.5	39.4	11.3
Would You Have Done Better at Old Location							
Total Per Cent	100.0	(100.0)	(100.0)	100.0	100.0	100.0	100.0
Yes	48.7	(53.3)	(45.8)	35.1	18.4	57.9	25.0
Uncertain	10.3	......	(16.7)	14.0	34.7	21.0	15.9
No	41.0	(46.7)	(37.5)	50.9	46.9	21.0	59.0
How Like Doing Business Here vs Old Location							
Total Per Cent	100.0	(100.0)	(100.0)	100.0	100.0	100.0	100.0
Like It Better Here	41.0	(53.3)	(30.4)	50.9	49.0	26.3	74.4
Both Areas the Same	17.9	(6.7)	(26.1)	19.3	28.6	18.4	9.3
Liked Old Area Better	41.0	(40.0)	(43.5)	29.8	22.4	55.3	16.3

erly assess the amount of business that will be done at a selected location. It may also be that many businesses underestimated the negative effects of the move. Actually the move may have been much more disruptive than expected. It is noted further that the types of businesses most likely to over-estimate the volume of business that they would do at the new location were the units that were predominantly dependent on a very localized neighborhood market area. This is particularly the case for the food-related retail units.

The level of satisfaction with the progress made at the new location seems to be closely related to how the amount of business done compares with expectations. At least the level of satisfaction follows the same pattern of difference by type of business. Service and food-related retail units have the largest proportion that are dissatisfied with progress made at the new location. Service units have an unusually larger proportion that are dissatisfied. Whereas only one-third of these units and those in the food-related retail category report a high level of satisfaction with the progress made since the move, approximately three-fifths of the non-food related retail and those in the "other" category are found at this satisfaction level. Of the latter units only a small minority reports dissatisfaction. Such responses are much more frequent among the jewelry firms, but this is probably not due to any shortcomings of the present site but rather, as already noted, to the unfavorable economic condition of the industry at the time of the study.

Here again we find large differences within the food-related category. The businesses from the Willard Center project area are disproportionately concentrated in the middle-satisfaction category. Here we find three-fifths of these units, as compared with only one-fifth of all other food-related retail establishments. The latter are more extreme in their responses in that they have a much larger proportion in both the high-satisfaction and in the dissatisfied categories. These units apparently vary widely in their reaction to the new site. Undoubtedly responses differ according to the progress made at the new location. While two out of five are in the high-satisfaction category, a nearly equal number are dissatisfied. The latter is exceeded only by the service units. It is noted that these food-related retail units were much more dependent on a local neighborhood market than were the units displaced from the Willard Center project area. Thus the move would cause more of a disruption. It is to be expected that the owners would be less satisfied with the progress made at the new site. It will be recalled that more than two-fifths of those units experienced a decline in volume after the move, while the Willard Center project businesses that relocated in the new shopping center not only retained their former customers but also gained new customers from among the Negroes who were moving into the area.

The responses to the question of how the businesses would have done had they remained at the old location follow the same general pattern of difference by type of business, already observed, regarding levels of satisfaction with the progress made at the present site. Nearly half of the food-related retail units and three-fifths of the service units report that they would have done better had they continued at the old site. That is, they would be better off if they had not been displaced. This, of course, is based on the contingency that the character of the old area would have remained unchanged. Consequently the relative evaluation is hypothetical but nonetheless represents a general attitude concerning the forced movement. It is noted, however, that except for service units, at least two-fifths of the businesses report that they would not be any better off even if they had not moved. Many of the units are uncertain. The proportion is particularly high among jewelry units, but again this is likely due in large part to the general uncertainty of the jewelry industry, and may be unrelated to the move. That this is the case is suggested by the low proportion of units reporting that they would be better off if they had remained at the old location. Jewelry firms are less likely to feel that the move was detrimental to their business than are other business types. This is due in large part to the relative unimportance of a specific location for jewelry manufacturing firms as long as it is in the jewelry district, since they do not cater to a small local market. More than any other type of business, they cater to a regional and more particularly to a national market. Thus movement, as far as location is concerned, would have only a minimum effect on such businesses. However, cost of building and the cost of relocation may be factors of paramount importance.

A majority of the non-food-related retail units and those in the manufacturing, wholesale, and construction category do not feel that they would have done any better even if they had remained at the original site. These are the units that also have the largest proportion who report high satisfaction with the progress made at the new site. Apparently the move was much less disruptive for businesses that are not predominantly dependent on a neighborhood market. However, the move would be expected to disrupt the customer relationships of food-related retail and service establishments. Thus it is not surprising that a large proportion of these units report that they would be better off had they not moved and had conditions continued as they were prior to the displacement.

Many businesses like their present location better than the one occupied previously. But as is evident from the data, this varies significantly among different kinds of businesses. Approximately half of the units prefer their present location as a place to do business over the old site, but the proportion ranges from only one-fourth of the service units to three-fourths of the establishments in the "other" category. Approximately half of the nonfood-related retail units and the jewelry firms prefer doing business at the present site. Jewelry firms have the largest proportion of units (29 per cent) that have no preference for either location. This is likely due to the high proportion remaining in the jewelry manufacturing district; thus in effect there was no change. Less than one-fifth of any of the other units do not state a preference. Service establishments, and to a lesser extent food-related retail units, have the largest proportions that state a preference for the old location. The proportions doing so are 55 per cent and 41 per cent respectively. The lowest proportion is found among those in the "other" category where only 16 per cent prefer the old site.

Large differences are found within the food-related group. More than half of the units from the Willard Center project state a preference for the present site, as compared with less than one-third of all other similar type units. However, a large proportion in both sub-groups report that they liked doing business at the old location better than at the present site. This is exceeded only by service units, where a majority states a preference for the old location. Thus it is evident that there is considerable variation in the reaction to the new site as compared with the original location. While a substantial number of units within each type of business report favorably regarding the present location, or make no distinction as to the relative merits of the two sites, it is nonetheless clear that the reaction of many of the units is a negative one. Such a reaction is likely to be more frequently stated by businesses that serve predominantly a circumscribed local market. Thus an unfavorable appraisal of the present site is most likely to come from service establishments, and to a lesser extent from the food-related retail units. It is the manufacturing, wholesale, and construction units that are most likely to view the new site favorably. Non-food-related retail units also tend to view the new location favorably, while among jewelry firms there is less consensus in their appraisal. The negative reaction expressed by some of the latter units may come disproportionately from those establishments that moved out of the jewelry district and thus lost the advantage of being in close proximity to similar-type units.

From the point of view of the general objectives of business, the ultimate question pertains to the relative income before and after the move. It is likely that to the individual businessman this is the most meaningful measure of the effects of displacement and relocation. To the extent that this is so, we can conclude generally that the move had harmful and disruptive effects, particularly for the food-related retail and service establishments. As is shown in Table 8-5, more than half of the former and nearly two-thirds of the latter report less income following relocation than prior to displacement. Repeatedly throughout the discussion we have noted that in the new location these businesses compare unfavorably with all other business types. The data concerning changes in income further support this general theme. Only in a minority of cases does income increase for the owners of these businesses after the move. Income remained about the same for approximately one-fourth of the units.

Jewelry firms also have a large disproportionate number of units with less income after the move, but it is uncertain as to how much of this decrease can be attributed to the disruptive effects of displacement and how much to the dip in business generally. The impression gained in the interview situation was that much of the decline was independent of the move. However, as noted earlier, this pertains only to the jewelry industry. Non-food-related retail and "other" businesses have the largest proportions,

TABLE 8-5

RELATIVE INCOME FOLLOWING RELOCATION BY TYPE OF BUSINESS

Income Has:	Food – Related Retail			Other Retail	Jewelry Mfg.	Service	Other
	Total	W. C.	Other				
Total Per Cent	100.0	(100.0)	(100.0)	100.0	100.0	100.0	100.0
Increased	17.9	(20.0)	(16.7)	29.8	22.4	13.2	27.9
Remained the Same	28.2	(26.7)	(29.2)	35.1	30.6	23.6	48.8
Decreased	53.8	(53.3)	(54.2)	35.1	46.9	63.2	23.3

30 per cent and 27 per cent respectively, whose income increased following the move. But even among these units, a substantial minority, from one-fifth to one-third of the units, experienced a decline. Thus it is abundantly evident that the move at least temporarily reduced the income of more than four units out of every ten; however this ranges as high as six units among the service establishments and down to only two units among the businesses in the manufacturing, wholesale, and construction category.

SUMMARY

The problems and consequences of relocation differ by type of business. The move seems to have been most disruptive as well as costly for service establishments and food-related retail units. In all aspects of relocation, these are the types of businesses that are most sensitive to the disruptive effects of the move. The major exception to this is found among the Jewish-owned kosher markets that relocated in the shopping center in one of the renewal areas. Because of the highly specialized products involved, these businesses were able to retain even those customers who had moved out of the area. This, of course, was not the experience of other-type food-related retail units.

We find that food-related retail units and service establishments had very similar experiences in moving to a new site. Because of their greater dependency on localized trade, both tended to move only short distances in an attempt to retain their original customers. However, this was not effective since the areas also changed. Other-type businesses, which were much less dependent upon a small market area, moved greater distances. In selecting a new location these units were able to place much more stress on the characteristics of the site as such. Thus they emphasized space, parking accommodations and attractiveness of the building to be occupied. However, food-related retail and service establishments placed much more stress on type of neighborhood, accessibility to customers, and proximity to the original location. Consequently such units show much less improvement in site characteristics. Although there is a general upgrading of sites, it is the non-food-related retail, manufacturing, wholesale, and construction establishments that show the most improvements.

The experiences of the jewelry manufacturing establishments were quite unique. Although they had been displaced from an area that was already in an advanced stage of disrepair, they nonetheless attempted to relocate in close proximity. This they did because they wanted to remain in the jewelry district, in spite of the rather widespread deterioration of the area. Such a location offered advantages for manufacturing because of the interdependence of separate units. Also, being in the jewelry district provided marketing opportunities which would not be available elsewhere. The older buildings also provided the space that such units needed at relatively lower rents than would be charged for comparable space in new buildings in better areas.

Jewelry units experienced a decline in business following the move and are generally not satisfied with the progress they have made since the move. However, little of this is attributed to the move as such, but rather to changes that have taken place in the market generally. The jewelry industry in this area was at a low point in a long-run slump. The move did not hurt the businesses but did come at an inopportune time, in that, due to a declining market, the units could ill afford the added cost and inconvenience of relocation.

The most unfavorable appraisals of the consequences of displacement and relocation are found among the service establishments and, to a lesser extent, among food-related retail units. This of course is due in large part to the greater dependence of these units on a recurrent and frequent relationship with established and regular customers living in close proximity. At the original location, these units were largely dependent on a neighborhood-type market, and thus were particularly sensitive to the disruptive effects of the move. It is only among these units that a distinct majority experienced a decline in income after the move. These units are dissatisfied with the progress made at the new site, and not only do they prefer the old location as a place to do business, but they think they would be better off if they had not been forced to move. On the other hand, the most favorable responses regarding the present site are found among the manufacturing, wholesale, and construction establishments. The latter are satisfied with the progress they have made and prefer the new location over the previous site as a place to do business. The move seems to have been largely to their advantage.

CHAPTER 6

SIZE OF BUSINESS

THIS chapter is devoted to a discussion of the problems or relocation by size of business establishment. Size is measured in terms of the number of employees prior to displacement. Specifically we are concerned with how problems, needs, and adjustment vary by size. We have already observed the close relationship between the rate of survival following displacement and size; however, the present analysis is limited only to those business units that moved to a new location and continued in business. The present chapter will investigate the extent to which size is a significant variable that deserves special consideration, in an attempt to understand the complex problems associated with programs of displacement and relocation of commercial establishments. Our discussion will follow the same general pattern as the previous chapter on type of business. For purposes of analysis, we have divided our sample of businesses into three groups, so as to have an approximately equal number of units in each size category. The units designated as small had only one or no employees;[1] medium-sized businesses had between two and seven workers prior to dislocation, while the large units employed eight or more workers. This is a rather crude measure

1 Nearly half of these units (47 per cent) did not have any employees, while 53 per cent employed one worker.

of size; however, if size of establishment is a significant variable in relocation, differences should be evident even on this general breakdown.

SELECTED CHARACTERISTICS

Before considering problems of relocation, attention is focused on the characteristics of persons operating different-sized establishments. The age composition of the business owners varies by size of establishment, but the pattern of difference is not continuous. Thus, whereas differences are found between the small and large units, it is the age composition of medium-sized units that differs most markedly. There are relatively few owners of small units in the younger ages. Only one in five is less than forty-five years of age. However, among the medium-sized businesses we find that one in three is of this age, and approximately the same proportion is found among the large establishments.[2] It is among the owners of the small units that we find the largest concentration of older persons. Nearly half of the owners are over fifty-five years of age. However, among the large units, only slightly more than one-third of the owners are of this age and among the medium-size establishments the proportion declines to approximately one-fifth. Thus the medium-sized businesses have the lowest proportion of owners in the older age groups. The owners of these units are disproportionately concentrated in the age group forty-five to fifty-four years. Nearly half are in this age group, as compared with less than one-third of the owners of either small or large establishments.

It is of particular interest to note the high proportion of owners among the small units who are beyond the normal retirement age. Among these units, one in five has reached the age of retirement, which is more than double the proportion in any other size category. A more detailed analysis showed that more than 30 per cent of those with no employees were beyond retirement

2 In a more detailed breakdown by size, there was a continuous increase in the proportion under forty-five years of age, starting with only 15 per cent of those without any workers and extending to 33 per cent of those with ten or more workers.

age, as compared with only 9 per cent of those with ten or more employees. In no other size of business class did the proportion exceed 10 per cent.

Perhaps the owner-operators of very small businesses have no other meaningful alternative but to continue in business in order to be able to support themselves economically, since many would not be covered by any formal retirement system. Also, their past ability to accumulate sufficient funds to provide for retirement, because of the size of their business operation, probably would have been quite limited. This is undoubtedly one of the major economic problems faced by the very small businessman, but this of course is quite independent of displacement and relocation. The day-to-day operations of the business may provide an income sufficient for the daily requirements of life, but do not provide a surplus for savings out of which they could provide for retirement at the customary age. Thus they must continue in business as long as possible. This suggests that when such units cannot successfully relocate, and it is this group that is least likely to be able to do so, the owners are faced with the problem of not being prepared financially for retirement. This is obviously a significant area in which research is needed.

There is a clear and consistent relationship between size of business and level of education of the owner, that is, as the size of unit increases, the level of education also increases. This of course is in part a function of age, particularly the low level of education among the owners of the smaller establishments. Among the owners of the small businesses, nearly one-fourth have less than seven years of formal education, but this proportion declines to less than 3 per cent among those in the other two business size classes.[3]

We note further that nearly half of those with less than two employees have not gone beyond the grade school level, but this drops to less than one-fifth among those with two or more employees. At the other end of the educational scale, we find that none of the businessmen with no employees had attended college. However, for the combined units with less than two employees, we find that 7 per cent had attended college, but the

3 Again, if we separate out those with no employees, we find that more than one-third have less than seven years of formal schooling.

proportion with college training increases to 26 per cent of those in the medium-sized class, and to 35 per cent among those with eight or more employees. The median level of education ranges from a low of 8.5 years among the small establishments to 12.5 among the large units. It is evident that these marked educational differences must be kept in mind as we view the problems of displacement and relocation by size of business.

Among our respondents, the type of preparation for operating a business varies by size of establishment. As expected, the larger units have the largest proportion who had some special training for business. This, of course, is largely due to formal education. Among those with eight or more employees, approximately one in five report that they had learned to run a business through some form of special training. This proportion decreases to only about one in ten among those in the medium or small business categories. Among the small establishments, that is, those with less than two employees, a majority report that they learned to operate their business by picking it up on their own. This proportion declines steadily by size of business.[4] In each size class approximately one-fourth learned the business from other family members. Another 10 per cent learned to run the business while working for someone else. Thus the major difference by size of business is that, disproportionately, the owners of the small establishments learned to operate their businesses by "just picking it up on their own," whereas those with larger units had "special training." Since the latter is due largely to formal education, it is likely that the owners of the larger businesses are persons who disproportionately entered business directly from college.

Differential preparation to operate a business is also found in the close relationship between size of business and type of job held prior to entering business. The small units are operated by persons who came predominantly from manual occupations. More than half held manual jobs before entering business, as compared with approximately one-fourth of those with eight or more employees. The latter were more likely to have come from

4 In a more detailed analysis, the proportion ranged from a high of 53 per cent among those with no employees to only 34 per cent of those with ten or more workers.

white-collar occupations or not to have been in the labor force prior to entering business. Of the latter, many entered business directly from college, which accounts for the higher proportion in the upper levels of education, as well as the higher proportion with special training which we have already noted.

Although there is considerable overlapping of chracteristics found in different-sized classes, it seems evident that the smaller units are owned and operated by quite different kinds of persons than those operating the larger units. In short, the smaller establishments are owned predominantly by older persons, the less well-educated who previously held manual jobs and who had no special training for running a business but largely learned to do so by picking it up on their own. These characterizations change generally as size of unit increases, even though the change is not always a continuous one. Nonetheless the larger units are owned and operated by younger persons, the college-educated with special training for running a business, who either had prior experience in white-collar work or entered business directly from college.

All of the businesses in our study can be properly classified as "successful operations," for they have continued in business beyond the period when the drop-out rate is highest. As already noted, more than 90 per cent of the units had been in business for at least five years. Nearly half of the small units and two-fifths of the large ones have been in business for more than twenty years. The questions of concern here pertain to the differential ability of different-sized units to cope with the problems of displacement and relocation. It would seem as though the larger units would be better equipped to absorb the disruptive effects of such a move. However, this is essentially an empirical question. It is to these problems that we now turn our attention.

SITE SELECTION

More than half of the displaced establishments interviewed report that they had considerable trouble in finding a new location. However, the proportion varies by size of business. Among the smaller units, 45 per cent report that they had difficulties, but among the large units this increases to 61 per cent. The medium-sized units are nearly midway between these two proportions. On the other hand, more than half of the small units and nearly two-fifths of the large units did not perceive themselves as having any trouble in finding a new location. However, when more specific questions were asked, as is shown below, the proportion reporting no problems in getting relocated drops substantially.

In response to the question as to how they found their present site, we find rather marked differences by size. In general, the pattern of difference tends to vary continuously in relation to number of employees. These data are shown in Table 1-6. A close inspection of these responses indicates clearly that the smaller units were more likely to find the new location through their own efforts and to do so informally, whereas the larger units tended disproportionately to turn to formal specialized agencies. For example, the proportion of larger units (19 per cent) that found their present site through a real estate agent is more than six times the proportion of small units that used this method. Similarly the proportion that found their new site through the governmental relocation agency varies in the same

TABLE 1-6

METHOD USED TO FIND SITE BY SIZE OF BUSINESS

Method Used to Find Site	Size of Business		
	Small	Medium	Large
Total Per Cent	100.0	100.0	100.0
Located by Self	58.8	56.0	48.0
Through Friends	10.3	13.1	5.3
Landlord Contacted Me	7.4	3.6	4.0
Real Estate Agent	2.9	11.9	18.7
Other Businessmen	10.3	1.2	2.7
Relocation Agency or State	1.5	3.6	10.7
Other	5.9	8.3	8.0
No Answer	2.9	2.4	2.7

direction. The range is from less than 2 per cent of the small units to more than 10 per cent of the large establishments. Altogether only about one unit in twenty reports that it found its present location through the official relocation agency that is charged with this responsibility. However, when the question was asked as to who had tried to help them find a new site, the proportion reporting the relocation agency more than doubled. This suggests in part that some of those who report that they found the present location by themselves may well have done so by following up addresses of available units provided to them by the relocation agency. At any rate, it is of particular interest to note the low proportion reporting that they found their present site through this agency. Our data do not permit us to determine whether the higher proportions among the larger units are due to more accurate reporting or to more frequent use. But whatever the cause, the larger units give credit to this agency seven times as often as do the small units.

If we combine categories on the general criteria of whether formal or informal means were used to find the present site, we find a marked and consistent difference by size of business. Thus, 87 per cent of the small units report that they found their present site by themselves, through friends or other businessmen, or through personal contact with the landlord, as compared with 74 per cent of the medium-sized units and only 60 per cent of the large units. However, those who found their present site through either real estate agencies or the relocation agency range from only about 4 per cent of the small units to 29 per cent of the large units – a seven-fold difference. Thus it is evident that in the process of relocation small and large businesses employ quite different techniques in their efforts to find a new site.

According to the data presented in Table 2-6, the kinds of problems encountered in trying to find a new location also vary significantly by size of establishment. The proportion reporting that no major problem was encountered is highest among the small units and is lowest among the large units. The range is from 37 per cent to 24 per cent. However, the opposite pattern of difference is found in the proportion reporting the high "costs" of a new location as a major problem. This was the major problem most frequently encountered by the small estab-

TABLE 2-6

MAJOR PROBLEM IN FINDING A NEW LOCATION AND LENGTH OF TIME REQUIRED BY SIZE OF BUSINESS

Major Problem and Length of Time	Size of Business		
	Small	Medium	Large
Major Problem			
Total Per Cent	100.0	100.0	100.0
None	36.8	25.0	24.0
Rents or Building Costs Too High	27.9	19.0	13.3
Zoning and/or License Problems	10.3	11.9	5.3
Wanted to Stay in Same Neighborhood	5.9	10.7	4.0
Could Not Find Suitable Building	7.4	12.0	29.3
Could Not Find Suitable Area	2.9	9.5	6.7
Other	8.8	11.9	17.4
Length of Time			
Total Per Cent	100.0	100.0	100.0
Less Than 2 Weeks	27.7	20.7	15.7
2 Weeks to 3 Months	24.6	23.2	14.2
3 Months to 6 Months	18.5	22.0	24.3
6 Months or More	29.2	34.1	45.8

lishments. Whereas this is reported by 28 per cent of the small units and by 19 per cent of the establishments in the medium-sized group, the proportion declines to only 13 per cent of the large units. Finding a suitable building is the major problem reported most frequently by the latter establishments. This is the response given by 29 per cent of the large units but by only 7 per cent of the small establishments. Thus, as the size of business increases, the major problem in finding a new location shifts from a primary concern with "costs" to the problem of finding an "adequate building." The larger units also face a greater variety of problems, as is evident from the much larger proportion of responses in the "other" category. Small and medium-sized businesses more frequently faced zoning and licensing problems than did large units. This difference is largely due to the type of businesses involved. The smaller units are made up disproportionately of businesses that would seek a site in or near a residential area so as to be close to their customers. License transfers are also a frequent problem for the small units because of the large number of liquor establishments found in this size category.

The smaller units required much less time than the larger units to find a new site. In response to the question as to how long it took to find their present site, 27 per cent of the small units report that they found it in less than two weeks, as compared with 20 per cent of the medium-sized units and only 15 per cent of the large units. In the next length of time category, that is, those that required between two weeks and three months to find a new site, we find 25 per cent of the small units but only 14 per cent of the large establishments. Thus while more than half of the small units were able to find a new location within three months, only three out of ten of the large units were able to do so. Of the latter establishments 46 per cent were unable to find a new location within a period of six months, but this declines to 34 per cent of the medium-sized units and to 28 per cent of the small units. Apparently the larger units require much more time to relocate than do the smaller establishments. This is likely due to the more specific building requirements of the larger units and to the more limited availability of such buildings. While the larger establishments seem to have a wider range of choice geographically, the alternative locations are nonetheless limited or at least have proven to be difficult to find.

THINGS LOOKED FOR IN A SITE

In Table 3-6 are shown the particular things looked for in selecting a new location. These are the responses to the very general question: In looking for a new location, what particular things did you look for? Again we find that the small units place much more stress on the costs factor than do the larger units. It seems likely that the range in costs that can be tolerated is much narrower in the case of the small units; thus it

TABLE 3-6

PARTICULAR THINGS LOOKED FOR IN SELECTING NEW LOCATION BY SIZE OF BUSINESS

Things Looked For	Size of Business		
	Small	Medium	Large
Total Per Cent	100.0	100.0	100.0
Low Rent or Costs	19.1	14.3	4.0
More Room	4.4	7.1	18.7
Place Near or in Old Area	20.6	14.3	2.7
Proper Zoning	5.9	3.6	2.7
Parking Facilities	2.9	4.8	8.0
Near Downtown Area	5.9	1.2	4.0
Good Location, Accessibility to Customers	11.8	21.4	10.7
Attractiveness of Building	4.4	13.1	24.0
Nothing in Particular	7.4	6.0	2.7
Other	17.6	14.2	22.6

becomes a dimension of major concern. It will be recalled that this was one of the major problems frequently encountered by the small units in trying to find a new location. Our data show that one unit in five reports "low costs" as the thing looked for in a site, but among the large units this drops to less than one in twenty. The opposite is found in respect to the proportion that placed primary attention on getting more space. This increases from only 4 per cent of the small units to 19 per cent of the large units.[5] It is of particular interest to note that, as the size of unit increases, the proportion placing emphasis on wanting a place "in or near" the original location decreases. The proportion seeking this in a new site declines from 21 per cent of the small units to only 3 per cent among the large establishments. The small units apparently wanted to minimize the

5 Large units were more likely to use relocation as an opportunity to expand their business, hence the emphasis on more room in looking for a new site.

disruptive effects of the move by trying to maintain their established position in the old area. This does not seem to be important for the larger units. Again we find that small establishments are more likely to stress proper zoning than are the medium or large units. This emphasis is likely due to the concentration of food-related retail units that wanted to locate in residential areas which would ordinarily not be zoned for commercial use. Yet such a location may be crucial for these units because of their dependence on a neighborhood trade.

The proportion reporting parking facilities as something looked for in a new site varies directly with size of establishment, as does the emphasis placed on the attractiveness of the building. The latter is reported by only 4 per cent of the small units and 24 per cent of the large units. Medium-sized establishments, in particular, place special attention on a good location that is accessible to customers. In general, the small units look for a low-cost site in or near the original location, whereas the larger units place particular stress on space and attractiveness of the building. Thus it is apparent that relocation needs vary markedly by size of business.

This is further evident from the data presented in Table 4-6. Respondents were asked to report the amount of importance they placed on a number of selected site characteristics in look-

TABLE 4-6

PROPORTION OF UNITS REPORTING SELECTED SITE CHARACTERISTICS AS NOT IMPORTANT BY SIZE OF BUSINESS

Selected Characteristic	Size of Business		
	Small	Medium	Large
Amount of Space in Building	10.3	9.5	5.3
Amount of Space in Land	60.3	52.4	25.3
Type of Neighborhood	25.0	29.8	48.0
Type of Business Area	47.1	44.0	64.0
Parking Accommodations	29.4	15.5	13.3
Accessibility to Customers	11.8	14.3	33.3
Nearness to Bus Lines	70.6	71.4	62.7

ing for a new location. Here we have presented only the proportion who report that the characteristic was considered as being *not important*. The complement of this percentage in each case would be the proportion who consider the specific characteristic as either quite or very important. It is readily apparent that nearly all of the businesses report that the amount of space in the building was an important consideration in looking for a place to move. Only 5 per cent of the large units and 10 per cent of the small units indicated that this was not important. However, when viewed from a different perspective, we find that only one-fourth of the small units rated this as very important, as compared with three-fifths of the medium-sized units and more than three-fourths of the large establishments. Marked differences are also found by size of business in respect to the importance attached to land area around the building. Three-fifths of the small units did not consider this important, as compared with only one-fourth of the large units. Among medium-sized units, about half did not consider this aspect of space important.

Small businesses are apparently much more concerned about the type of neighborhood and type of business in the area in looking for a new location than are the large units. The small units are more neighborhood-oriented, whereas the large units seem to operate on the assumption that the immediate surroundings are not of major significance. They can do this since they are less dependent on a localized market for customers. This, however, will be explored more fully below. At any rate, only one-fourth of the small units report that type of neighborhood is not important, as compared with nearly half of the large units. Although not shown here, nearly half of the small units reported that the type of neighborhood was considered to be very important, but less than one-fourth of the large units placed an equal amount of emphasis on this as a feature of the new location.

It is of interest to note that type of neighborhood is considered to be a more important characteristic of a site than types of businesses in the area by all sized units. But again we note that the type of business in the area is more likely to be considered as not important by the large units than the small ones. Half of the latter do not consider it important, as compared with two-thirds of the former. The small units probably place more emphasis on this since they may be more dependent on other businesses attracting potential customers to the area. Large units, on the other hand, can more effectively attract their own customers and are thus less concerned about complementary activities in the area. We find partial support for this in the responses to the importance of "accessibility to customers" as a site characteristic. Here we find that only 12 per cent of the small units consider this as not important in looking for a new location, as compared with one-third of the large units. Both small and medium-sized units place much more emphasis on accessibility to customers than do the large units. These data suggest that when a certain minimum size is reached, a business can tolerate a much broader range of choice in selecting a location, that is, large units have a kind of independence in their location that is not enjoyed by the small establishments. The latter have to be much more cautious and selective, in that the business operation must seek every available location advantage. Consequently, these businesses in selecting a site are much more sensitive to the character of the area. According to the smaller units, accessibility to customers is one of the most important and crucial aspects of a business location. Our data show that, for small units, this characteristic has the lowest proportion that did not consider it important, and the highest proportion that reported that it was very important. The larger units place less stress on accessibility to customers as such, but are much more concerned about parking accommodations. This, of course, is also a form of accessibility, even though it differs in type. Thus we find that the proportion reporting that parking was not important declines from 29 per cent of the small units to only 13 per cent of the large units. On the other hand, only one-third of the small establishments report that parking accommodations around a site are very important, but this increases to more than half of the large units.

That business is oriented predominantly around the automobile is clearly evident from the importance that is placed on parking facilities and the general lack of emphasis on being near to the bus lines. A substantial majority of all sized units doesn't consider nearness to the bus line as important in looking for a new location. However, the larger units were more concerned about this than the small ones. Only 7 per cent of the latter report it as very important, as compared with 27 per cent of the large units. Medium-sized establishments also place little emphasis on this characteristic. Unfortunately our data do not permit us to determine whether the large units want to be near the bus line so as to attract customers or in order to have a mode of travel for their employees. It is probably the latter, since many of these units are in jewelry manufacturing as well as other-type manufacturing. Such businesses employ a large number of females who are largely secondary family workers, and thus would tend disproportionately to be dependent on the bus as a mode of travel to work.

Our data clearly show that, in seeking a new location, the emphasis placed on selected site characteristics varies markedly by size of business. The smaller units tend to place particular emphasis on the type of neighborhood and accessibility for their customers. To a lesser extent, they are also concerned about the type of business in the area, at least more so than larger businesses. The latter are particularly concerned with space, both within and adjacent to the building, and with parking accommodations. Large units seem to be much less concerned about type of neighborhood or type of business in the area. Hence these data suggest that the larger units place more emphasis on the site itself, whereas the smaller units tend to look more to the general character of the area. The smaller establishments want to be near to their customers, whereas for the larger units a good business location is one that has an attractive building with ample space and parking accommodations. Given these conditions, they apparently feel that they can attract customers independently. The larger units are, of course, much less dependent on local customers, in that many serve a non-local market; therefore the specific location in the community becomes less important.

REASONS FOR SELECTING PRESENT LOCATION

That different-sized establishments vary in the amount of emphasis placed on certain site characteristics is further evident from the reasons given for selecting their present site. As is evident from the data presented in Table 5-6, the small units are much more likely to have selected their present site for cost reasons. In respect to this, we find more than a three-fold difference between the small and large units. Among the small establishments, 16 per cent report that they selected the present site for cost reasons, as compared with only 5 per cent of the large units. The latter selected the present site largely because they thought it would be a good business location, without specifying any particular characteristic of the site which would make it so. However, the major differences of significance by size of establishment are found in the proportion that selected the present site because of its proximity to the original location and those who picked the present site because of the attractiveness of the building. The latter was the reason given by 28 per cent of the large units, but by only 6 per cent of the medium-sized units and less than 2 per cent of the small establishments. The small units placed particular stress on staying in the same general area from which they had been displaced. This is the reason given for selecting the present site by 31 per cent of the small

TABLE 5-6

GENERAL REASONS FOR SELECTING PRESENT LOCATION BY SIZE OF BUSINESS

Reason	Size of Business		
	Small	Medium	Large
Total Per Cent	100.0	100.0	100.0
Costs, Rent or Price	16.2	14.3	5.3
Near Old Location	30.9	23.8	6.7
Only Thing Available	16.2	16.7	13.3
Good Business Location	8.8	25.0	36.0
Attractiveness of Building	1.5	6.0	28.0
Owned by Self or Family	5.9	1.2	1.3
Other	20.6	13.1	9.4

TABLE 6-6

DISTANCE MOVED BY SIZE OF BUSINESS

Distance (Miles)	Size of Business		
	Small	Medium	Large
Total Per Cent	100.0	100.0	100.0
Within 1/10	25.0	20.2	8.0
1/10 – 1/2	41.2	35.7	21.3
1/2 – 1 1/2	22.0	27.4	42.7
1 1/2 and Over	11.8	16.6	28.0

units but by only 7 per cent of the large establishments.[6] However, for a substantial minority in each size class, the present site was selected only because no other alternative was available. Again we find that the smaller units placed emphasis on the area as such, whereas the large units placed more emphasis on the features of the building, that is, that they wanted it to be attractive. Earlier we noted that they also wanted it to be spacious. The small units were more variable in the reasons given for selecting the present site, as is indicated by the large proportion in the "other" category.

DISTANCE MOVED

Since the smaller units clearly state a preference for remaining in or near the original area, and also frequently give this as the reason for selecting the present site, we would expect to find that the distance moved would be less for small units than for the larger establishments. The distances moved by size of business are shown in Table 6-6. It is strikingly evident that the

6 In an earlier chapter it was found that the units displaced from the Willard Center project tended to relocate in the same area. Thus we ran a separate analysis excluding these units but found that the marked tendency for small businesses to select a site because of its proximity to the original location persisted. The pattern of difference remained unchanged, but the range of difference declined.

small units did relocate in close proximity to the original location. Among these units, one-fourth moved within a radius of one-tenth of a mile, as compared with one-fifth of the medium-sized establishments and only 8 per cent of the larger businesses. In the next distance zone, that is, from one-tenth to one-half mile, we find 41 per cent of the small businesses, but this declines to one-half that proportion among the large establishments. Thus two-thirds of the small establishments relocated within a radius of less than one-half mile of the original location, as compared with less than 30 per cent of the large units. On the other hand only 12 per cent of the small units moved more than one and one-half miles, whereas 17 per cent of the medium-sized units and 28 per cent of the large units did so. Thus it seems that the small units have attempted to hold on to the established advantages of the past, in that they have attempted to minimize the disruptive effects of the move by remaining in or near the old location. However, the larger units have tended to make a clear and distinct break with the past by selecting a site in a new or different area quite some distance removed from the original location. Such units are, of course, much less dependent on a localized market area, as already noted; thus there is no need to remain in the same general area. Rather, they can use displacement as an opportunity to gain certain location advantages. The significance of distance moved is to be considered more fully in Chapter VII.

THINGS LIKED AND DISLIKED: NEW AND OLD LOCATION

We turn now to a discussion of the things liked and disliked about both the present and the former location. According to the data shown in Table 7-6, the characteristics about each location that are viewed positively differ substantially by size of business. It is readily apparent that the larger units view the present site more favorably, whereas the smaller units are more likely to express specific likings for the former location.

Approximately one-third of the small units do not find anything to their liking in evaluating the present location. This type of response declines to less than 20 per cent of the medium-

TABLE 7-6

THINGS LIKED ABOUT PRESENT AND FORMER LOCATION BY SIZE OF BUSINESS

Things Liked About Location	Size of Business		
	Small	Medium	Large
		Present Location	
Total Per Cent	100.0	100.0	100.0
None	33.8	19.0	9.3
Better Neighborhood	10.3	8.3	.....
Parking Accommodations	2.9	14.3	16.0
Attractiveness of Building	26.5	29.8	46.7
Good Business Location	7.4	15.5	14.7
Convenient for Self	11.8	3.6	1.3
Other	7.4	9.5	12.0
		Former Location	
Total Per Cent	100.0	100.0	100.0
None	7.4	15.5	26.7
Good Location—Accessibility	13.2	23.8	20.0
Parking Accommodations	7.4	4.8	2.7
Good Trade—Established	36.8	25.0	14.7
Attractiveness of Building	11.8	8.3	14.7
Low Costs	5.9	10.7	13.3
Liked Everything	8.8	7.1	5.3
Other	8.8	4.8	2.7

sized units and to less than 10 per cent among the large establishments. Just the opposite is found in their appraisals of the former site. Only 7 per cent of the small units report that there was nothing to their liking in evaluating the original location, as compared with 16 per cent of the medium-sized and 27 per cent of the large establishments. Viewed in another way, we find that 93 per cent of the small units report a specific liking for the old location, but only 66 per cent do so in reference to the present site. The comparable proportions among the large establishment change from 73 per cent to 91 per cent respectively.

While some of the small and medium-sized establishments report their present location is in a better and more attractive neighborhood, this feature is not even mentioned by the large units. The latter, however, are much more likely to stress parking accommodations as the thing liked best about the present site. While this is reported by only 3 per cent of the small units, it is mentioned by 16 per cent of the large businesses. The attractiveness of the building is mentioned as the thing liked best about the present location by nearly half of the large units, but by only one-fourth of the small ones. This is to be expected in view of the stress large units placed on the characteristics of the building in selecting a site. The larger units are also more likely to view the present site as a good business location, but an even larger proportion mentions this as the feature liked best about the former site. The smaller units tend to view this as an attractive feature of the former location only. Perhaps this is due, in large part, to a decline in volume of business at the new location. This is suggested by the fact that small units in particular stress that they had a good trade established prior to displacement. Nearly two-fifths of the small establishments and one-fourth of the medium-sized units report that this is what they liked best about the former location, but this feature is reported by only 15 per cent of the large units. The latter are more likely than the small units to view the low costs of rent and overhead as an attractive feature of the old location.

The smaller units express more of a liking for the old location than for the present site; however, the size of this difference declines among medium-sized units, and the pattern reverses sharply among the larger businesses. This is further supported by the data on things disliked about both locations. The close emotional attachment to the former site among the small businesses is suggested by the high proportion who state that they did not dislike anything about that location. While nearly half of the small units express this regarding the former location, the proportion declines to less than one-fifth in terms of the present site. Thus nearly 85 per cent of these units express a specific dislike for the present site, whereas only slightly more than half do so in regard to the former location. The opposite is found among the large units. Only 20 per cent report no dislikes concerning the old site, but more than one-third respond thusly when asked to evaluate the present location. These data are shown in Table 8-6.

The specific dislikes of the old area which are most frequently mentioned pertain to the "poor neighborhood" or to the "unattractiveness of the building" which the business had occupied. It is the small units that disproportionately focus their dislike on the "poor neighborhood." However, the "unattractiveness of the building" is the characteristic of the site disliked most frequently by the larger units. This feature of the old site is reported as disliked by only 7 per cent of the small units but by

TABLE 8-6

THINGS DISLIKED ABOUT PRESENT AND FORMER LOCATION BY SIZE OF BUSINESS

Things Disliked About Location	Size of Business		
	Small	Medium	Large
	Present Location		
Total Per Cent	100.0	100.0	100.0
None	16.2	27.4	36.0
Poor Business	17.6	4.8	4.0
Inaccessibility	13.2	9.5	14.7
Parking Problems	10.3	10.7	4.0
Rental Costs	5.9	6.0	9.2
Unattractiveness of Building	17.6	13.1	9.2
Poor Area in Transition	10.3	9.5	6.7
Everything	2.9	6.0	1.2
Other	5.9	13.1	15.0
	Former Location		
Total Per Cent	100.0	100.0	100.0
None	47.1	33.3	20.0
Poor Parking	14.7	14.3	14.7
Poor Neighborhood	22.1	15.5	14.7
Unattractive Building	7.4	27.4	36.0
Other	8.8	9.5	14.7

27 per cent of the medium-sized units and by 36 per cent of the large establishments.

There is greater variety of dislikes reported concerning the present location. Small establishments in particular complain about the "poor business" that they are doing at the present site. This is reported by 18 per cent of the small establishments but by only 4 per cent of the large units. Small businesses, as compared with the larger units, more frequently report that they dislike the parking problems of the present site, the unattractiveness of the building occupied, and the poor condition of the neighborhood. These are all consequences of relocating in close proximity to the original location. On the other hand, the large units are less likely to have any dislikes at all. The only specific dislike reported more frequently by the large units than by other-sized businesses pertains to the rental costs of the present site. The new location obviously has advantages for the larger units but owners are nonetheless concerned about the higher rental costs. There is less uniformity among the larger units in things disliked, as is indicated by the higher proportion of responses in the "other" category.

The smaller units have a much more favorable view of the former location and a less favorable view of the present site than do the larger businesses. Whereas the specific dislikes decrease following the move among the larger units, they increase among the small businesses. Conversely the likes increase among the large units following relocation but decrease among the small establishments.

CHANGES IN SELECTED SITE CHARACTERISTICS

In Table 9-6, we find a comparison of selected site characteristics before and after the move. It is apparent that a majority of all-sized businesses moved to larger quarters than they had occupied prior to displacement; however, the proportion that did so increases with size of business. On the other hand, a substantial minority, that is, from one-fourth to one-fifth of all businesses in each size class, moved to a building with less space. Small and medium-sized businesses were more likely than large

TABLE 9-6

SELECTED CHARACTERISTICS OF SITE BEFORE AND AFTER MOVE BY SIZE OF BUSINESS

Selected Characteristics	Size of Business		
	Small	Medium	Large
Amount of Space			
Total Per Cent	100.0	100.0	100.0
More Here	57.4	59.5	68.0
Same	17.6	17.9	10.7
Less Here	25.0	22.6	21.3
Age of Building			
Total Per Cent	100.0	100.0	100.0
Present One Newer	44.8	46.4	60.0
About Same Age	20.9	34.5	25.3
Present One Older	34.3	19.0	14.7
Condition of Building			
Total Per Cent	100.0	100.0	100.0
This One Better	45.6	54.8	69.3
About Same	20.6	27.4	22.7
This One Worse	33.8	17.9	8.0
General Condition of Area			
Total Per Cent	100.0	100.0	100.0
This Is Better	42.6	50.0	58.7
About Same	27.9	35.7	30.7
This Is Worse	29.4	14.3	10.7

businesses to move to the same amount of space as previously occupied, but in each size group such a move was made by less than one unit in five. Most of the businesses increased their space with the move. For many, the move was also to a newer building. The proportion that moved to newer quarters increases directly by size of business. The range is from 45 per cent of the small units to 60 per cent of the large establishments. On the other hand, more than one-third of the small businesses moved to an older building, as compared with 19 per cent of the medium-sized and 15 per cent of the large units. In short, the medium-sized businesses were most likely to move to another building about the same age as the one previously occupied, whereas the small businesses had the largest proportion moving to an older building, and the large businesses were most likely to move to newer quarters. Part of this difference is due to the small businesses remaining close to the original area where the physical environment was similar, whereas the larger units moved further and more frequently to the suburbs.

The proportion of businesses moving to a building in better condition than the one vacated also increases consistently with size. This, of course, is not unrelated to age of building. The proportion moving into a better building ranges from 46 per cent of the small units to 55 per cent of the medium-sized establishments and to 69 per cent of the large units. Thus a substantial majority of the large units, in particular, moved to a better building than the one occupied prior to displacement. This is further evident when we note the proportion that moved to a building in worse condition. We find that only 8 per cent of the large businesses did so, as compared with 18 per cent of the medium-sized and 34 per cent of the small establishments. For the latter units, which constitute a sizable minority, displacement placed them in a less desirable structure than the one from which they had been forced to move.

The same pattern is observed in respect to the general condition of the two areas. There is evidently a general upgrading in the condition of the area following the move, but it is the large units that show the most improvement. Nearly three-fifths of these moved to a better area, as compared with only half of the medium-sized and slightly more than two-fifths of the small establishments. On the other hand, nearly one-third of the latter moved to an area in worse condition than the one vacated, but only one-tenth of the large businesses did so.

Thus it seems that all-sized businesses in the aggregate are better off in respect to each site characteristic, but the amount of improvement varies significantly by size. For a substantial majority of the large units, the move was to a larger, newer, better building in a better area than had been occupied prior to displacement. Comparable improvements are found for nearly half of the small establishments also. But for a large proportion of the latter, the move was to a less attractive site, while this type of move is found among only a minority of the large units. In most instances the medium-sized establishments show more improvement than the small ones but less than the large units.

Another measure of the relative attractiveness of the two areas is to be found in the number of business vacancies within the same block. It is assumed here that vacancies detract from the quality of an area as a business location, since they tend to depreciate values. Also they tend to be symptoms of decline. Our data show that there is a marked decline in the proportion of business vacancies in close proximity following the move, that is, vacancies are much less prevalent around the new locations. Although there is a decline in all size classes, the difference is least among the small units. At the original locations, there were only slight variations in vacancy rates by size, but following the move the small units are located in blocks with a much higher vacancy rate. We find that 46 per cent of the small units, but only 29 per cent of the large units, report that there are vacancies within the block where they are currently located. Prior to the move, more than half of the units in each size class reported comparable vacancies. This dimension also represents an improvement for units in each size class, but again it is most marked among the large establishments.

NEW CONSTRUCTION AND SIZE OF BUILDINGS

A majority of units in all size classes moved into existing structures, as is shown in Table 10-6. Less than one business in four actually had a new building constructed for its own use. Other units may have moved into new buildings also, but they would have been existing structures which were available on the market at the time. It is the large establishments that were most likely to have a building constructed specifically for their own use.

TABLE 10-6

PROPORTION HAVING BUILDING CONSTRUCTED AND SIZE OF BUILDING OCCUPIED BY SIZE OF BUSINESS

Have Building Constructed and Size of Building	Size of Business		
	Small	Medium	Large
Have Building Constructed			
Total Per Cent	100.0	100.0	100.0
Yes	19.1	19.0	32.0
No	80.9	81.0	68.0
Size of Building Occupied			
Total Per Cent	100.0	100.0	100.0
Under 500	41.5	8.8	2.7
500 – 999	20.0	22.5	4.0
1,000 – 2,999	27.7	32.5	12.2
3,000 – 4,999	9.2	18.8	18.9
5,000 – 9,999	1.5	15.0	28.4
10,000 and Over	.....	2.5	33.8
Median	712	2,154	7,145

Nearly one-third of these units did so, as compared with less than one-fifth of the small and medium-sized units. It is noted, however, that the pattern of variation by size is partially lost here, since in a more detailed analysis the proportion increased consistently as size increased. The units least likely to have a new structure built are those with no employees. Part of the differences by size are likely due to differences in area of relocation. The smaller units disproportionately relocated in the city where available land sites were already occupied by a building, whereas the larger units disproportionately moved to the suburbs where the opportunities for new construction were greater. Since the latter units were particularly concerned with the attractiveness of the building as a site characteristic, they tended to use this as an opportunity to have a new structure built. Also their space needs may have been such that available structures were very limited. The age of the owner may also have been a significant factor here, since we would expect the older owners of the smaller units to have been less inclined to put up a new building which would probably require an added investment than the younger owners of the larger establishments.

As expected, the size of the structure occupied varies markedly by size of business. Among the small establishments, 42 per cent occupy less than 500 square feet, but among the large units this declines to less than 3 per cent. Nearly 90 per cent of the small units occupy less than 3,000 square feet of floor space, as compared with approximately two-thirds of the medium-sized establishments and less than one-fifth of the large units. At the other extreme, none of the small units and less than 3 per cent of the medium-sized establishments occupy 10,000 square feet or more. But among the large units, we find one-third in buildings of this size. The close relationship between size of structure occupied and size of business is strikingly evident from the average size of structure in each size class. The median amount of floor space occupied by the small establishments is only 712 square feet. This increases three-fold to 2,154 among medium-sized units and ten-fold to more than 7,100 square feet for the large businesses. Thus it is readily apparent that the amount of space needed varies and the range by size is substantial. Among large units, a majority occupies more than 5,000 square feet, whereas among the small establishments, a similar majority of more than 60 per cent occupies less than 1,000 square feet.

PARKING ACCOMMODATIONS

That all-sized businesses improved their parking facilities with the move is clearly evident, but again we find that the improvement was most marked for the larger establishments. These data are presented in Table 11-6. Concerning the former site approximately half of the small units, but only one-fourth of the large units, report that parking was adequate. However, following the move, the proportions with adequate parking are two-thirds and three-fourths respectively. The move afforded the large units in

TABLE 11-6

PARKING ADEQUACY AT FORMER AND PRESENT LOCATION BY SIZE OF BUSINESS

Adequate Parking	Size of Business		
	Small	Medium	Large
		Former Location	
Total Per Cent	100.0	100.0	100.0
Yes	53.3	40.6	24.0
No	46.7	59.4	76.0
		Present Location	
Total Per Cent	100.0	100.0	100.0
Yes	66.6	70.3	76.0
No	33.4	29.7	24.0

particular an opportunity to obtain a site which would provide adequate parking. The need for improvement is apparent when we note that three-fourths of these units did not have adequate parking at the original location. The medium-sized units also show a marked improvement following the move. The proportion reporting adequate parking increased from 40 per cent at the old location to 70 per cent after the move.

It was observed earlier that the amount of importance placed on parking facilities in selecting a site increased directly by size of business. These data suggest that present sites were selected, particularly by the larger units, with attention being focused on this characteristic, even though this did not frequently constitute the main reason for selecting the present site. Nonetheless the marked improvements found would have resulted only from deliberate effort. The perennial problem of providing adequate parking was apparently resolved successfully by a majority of the business units. At the new location, only a minority finds facilities to be inadequate. It is the small units that are most likely to do so. These findings are consistent with our earlier observation that parking problems are more likely to be reported as a dislike of the present location by small units than by large ones.

AREA SERVED

We turn now to a discussion of the extent to which the move changed the size of the area from which the businesses predominantly attract their customers. It is expected that the largest changes would be found in respect to the proportion of businesses that serve only a neighborhood area, since displacement is likely to have its most profound effect on businesses that are largely neighborhood-oriented. The area served is thought to be such an important factor in the whole relocation problem that special attention will be focused on this in a later chapter. At this point, however, we are concerned only with the change in area served that resulted as a consequence of the move and the extent to which this change varies by size of business. As shown in Table 12-6, it is the small units in particular that report serv-

TABLE 12-6

AREA SERVED AT FORMER AND PRESENT LOCATION BY SIZE OF BUSINESS

Area Serviced	Former Location			Present Location		
	Small	Medium	Large	Small	Medium	Large
Total Per Cent	100.0	100.0	100.0	100.0	100.0	100.0
Immediate Neighborhood	47.1	28.6	10.7	30.9	19.0	4.0
Same Side of Town	10.3	11.9	4.0	13.2	14.3	12.0
Larger Community	32.4	36.9	30.7	41.2	42.9	30.7
Region – Other	10.3	22.6	54.7	14.7	23.8	53.4

ing only a neighborhood area at both locations. The proportion of units that did so prior to displacement ranges from 47 per cent of the small units to only 11 per cent of the large establishments. After the move, the proportion serving only a neighborhood area declines substantially, and the change is observed within each size class. Following the move, the proportion attracting customers from a neighborhood area only declines to 31 per cent of the small businesses, and to only 4 per cent of the large units. On the other extreme, at the former location there was a close relationship between size of business and the proportion attracting customers from outside of the local community area. While only one-tenth of the small businesses catered primarily to this more inclusive area, the proportion increased to nearly one-fourth of the medium-sized units and to more than half of the large units. This changed little following the move. Thus the major changes in area served are found in the shift away from a neighborhood area by many of the smaller units. This may account for much of their decline in volume of business following the move. The move likely had serious consequences for these businesses because of their dependence on a specific location in the local area. A move would be particularly disruptive under such conditions. Among the large businesses, the move would be much less disruptive, in that it would probably not appreciably alter their usual relationship with their customers, since they did not live in close proximity. In short, for businesses serving a large geographical area, the specific location of an establishment is of much less significance.

CHANGES IN VOLUME AND VALUE OF BUSINESS

A question of crucial concern, particularly from the point of view of the individual business establishment, pertains to the consequences of the move in respect to changes in the volume of business and changes in value. Although these two dimensions may be closely related, it is possible for the two variables to vary independently, since volume of business is subject to wide fluctuations depending on the temporary conditions of the market, whereas the value of the business is likely to be more stable and more closely related to investment. Value represents not only volume of business but physical characteristics of the site as well as other factors. It is assumed here that the changes in value observed following relocation would be due largely to changes in site characteristics.[7] Thus if the business moved into a better building

7 This assumption has an empirical base. The units reporting an increase in value after the move were asked: How do you account for this change? Approximately 12 per cent reported that they now "owned their building," and nearly four-fifths (78.6 per cent) of the responses included such site characteristics as "better building," "more space," "better business location," and "accessibility."

in a better area, we would expect value to increase even though volume of business may have remained the same or even decreased. Conversely, if the site were less attractive, we would expect the value of the business to decrease.

At this point, we are interested in how both volume of business and value changed following relocation. The data in Table 13-6 show the amount of business and value of business at the present location as compared with the former site. It is readily evident that the move had a differential effect by size of establishment. The medium-sized businesses show the largest relative gains in volume of business following displacement. More than two-fifths report that they are doing more business now than while at the old location; however, the proportion reporting an increase in business declines to one-third among the large units and to only one-fifth of the small establishments. These data clearly show that at least for a substantial minority there was an increase in business following the move. For nearly one unit in three in each size class, the move had no apparent effect on

TABLE 13-6

CHANGES IN VOLUME AND VALUE OF BUSINESS FOLLOWING RELOCATION BY SIZE OF BUSINESS

Volume and Value of Business	Size of Business		
	Small	Medium	Large
Volume of Business			
Total Per Cent	100.0	100.0	100.0
More Business Here	20.6	43.9	33.8
About Same	32.4	29.3	36.5
Less Business Here	47.1	26.8	29.7
Value of Business			
Total Per Cent	100.0	100.0	100.0
Worth More Here	22.1	52.4	52.0
About Same	50.0	35.7	32.0
Worth Less Here	27.9	11.9	16.0

business, for the volume remains the same as prior to the move. But for a large number of the small establishments, the move was detrimental, in that a loss of business is reported. Nearly half of the small units are doing less volume now than they had done at the old location prior to displacement.

The move was apparently less damaging to the medium- and large-sized establishments, for less than three out of ten experienced a decline in volume of business following displacement. No doubt the differential effects of displacement by size of business are due in large part to differences in area served and how a change in location would affect customer relationships. The small units, catering predominantly to a local neighborhood market in the old area, experienced a real change in their proximity to their customers, and this resulted in a decline in business for nearly half of the establishments involved. It is noteworthy, however, that the move did not result in a decline in business for more than half of the small businesses and for more than seven out of ten of the medium- and large-size establishments. In many instances, the business units experienced an actual increase in volume. But among small units, more lost because of the move than gained. However, among both the medium and large businesses, the proportion that increased their volume exceeded the proportion that experienced a decline.

A rather favorable adjustment in the new location on the part of many is further reflected in the comparative value of the business reported before and after the move. More than half of the medium and large units report that their business is worth more now than prior to displacement. However, among the small businesses, only slightly more than one-fifth report such an increase. But even among the small establishments, half of the businesses report no change in value after the move. One-third of the other-sized businesses also remained about the same in value. It is only in a minority of the cases that value declines, but this constitutes a substantial minority (28 per cent) among the small businesses. Medium-sized units are the least likely to experience a decline in value. It is noted with particular emphasis that, for at least seven out of ten businesses, the move reportedly did not have any negative effect on what the business is worth. And more particularly a majority of the medium and large units report an absolute increase in value.

REACTION TO NEW LOCATION

For a majority of the establishments, business after relocation turned out to be about what they had expected. As is evident from Table 14-6, this proportion does not vary by size. However, the proportion that either over- or underestimated the

TABLE 14-6

REACTION TO NEW LOCATION BY SIZE OF BUSINESS

Reaction to Present Location	Size of Business		
	Small	Medium	Large
Volume of Business Compared with Expectations			
Total Per Cent	100.0	100.0	100.0
Better Than Expected	8.8	21.4	21.3
About What Expected	54.4	59.5	57.3
Less Than Expected	36.8	19.0	21.3
Satisfaction With Progress at New Location			
Total Per Cent	100.0	100.0	100.0
Very and Quite Satisfied	29.5	46.4	57.4
Satisfied	41.2	29.8	26.7
Very and Quite Dissatisfied	29.4	23.8	16.0
Would You Have Done Better at Old Location			
Total Per Cent	100.0	100.0	100.0
Yes	51.5	33.3	24.0
Uncertain	17.6	16.7	24.0
No	30.9	50.0	52.0
How Like Doing Business Here vs Old Location			
Total Per Cent	100.0	100.0	100.0
Like It Better Here	26.5	56.6	61.3
Both Areas the Same	23.5	16.9	17.3
Liked Old Area Better	50.0	26.5	21.3

amount of business to be expected at the new location does vary by size of establishments. The small units were most likely to overcalculate the amount of business that would be done at the new location. Nearly two-fifths report doing less business than they had expected, but this declines to approximately one-fifth among the medium and large establishments. On the other hand, less than one-tenth of the small units are doing more business than expected, whereas more than one-fifth of the medium and large establishments are doing so. These data suggest that the smaller units may have been either over-optimistic or unrealistic as to the merits of the present location. Apparently they did not foresee the consequences of losing their established contacts with their customers. It is also likely that they did not properly assess their dependence on the local neighborhood areas prior to dislocation. They may also have failed to realize that it requires time to attract customers at a new location. At least for a large minority (37 per cent) of the small establishments, business at the present site fell short of expectations. Consequently we would expect the small units to be the least satisfied with the progress made since the move. It is to this question that we now turn.

The level of satisfaction with the progress made following relocation varies significantly by size of business. When the respondents were asked to evaluate their progress at the new location on a five-point scale, only 7 per cent of the small establishments reported that they were "very satisfied," while 31 per cent of the large units did so. When the "very" and "quite" satisfied categories are combined, we find 30 per cent of the small units at this level of satisfaction, but this increases to 46 per cent of the medium-sized and to 57 per cent of the large establishments. Thus the large units have nearly double the proportion of the small units that express this level of satisfaction with the progress made. However, even though the small establishments are less than enthusiastic about their progress, it is noted that at least seven out of ten do not express any dissatisfaction. The proportion of large establishments expressing dissatisfaction is only half as frequent as that found among the small units. Thus it is abundantly evident that the consequences of the move are viewed much more favorably by the larger establishments. This favorable reaction may well be due in large part to the substantial number that are doing more business at the new location than they had expected, whereas the larger proportion dissatisfied among the small units is unquestionably due to the decline in volume of business experienced by these units.

The level of satisfaction with the move is further evident from the responses to the question on whether the owners thought they would have done better had they continued at the old location. More than half of the small establishments express the opinion that they would be better off if they had not been forced to move. However, this response declines to one-third among the medium-sized businesses and to only one-fourth of the large establishments. On the other hand, at least half of the medium and large units report that they are better off now than they would have been had they remained at the original site. But among the small units, such responses are given by only three out of ten businesses. A substantial minority in each size class seems to be uncertain as to what their present status would have been if they had continued at the former site. Responses of this type are reported by 24 per cent of the large units and by 18 per cent of the small ones.

It is apparent that the small businesses continue to have a preference for what they had prior to dislocation. This is further supported by the responses to the question on how they like doing business at the present site as compared to the old location. Half of the small establishments report that they preferred doing business at the old location, but among the large businesses this proportion declines to only one-fifth. However, we find that 61 per cent of the latter state a preference for the present site, while only 27 per cent of the former do so. The medium-sized units also have a majority (57 per cent) who like doing business better at the present site than at the former location.

Thus, in response to a whole series of questions, the larger units consistently indicate a favorable reaction to the move, whereas the small establishments tend to view the move negatively. The latter express the general opinion that things would have been better for them if no change had occurred at all. Relocation seemed to have been much more to the advantage of the large units than to the small ones. The extent to which this is in fact the case is reflected in changes in income following the move.

A significant dimension of relocation is what happens to the amount of money businesses make after the move as compared to what they made prior to displacement. The extent to which the move is beneficial or harmful to the individual owner depends in large part on what effect it has on income. The general reaction to the whole program of displacement is likely to be intimately tied in with what happens to income following the move. In the light of our earlier observations regarding the reaction to the move, we would expect to find that the large units have made a more favorable economic adjustment in terms of this criterion than the small establishments. And this is what our data show. An inspection of Table 15-6 shows a marked variation by size of business in relative income following relocation. Among the small establishments, less than one unit in eight experienced an increase. However, one unit in four among the medium-sized

TABLE 15-6

CHANGES IN INCOME FOLLOWING RELOCATION AND PRESENT ANNUAL INCOME BY SIZE OF BUSINESS

Changes in Income and Present Income	Size of Business		
	Small	Medium	Large
Change in Income			
Total Per Cent	100.0	100.0	100.0
Increased	11.8	26.6	29.3
Remained the Same	27.9	36.1	36.0
Decreased	60.3	37.3	34.7
Present Income			
Total Per Cent	100.0	100.0	100.0
Under $2,000	23.3	9.7	1.9
$ 2,000 – $3,999	28.3	12.9	1.9
$ 4,000 – $7,499	31.7	32.3	20.8
$ 7,500 – $9,999	10.0	22.6	26.4
$10,000 and Over	6.7	22.6	49.1
Median	$3,880	$6,975	$9,910

businesses and nearly one in three of the large establishments report more income after relocation than prior to displacement. On the other hand, three-fifths of the small businesses suffered a loss in income. A decline is also reported by approximately one-third of the large units. Much of the dissatisfaction expressed above by the smaller establishments is likely due to this decline in income. And much of this decline may be due to the fact that many of the small units depended on neighborhood trade areas which were lost when the areas were cleared. The move would be much more disruptive for these businesses than for those that drew customers from a much larger area. And even though the small units seemed to have deliberately minimized the distance moved in order to maintain the advantages of the original location, the disruptive effects of relocation were nonetheless pronounced.

Further inquiry shows that the small units are also much less optimistic concerning the future than the larger units. Less than one-fourth expect next year's business to improve. However, more than half of the medium-sized units and nearly two-thirds of the large units look for an increase in business during the next year. It is noteworthy that more than two-fifths of the small establishments expect business to continue at about the same level during the next year. Although only a small minority of the establishments view the forthcoming year unfavorably, we do find that it is the small businesses that have the largest proportion who expect business to decline. But of special interest is the large number of small units that are uncertain or do not know what to expect during the coming year. While 22 per cent of the small establishments respond thusly, the proportion declines continuously to only 11 per cent of the large units. In short, large units not only are more satisfied with the move but also view the near future much more positively than do the small establishments.

Further evidence of the less favorable view of small businesses is found in the responses to a question on how the owners felt about forcing businesses to move to make way for public improvement programs. Although the question was asked in general terms, it is assumed that the attitudes expressed reflect, at least crudely, how the respondents feel about having been displaced. Again we note that marked and consistent differences are found by size of business, with the small units expressing negative opinions much more frequently than the large establishments. Thus more than one-fourth of the small businesses report that they are very much opposed to businesses being forced to move; however, less than one-tenth of the large units concur in this opinion. The latter, as well as the medium-sized establishments, are much more likely to be fatalistic concerning the whole idea. To them progress exacts its toll and displacement is inevitable as these necessary programs are developed. Many of the small units were less philosophical. We find that 27 per cent were very much opposed and another 15 per cent objected because it was an inconvenience and caused a hardship for the displaced units. But even among the small establishments, nearly two-fifths viewed forced movements, under such circumstances, favorably. More than one unit in four (26.5 per cent) approved of forcing businesses to move with no reservations. However, a much larger proportion of the large businesses reponded thusly. Of the latter, 44 per cent approve such displacements with no reservations. Altogether, three-fifths of the large units and nearly half of the medium-sized establishments approve of displacing businesses, but some of this approval is qualified with reservations attached.

Large units are likely to be in a much more favorable position to withstand the disruptive effects of the move, in that they may have more abundant resources available. Perhaps one of the reasons for the unsatisfactory adjustment among the smaller establishments in particular is due to the relative low income of the owners of these units. At any rate, as shown in Table 15-6, annual income varies significantly by size of business. Comparable data for the former locations are not available but we do know that the small units had the largest proportion that reported a decline. Obviously these businesses were the least able to afford such a decrease, for nearly one-fourth of the owners of small establishments report an annual income of less than $2,000. At this income level, we find less than 10 per cent of those with medium-size establishments and less than 2 per cent of the owners of the larger businesses. The proportion with income of less than $4,000 ranges from a high of 52 per cent among the small units to less than 4 per cent of the owners of the large establishments. When attention is focused on the higher income categories, we find that less than one-fifth of the owners of small businesses report an income of more than $7,500, as compared with slightly less than half of those with medium-sized units and more than three-fourths of the owners of large establishments. Half of the owners of the large businesses are in the top-income category.

The magnitude of these differences by size of business is dramatically shown in the variations of annual median incomes. These range from less than $4,000 to approximately $10,000. The owners of medium-sized businesses fall midway between these two extremes, with a median income of nearly $7,000. Thus income varies consistently and markedly by size of business. These data clearly show the rather precarious position particularly of the owners of the small establishments. A majority of these owners report an income substantially lower than the national average for laborers.[8] Owners of medium-sized business have an income higher than that of craftsmen but lower than that reported for sales workers.[9] The owners of such businesses have an income about 13 per cent above the national average for the self-employed in the manager, official and proprietors category.[10] Those with the larger establishments exceed this amount by more than 50 per cent. Thus, at least as far as income is concerned, the owners of the displaced businesses that relocated are above the national average; however, the owners of small establishments have incomes that are significantly below this average. And even though this income may not be atypical for such small businessmen, it is nonetheless the case that such units can tolerate only a very small margin of error. Thus the problems of displacement and relocation are less likely to be viewed favorably, in that these businesses are at best marginal, and the line between continuance and failure may well be a very thin one. It is little wonder then that they should be opposed to any program of displacements which would threaten to upset this minimal balance.

8 Median income for laborers in 1960 was $4,393. *Current Population Reports,* Consumer Income, Income of Families and Persons in the United States: 1960, Series P-60, No. 37, January 17, 1962, Table 8, p. 30.

9 *Ibid.* Craftsmen $6,660, Sales Workers $6,977.

10 *Ibid.* The income for this group is $6,138.

CHAPTER 7

ADJUSTMENT FOLLOWING RELOCATION

ONE of the most significant dimensions of the displacement-relocation process pertains to the relative adjustment the business establishment makes following the move. It is to this issue that the present chapter is directed. What constitutes adjustment is, of course, nebulous, but for our purposes it can be operationally defined. Since, for the most part, the primary objective of a business is to make money and the success of a business is expressed in whether or not it realizes a profit, the ultimate question of adjustment may well be measured in terms of the comparative income before and after the move. To the extent that the income has remained the same or increased, we can say that a satisfactory economic adjustment has been made. At least displacement has not been costly in terms of income from the business. On the other hand, a decrease in income would be viewed as an indication that, at least at this point in time, the business has not worked out a favorable adjustment in the new location. At any rate, adjustment would be less favorable than the level attained at the old location. However, to express adjustment only in terms of income would, in the writer's opinion, be an approach that is too narrow or limited. Income is of course important, but there are other aspects which are also of significance.

Apart from the economic consideration as to how the volume of business and the value of the business have changed following displacement, there are the psychological gains or losses as perceived by the businessmen involved. These are, of course, intangibles which cannot be measured, but for our purposes we have assumed that the evaluative and comparative attitudes expressed regarding the new location serve as an index of this dimension of adjustment after the move. Thus, as a part of the operational definition of adjustment in the new location, we are concerned with such variables as the level of satisfaction with the progress made, how the owners of establishments like doing business at the new location as compared with the old site, and whether the owners think their business would have been able to do better had they not been forced to leave the old area. Each of these will be considered separately. It may be that their economic position has improved, but they may think they could have done even better at the old location. To the extent that there is an expressed preference for the old area and a stated dissatisfaction with the progress that has been made since the move, we would view the adjustment to be unsatisfactory.

In earlier chapters it has been found that adjustment following relocation varies by both type and size of business. Also the business establishments that moved to the suburbs report a more favorable adjustment, both economically and psychologically, than the businesses that remained in the central city. The purpose of the present chapter is to investigate the influence of a selected number of variables on adjustment in the new location. Attention is first focused on the extent to which adjustment in the new location varies by the demographic characteristics of the owners.

DEMOGRAPHIC CHARACTERISTICS

The significance of age and education is clearly evident from the data presented in Table 1-7. Not only do the older businessmen and the less well educated have a much higher failure rate following displacement, as noted earlier, but even among those who remain in business, these persons show the least favorable economic and psychological adjustment in the new location. Al-

TABLE 1-7

ADJUSTMENT FOLLOWING RELOCATION BY AGE AND EDUCATION OF BUSINESS OWNERS

Adjustment	Age			Education		
	Under 45	45-54	55 and Over	Grade School	High School	College
Total Per Cent	100.0	100.0	100.0	100.0	100.0	100.0
Volume of Business						
More Here	46.1	39.5	16.7	21.7	38.0	39.6
About Same	30.8	28.4	38.4	23.3	33.3	39.6
Less Here	23.1	32.1	44.9	55.0	28.7	20.8
Value of Business						
Worth More Here	49.2	50.6	30.4	30.0	46.8	52.8
About Same	38.5	36.1	41.8	36.7	41.4	34.0
Worth Less Here	12.3	13.3	27.8	33.3	11.8	13.2
Satisfaction With Progress at New Location						
Very and Quite Satisfied	53.9	48.2	34.2	28.3	50.5	52.8
Satisfied	29.2	30.1	36.6	31.7	31.5	34.0
Very and Quite Dissatisfied	16.9	21.7	29.2	40.0	18.0	13.2
Would You Have Done Better at Old Location						
Yes	20.0	39.7	44.3	58.3	31.6	18.9
Uncertain	24.6	18.1	16.5	11.7	19.8	26.4
No	55.4	42.2	39.2	30.0	48.6	54.7
How Like Doing Business Here vs Old Location						
Better Here	56.9	51.2	40.6	31.7	50.9	67.9
Same	20.0	17.1	20.2	15.0	23.6	13.2
Better at Old Location	23.1	31.7	39.2	53.3	25.5	18.9
Change in Income						
Increased	30.8	25.3	14.0	10.2	28.0	28.3
Same	35.4	33.7	32.1	22.0	35.1	43.4
Decreased	33.8	41.0	53.9	67.8	36.9	28.3

though one-third of the units enjoyed more business after the move than before, this proportion ranges from a low of 17 per cent among those fifty-five years of age and over to a high of 46 per cent among those under forty-five years of age. Of the latter, less than one-fourth experienced a decline in the volume of business following displacement, but nearly half of those in the older group did so. Large differences are also observed by education. Twice as many in the college category experienced an increase in business as is found among those with only a grade school education. However, more than half of the latter group suffered a loss in volume of business, whereas only one-fifth of the college-trained did so. Thus those low in education were two and one-half times more likely to experience a decline in business than those in the highest educational category. A similar but less marked pattern of change by age and education is observed in reference to the relative value of the business before and after the move. Younger businessmen and those with college training were most likely to report that the value of their business increased following displacement. On the other hand, a substantial number of the older and less well educated actually experienced a decline in the value. One general impression that was gained in talking with the older respondents was that they were hesitant to invest in the new location because of their age. They were faced with the problem of having so little time left in which to recoup an investment. Many were still too young to retire, but they felt that they were too old to try to build up a business in a new location. Consequently, they decided to continue in business but to keep the operation at a level which would require the minimum amount of investment. Accordingly, we find that the volume and value of business declined disproportionately for this age group following displacement.

It is also the older businessmen and the less well educated who have the lowest proportion expressing high satisfaction with the progress they have made at the new location. In the high satisfaction category, we find only one-third of those fifty-five and over, but more than half of those under forty-five years of age. A similar marked difference is found by education. Only 28 per cent of those at the grade level are found in the high satisfaction category, as compared with 53 per cent of those with college training. Those low in education have a particularly high proportion who expressed dissatisfaction with the progress made following displacement. The proportion dissatisfied exceeds that at the college level three-fold. The high proportion dissatisfied among those fifty-five years of age and over is also worthy of note.

It is not surprising, in view of our observations so far, that the older respondents and those at the lower end of the educational scale should feel that they would have been better off if they could have continued in business at the old location. That is, they are the ones most likely to feel that they would have been better off if no change had occurred and the old areas had continued in existence as before. We find that while only 20 per cent of those under forty-five years of age and 19 per cent of those at the college level report that they would have been better off if they could have continued at the old location, this proportion increases to 44 per cent among those over fifty-five years of age and to 58 per cent of those at the grade school level. More than half of those in the younger group and of those with college training do not feel that they would be any better off if they had continued at the original location. This proportion, however, declines to 39 per cent of those fifty-five years of age and over and to only 30 per cent in the grade school category.

We find also that there are marked differences by age and education in the responses to the question on how they like doing business at the new location as compared to the previous site. Among the younger businessmen, 67 per cent prefer the new location, as compared to only 41 per cent of those in the oldest category. On the other hand, only 23 per cent of those under forty-five years of age liked doing business better at the old location, whereas 39 per cent of those in the oldest age category state such a preference. Approximately one unit in five at all age levels makes no distinction between the two areas.

It is among the college-trained that we find the largest proportion that prefers doing business at the new location. More than two-thirds state such a preference, as compared with less than one-third at the grade school level. On the other hand, more than half of those in the grade school category state a preference for doing business at the old location, but this declines to one-fourth at the high school level and to less than one-fifth at the college level. It is clearly evident from these data that the better educated and the younger businessmen have responded most favorably to the move. No doubt much of this is due to the more favorable economic adjustment experienced by businessmen with these characteristics. Not only have they enjoyed a disproportionate increase in volume and value of business following displacement, but they are also the ones most likely to enjoy an increase in income.

Nearly one-third of those under forty-five years of age report that they are making more at the new location than prior to displacement, but this drops to only 14 per cent of those fifty-five years of age and over. And while only one-third of the younger businessmen are making less than before the move, we find that more than half of those in the older group experienced a loss in income at the new site. Marked and consistent differences are also observed by education. While only 10 per cent of those in the grade school category are making more now than before the move, this increases to 28 per cent among those at both the high school and college levels. Conversely the proportion experiencing a loss in income after relocation declines sharply by educational levels. At the grade school level 68 per cent report a loss in income, but this declines to 37 per cent in the high school category and to 28 per cent of those with college training.

Thus it is apparent that the effects of displacement and relocation vary by the demographic characteristics of the businessmen involved. The younger and better educated seemed to have made the most favorable economic adjustment, and they also tend to view the new location much more positively than older businessmen and those at the lower educational levels. The latter are more likely to feel that they would be better off if things had remained as they were and they had not been forced to move. In terms of all of the variables considered in this analysis, it is these businessmen who have made the least favorable adjustment.

AREA SERVED

It is to be expected that the adjustment following relocation would be closely related to the geographical scope of the area served by the business units prior to displacement. Units catering primarily to a neighborhood market would be more sensitive to change than establishments whose customers were drawn from throughout the whole community or from outside of the local area. We would expect the adjustment to be most difficult for those units that were dependent on a neighborhood market, since displacement and relocation would tend to sever established relationships. The extent to which this hypothesis is valid is the topic to which we now direct our attention. The data on which this discussion is based are shown in Table 2-7.

Regardless of the type of area served prior to displacement, the volume of business after relocation exceeded the amount of business done at the old location for approximately one-third of the establishments. However, it is particularly worthy of note that more than half of the units which were largely neighborhood-type businesses actually experienced a decline in volume after the move, as compared with only one-fourth of those serving a larger market area. It is also the neighborhood-type businesses that have the largest proportion that report a decrease in the value of business following the move. However, many of the units that report a decline in volume of business did not report a decline in value. While only a minority of the establishments report their business to be worth less at the new location, the proportion is highest among the units that drew their customers predominantly from a neighborhood area.

The level of satisfaction with progress made at the new location is also found to vary markedly by type of area served prior to displacement. The neighborhood-type businesses are much more frequently dissatisfied with the progress made since the move than the units which attracted customers from the whole community or who served a regional or national market. Of those serving a neighborhood area, more than four out of ten units express dissatisfaction with the progress made at the new location. At the other extreme, we find that only 23 per cent of those that served a neighborhood market express a high degree of satisfaction, but this increases to 49 per cent among those who attracted customers from throughout the whole community, and to 60 per cent of those who catered predominantly to a non-local market.

It seems quite evident that it is the businesses that catered primarily to a local neighborhood area that are the ones least

TABLE 2-7

ADJUSTMENT FOLLOWING RELOCATION BY AREA SERVED PRIOR TO DISPLACEMENT

Adjustment	Neighbor-hood	Commu-nity	Non-Local
Total Per Cent	100.0	100.0	100.0
Volume of Business			
More Here	31.7	33.3	35.4
About Same	15.9	39.6	38.4
Less Here	52.4	27.1	26.2
Value of Business			
Worth More Here	39.1	43.8	46.3
About Same	28.1	46.8	37.3
Worth Less Here	32.8	9.4	16.4
Satisfaction With Progress at New Location			
Very and Quite Satisfied	23.4	49.0	59.7
Satisfied	34.4	37.4	22.4
Very and Quite Dissatisfied	42.2	13.6	17.9
Would You Have Done Better at Old Location			
Yes	62.5	25.0	25.4
Uncertain	15.6	22.9	17.9
No	21.9	52.1	56.7
How Like Doing Business Here vs Old Location			
Better Here	28.1	52.6	64.2
Same	14.1	26.3	13.4
Better at Old Location	57.8	21.1	22.4
Change in Income			
Increased	14.1	23.2	31.4
Same	20.3	41.1	35.8
Decreased	65.6	35.7	32.8

satisfied with the results of displacement. This is further evident from the responses to the question on whether or not the business establishments would be better off if they had remained at the old location. Nearly two-thirds of the neighborhood businesses report that they would be better off if they could have remained at the old location, as compared with only one-fourth of the other units. More than half of the establishments serving a non-neighborhood area report that they would not be any better off if they had continued at the old location. This drops, however, to only one-fifth of the neighborhood-type businesses. Nearly two units out of ten are uncertain as to whether or not the move was to their advantage. This varies only slightly by area served.

Neighborhood-type businesses state a very marked preference for the old area as a place to do business. Nearly three-fifths of the units report that they liked doing business better at the old location than at the present site, but this proportion declines to approximately one-fifth of the establishments that drew their customers from the larger community or from a larger market area. The latter, however, have a very distinct preference for the new location. While only 28 per cent of the neighborhood-type establishments report they prefer the new area, this increased to 64 per cent of those that catered predominantly to a regional or national market. Undoubtedly these responses differ in content. For the neighborhood-type businesses response is likely stated in reference to their proximity to and relationships with their customers, whereas the other-type businesses are more likely responding in terms of the quality of the building or the general condition of the area in which they are presently located, as compared with the old site. Also it is likely that the responses are due in part at least to changes in income following the move. Support for this is found in the relative incomes before and after displacement. Neighborhood businesses have the lowest proportion of units that report an increase in income following the move. While only 14 per cent of these units experienced a higher income after displacement, the proportion increases to 23 per cent of the units serving the whole community, and to 31 per cent of the establishments catering to a non-local market. However, two-thirds of the neighborhood-type businesses report a loss of income, but only one-third of the units serving a larger area are making less at the present site than they made prior to displacement.

That the move had a differential effect by type of area served is further evident from the responses to the question on how the amount of business at the new location compares with expectations. As the geographic scope of the market area increases, there is an increase in the proportion of units reporting more business than expected. Thus while less than 10 per cent of the neighborhood businesses report doing better than expected, this increases to 16 per cent among the units serving the whole community, and to 28 per cent of the businesses that served a regional or national market. The extent to which business fell short of expectation varies inversely with size of market area. While only one-tenth of the units serving a regional or national market report the amount of business to be less than expected, this increases to one-fourth of the units catering to the whole community, and to more than two-fifths of the businesses that were primarily neighborhood-oriented. It is apparent from these data that neighborhood businesses in particular tended to overestimate the amount of business potential of the new site, whereas the businesses catering to a larger market area disproportionately underestimated the business potential of the new location. It is likely that the neighborhood businesses did not realize the full extent of their dependence on the local area, and thus could not realistically appraise the business potential of the new area nor the loss that would result from losing contact with their regular customers. On the other hand, the larger businesses must not have realized the full advantages to be gained through a more attractive site, even though they emphasized this in looking for a new location.

It is consistently found that the least favorable adjustment is made by the kinds of businesses that predominantly served a neighborhood market prior to the move. Such units are most likely to suffer a decline in the volume and value of business as well as in income following relocation. A distinct majority state a preference for the old location as a place to do business and feel that they would be better off if they could have continued to operate at the old location. On the other hand, the business establishments that had served a non-local market made the most favorable economic adjustment. A clear majority expresses high satisfaction with progress that has been made since the move, and feel that they would not be any better off if they had remained at the old location. They also like doing business at the present site better than at the old location. These units appear to have improved their position with the move, whereas the neighborhood businesses were definitely hurt by displacement. It will be recalled that the neighborhood businesses also had the highest failure rate following the move.

The adjustment at the new location varies markedly by the familiarity of the relationship the businessmen had with their customers at the old location. The adjustment, both economic and psychological, is found to be least satisfactory for those who report that they knew "most" of their customers, and most satisfactory for those who knew "few or none." This difference largely reflects the type of area serviced. However, this lends further support to our interpretation regarding the special problems faced by neighborhood-type businesses. In short, those who knew most of their customers at the old location report that they would be better off if they had not moved, and they state a definite preference for doing business at the old location. It is also noted that they are making less money at the new location than they made before the move. At the other extreme, of those businessmen who knew "few or none" of their customers, a majority do not feel that they would be any better off if they had not moved, and nearly two-thirds like doing business better at the new location than at the old site. These businesses also have the largest proportion that experienced an increase in income following the move, as well as an increase in the value of their business. The pattern of difference according to how well the businessmen knew their customers at the old location is marked and consistent. The most favorable adjustment is reported by those businessmen who knew "few or none" of their customers, and the least favorable adjustment is made by those who knew "most" of their customers, whereas those who knew "some" tend to fall midway between the two. In short, businesses that were largely dependent on a frequent and recurrent relationship with customers who came predominantly from the neighborhood market area made the least favorable adjustment following the move.

PRESENT TENURE AND CHANGES IN TENURE

The adjustment at the new location varies markedly by tenure as well as by changes in tenure following the move. An overall inspection of Table 3-7 shows in general a more favorable adjustment in the new location for owners than for renters. Businessmen who currently own the building they occupy have a larger proportion who experienced an increase in volume of business after the move than is found among renters. While only 20 per cent of the owners report a drop in volume of business, this increases to 43 per cent of the renters. However, for the latter the range is from 40 per cent of those who were renters at both locations to 58 per cent of those who had previously owned the building from which they had been displaced. Thus the businesses that most frequently experienced a decline in volume after the move are those whose owners moved to rented quarters prior to relocation. Loss in business volume is least frequently reported by establishments that occupied their own building at both locations. Owners at the new location also have the largest proportion who report no change in volume of business. For more than two-fifths of these units, the move had no effect on the volume of business. This, however, was the experience of only one-fifth of the units that moved from "own" to "rent."

An even more marked relationship is found between present tenure as well as changes in tenure and changes in relative value of the business after the move. Nearly two-thirds of the present owners, but less than one-third of the renters, report an increase in the value of business following the move. The proportion reporting an increase ranges from a high of 67 per cent among the businesses moving from rentals to ownership to a low of only 26 per cent of those who moved from own to rent. Among the latter, 42 per cent report a decline in value, as compared with only 6 per cent of the former. While less than one unit in five which did not change tenure reports a decline in value, it is the business owners at the present location who have the lowest proportion reporting a decline, and the highest proportion reporting an increase. Obviously value of business is not viewed independently of the amount of investment in the building occupied. Thus to move from "own" to "rent" was to experience

TABLE 3-7
ADJUSTMENT FOLLOWING RELOCATION BY PRESENT TENURE AND DIRECTION OF TENURE MOVE

Adjustment	Present Tenure		Direction of Tenure Move			
	Own	Rent	Own to Rent	Rent to Rent	Own to Own	Rent to Own
Total Number	86	141	19	122	53	33
Volume of Business						
More Here	37.6	30.9	21.0	32.5	37.7	37.5
About Same	42.4	26.6	21.0	27.4	43.4	40.6
Less Here	20.0	42.5	58.0	40.1	18.9	21.9
Value of Business						
Worth More Here	62.8	31.2	26.3	32.0	60.4	66.7
About Same	26.7	46.1	31.6	48.3	26.4	27.3
Worth Less Here	10.5	22.7	42.1	19.7	13.2	6.0
Satisfaction With Progress at New Location						
Very and Quite Satisfied	54.6	39.0	31.6	40.1	52.8	57.6
Satisfied	33.8	31.2	26.3	32.0	34.0	33.3
Very and Quite Dissatisfied	11.6	29.8	42.1	27.9	13.2	9.1
Would You Have Done Better at Old Location						
Yes	30.2	39.0	68.4	34.4	28.3	33.3
Uncertain	15.1	22.0	5.3	24.6	15.1	15.2
No	54.7	39.0	26.3	41.0	56.6	51.5
How Like Doing Business Here vs Old Location						
Better Here	61.7	41.4	33.3	42.6	56.7	69.6
Same	15.7	20.7	16.7	21.3	16.9	15.2
Better at Old Location	22.6	37.9	50.0	36.1	26.4	15.2
Change in Income						
Increased	28.2	19.9	10.5	21.3	30.8	24.2
Same	36.5	31.9	31.6	32.0	36.5	36.4
Decreased	35.3	48.2	57.9	46.7	32.7	39.4

a decrease in value, whereas an increase in value resulted from a change from "rent" to "own."

We also find that those who own the building they occupy have the largest proportion who are satisfied with the progress made since the move. Among such units, 55 per cent are high on the satisfaction scale, as compared with only 39 per cent of the renters. Conversely, only 12 per cent of the former but 30 per cent of the latter express dissatisfaction. However, the proportion dissatisfied varies even more significantly by changes in tenure following displacement. The proportion dissatisfied ranges from a low of only 9 per cent of the former renters who became owners after the move to a high of 42 per cent of the previous owners who moved to rented quarters. The businessmen who owned the building they occupied at both locations are only half as likely to be dissatisfied with the progress made since the move as the businesses who rented both before and after the move. The proportions dissatisfied are 13 per cent and 28 per cent respectively. On the other hand, the proportion expressing a high level of satisfaction at the new location ranges from a low of less than one-third of the renters who formerly owned, to a high of nearly three-fifths of those who own now but had rented the building previously occupied at the former site. A further inspection of these data shows that, while 53 per cent of those who owned at both locations express a high level of satisfaction with the progress made since the move, the proportion drops to only 40 per cent of the renters. Thus it seems that the move is viewed more favorably by those who own their building than by those who have moved to rented quarters. It is the businesses that owned prior to displacement, but which now rent, that express the least amount of satisfaction with the progress they have made at the new site. However, the consequences of the move are viewed most favorably by the former renters who bought the building they now occupy.

When asked if they would be better off had they continued at the old location, the owners are less likely to respond negatively than the renters. The proportions doing so are 55 per cent and 39 per cent respectively. Here too we find that the responses vary by the direction of the tenure move. Only one-fourth of the establishments who moved from "own" to "rent" report that they would not be any better off if they had continued at the old location; however, this increases to two-fifths of the renters at both locations, and to more than half of those who changed from "rent" to "own," and of those who owned at both locations. But it is worthy of note that more than two-thirds of the movers from "own" to "rent" report that they would be better off if they had remained at the old site. This declines to only one-third of the "rent" to "rent" and the "rent" to "own" businesses, and to less than one-third among those who owned both before and after the move. Thus it is only among the businesses that owned at the old location and now rent that a substantial majority feel that they would be better off if they had not been displaced. Among those who own their present building, regardless of their previous tenure, a majority reports that they are better off now than they would have been if they had not been forced to move.

Owners are also more likely than renters to prefer the present site over the old location as a place to do business. While 61 per cent of the owners state a preference for the present site, only 41 per cent of the renters respond thusly. On the other hand, 38 per cent of the renters express a preference for the former site as a place to do business, as compared with 23 per cent of the owners. Preference for the present site also varies substantially by changes in tenure following displacement. The units that moved from "own" to "rent" have the smallest proportion who prefer the present site, whereas those who rented formerly but who now own have the largest proportion who state a preference for the present location. These proportions are 33 per cent and 70 per cent respectively. Those who owned at both locations have a larger proportion who prefer the present site than is found among those who rented at either or both locations. But the point of particular interest is that 50 per cent of the units changing from "own" to "rent" report that they liked doing business better at the former site, whereas this declines to only 15 per cent of those who now own but who had rented prior to the move. Renters at both locations are more likely than owners to state a preference for the old location as a place to do business. But one-fifth or less in all tenure status categories are unable to rate one area over another. To these businesses the move seems to have been of little significance.

Income after the move as compared to income at the old location also varies by tenure and by changes in tenure. Owners have a larger proportion who report an increase in income following relocation, whereas the renters are more likely to have experienced a decrease. The businesses with the lowest proportion reporting an increase in income after the move are the units who owned the building prior to displacement but currently occupy rented quarters. Only 10 per cent of these units report an increase in income, while nearly 60 per cent report a loss at the new location. This compares very unfavorably with businesses that owned at both locations. The latter are three times as likely to experience an increase, and are only half as likely to experience a decline in income following the move. Owners at both locations have the lowest proportion who experienced a decline after the move. Again we find that the businesses moving from "rent" to "own" make a more favorable adjustment in terms of income, at the new site than either rentals at both locations or those who formerly owned but now rent.

In terms of all of the variables considered here, it is evident that owners make a more favorable adjustment following displacement than do renters. The least favorable adjustment is made by the businessmen who moved from "own" to "rent," and the most favorable adjustment is made by businessmen who formerly rented but now own. Also those who owned at both locations apparently have made a more favorable adjustment than those who occupied rented quarters both before and after the move. We turn now to a discussion of how adjustment varies by changes in selected site characteristics.

CHANGES IN SITE CHARACTERISTICS

In selecting a new site, a majority of the establishments moved to larger quarters than they had previously occupied, whereas a minority moved either to a location about equal in size or to a site which was smaller than the one from which they had been forced to move. The purpose of this discussion is to examine how changes in space are related to the adjustment of the business units in the new location. Similarly we are concerned with how adjustment varies by the relative age of the building occupied, as well as by changes in the quality of the area following the move. In short, how does adjustment vary by changes in selected site characteristics? These data are shown in Table 4-7.

It is evident that those who moved to larger quarters have the largest proportion who experienced an increase in volume and value of business following relocation. They also have the smallest proportion who experienced a decline. Conversely units that have less space after the move are the ones most likely to report a loss in volume and a decline in value. Such units have the smallest proportion who report increases. It is also noted that the highest proportion reporting no change in volume and value of business is found among those businesses that maintained approximately the same amount of space after relocation as prior to the move.

Of those that moved to larger quarters, 43 per cent report an increase in volume of business, but this proportion declines to 26 per cent among those that continued to occupy the same amount of space, and to only 14 per cent of those that moved to less space. Among the latter, however, 56 per cent report a decline in volume of business, as compared with only 26 per cent of those that moved to larger quarters. This compares with an average of about one-third for all businesses. Reported values also show a consistent pattern in relationship to changes in space. More than half of those with more space report an increase in value, but this declines to less than one-fourth of those which have less space after the move. Of the latter, 40 per cent report their business to be worth less now than before the move, whereas only 11 per cent of the former do so. Less than one-fifth of all businesses report a decline in value.

It is only the businesses that moved to larger quarters that have a distinct majority expressing high satisfaction with the progress made since the move. Nearly three-fifths do so, as compared with only about one-fourth of those who moved to the same-sized place or to less space. The latter are much more likely to express dissatisfaction with the progress made. More than one-third of the units, that is, 35 per cent, moving to less space report dissatisfaction, as compared with only 17 per cent of those who have more space now than at the old location. Further sup-

TABLE 4-7

ADJUSTMENT FOLLOWING RELOCATION BY CHANGES IN SITE CHARACTERISTICS

Adjustment	Changes in Space			Age of Building			Condition of Area		
	More	Same	Less	Newer	Same	Older	Better	Same	Worse
Total Per Cent	100.0	100.0	100.0	100.0	100.0	100.0	100.0	100.0	100.0
Volume of Business									
More Here	43.1	25.7	13.5	40.2	31.3	22.0	44.3	26.8	15.0
About Same	31.3	40.0	30.8	33.9	29.6	34.0	34.4	29.6	32.5
Less Here	25.6	34.3	55.8	25.9	39.1	44.0	21.3	43.6	52.5
Value of Business									
Worth More Here	53.6	31.4	23.1	58.8	29.0	26.0	59.2	29.2	22.5
About Same	35.7	54.3	36.5	30.7	48.4	46.0	33.0	47.2	40.0
Worth Less Here	10.7	14.3	40.4	10.5	22.6	28.0	7.8	23.6	37.5
Satisfaction With Progress at New Location									
Very and Quite Satisfied	57.2	22.8	26.9	57.0	32.2	34.0	63.5	31.9	15.0
Satisfied	25.7	48.6	38.5	28.1	33.9	40.0	27.8	33.3	42.5
Very and Quite Dissatisfied	17.1	28.6	34.7	14.9	33.9	26.0	8.7	34.8	42.5
Would You Have Done Better at Old Location									
Yes	27.1	37.1	57.7	32.5	40.3	36.0	20.0	43.1	67.5
Uncertain	20.7	20.0	15.4	15.8	24.2	22.0	19.1	25.0	10.0
No	52.1	42.9	26.9	51.8	35.5	42.0	60.9	31.9	22.5
How Like Doing Business Here vs Old Location									
Better Here	59.0	42.9	26.9	60.6	40.3	34.7	65.8	40.3	17.5
Same	15.8	25.7	23.1	17.5	14.5	28.6	19.3	20.8	15.0
Better at Old Location	25.2	31.4	50.0	21.9	45.2	36.7	14.9	38.9	67.5
Change in Income									
Increased	29.3	20.0	7.8	29.2	19.4	14.0	34.2	13.9	7.5
Same	35.7	37.1	25.5	31.0	37.1	36.0	34.2	31.9	35.0
Decreased	35.0	42.9	66.7	39.8	43.5	50.0	31.6	54.2	57.5

port for the importance of space is evident in the responses to the question on whether or not the businessmen would be better off if they had remained at the old site. We find that 58 per cent of those with less space feel that they would be better off if they had not been forced to move. However, only 27 per cent of those with more space concur in this response. More than half of the latter businesses, 52 per cent, respond negatively to this question, as compared with 43 per cent of those with the same amount of space, and only 27 per cent of those with less space.

It is also the businesses in larger quarters that have the largest proportion preferring the present site as a place to do business. About three-fifths state a preference for the new location. This response declines to two-fifths among those with the same amount of space, and to only one-fourth of the units that moved to less space. The opposite proportions are found in terms of those that liked the old location better. Half of those with less space report that they liked doing business at the old location better than at the present site.

Changes in income following relocation are also found to be closely related to changes in the amount of space occupied. We find that 29 per cent of the establishments that increased their space have a higher income after the move, as compared with only 8 per cent of those that have less space. However, two-thirds of the latter experienced a loss in income, while only one-third of the former did so.

In terms of all of the variables considered, the most favorable adjustment at the new location is reported by the business units that used displacement as an opportunity to increase the amount of space available for the operation of their business. Those who moved to the same amount of space made a less favorable adjustment than those who moved to larger quarters, but a more favorable adjustment than did the businesses having less space than they had prior to displacement. It is unlikely that these differences are due either to the size or type of businesses involved in the movement to larger or smaller quarters. Although changes in space did differ by type and size of business, the differences were not sufficiently large to account for the marked variations in adjustment in relation to changes in space before and after the move.

For the most part, displacements for both urban renewal and highway construction projects have involved properties which were old and in areas that were in the process of deterioration. Many of the structures in these areas had already reached advanced stages of disrepair, but, as noted earlier, most of the businesses were established and had been in operation in these areas for many years. The question of concern here is how adjustment in the new location varies by the relative age of the buildings occupied after the move, as compared to the one from which they had been displaced. These data are also presented in Table 4-7. At first blush, it is immediately evident that the adjustment is most favorable among the establishments that moved to newer buildings. This applies in terms of all of the variables studied. Such moves were made by half of the establishments, whereas less than one-fourth of the businesses moved into older structures.

Of the businesses that moved to a newer building, two-fifths report an increase in the volume of business, as compared with half this proportion among those that moved to an older structure. On the other hand only one-fourth of the former but more than two-fifths of the latter report a decrease in volume of business following the move. Changes in value of business are also closely related to relative age of the building presently occupied. Three-fifths of those in a newer building but only one-fourth of those that moved into an older structure report that the value of their business has increased following relocation. And while only 10 per cent of those in a newer building report a decline in value, this proportion increases nearly three-fold among the units that moved to an older building than they had occupied prior to displacement.

Businesses in the newer structures have the largest proportion that are satisfied with the progress they have made since the move. Also such units have the largest proportion that report that they would not be any better off if they had remained at the old location. It is of particular interest to note that 61 per cent of the establishments in newer buildings prefer doing business at the present site over the old location, but this declines to 40 per cent of those in the same-aged building, and to 35 per cent of those who moved to an older building. Of the latter, more than one-third state a preference for doing business at the old location, while less than one-fourth of those in a newer building do so.

The favorable responses noted here are likely due in large part to the relative changes in income by age of building occupied. The proportion of units reporting an increase in income at the new location is highest for those in newer buildings and lowest for the businesses that moved into older structures. The highest proportion reporting a decline in income following relocation is found among the units that moved to an older building than they had previously occupied. Thus the businesses that had the necessary resources which permitted them to use displacement as an opportunity to move into newer structures are the units that have made the most favorable adjustment and are most likely to view the move positively, whereas those who moved to older buildings tend disproportionately to view the present location negatively. In short, they apparently have made a less favorable adjustment in the new area. Similar, but even more marked, differences are found in respect to the general relative quality of the area into which the businesses moved.

Of the businesses that relocated, slightly more than half upgraded their physical surroundings by moving to an area where the general conditions were better, in their own judgment, than was the area from which they had been displaced. Less than one-fourth moved to the same quality area and approximately one-fifth to an area that is in worse condition. In a sense, this movement can be viewed as a form of mobility. Those moving to a better area can be classified as being upwardly mobile, while those who moved to a less attractive area are downwardly mobile. The question of concern here pertains to how adjustment at the new site is related to the direction of mobility. The quality of the area is likely closely related to the age of the building occupied, but the relationship would only be approximate; thus a separate treatment is justified.

That adjustment at the new site varies markedly by direction of mobility is readily apparent. The businesses which were upwardly mobile have a much larger proportion that report a favorable adjustment than is found among those that were either downwardly mobile or remained at the same level. The differences observed are consistent in respect to each of the indices of adjustment employed. Among those who were upwardly mobile in respect to the physical conditions of the area in which their business is located, 44 per cent experienced an increase in volume of business. However, this decreases to 27 per cent among the non-mobile and to only 15 per cent of those who were downwardly mobile. On the other hand, a decrease in volume is reported by only one-fifth of the upwardly mobile, as compared with more than half of those whom we have classified as downwardly mobile, that is, those who moved to a poorer area. Among the upwardly mobile, 59 per cent report their business to be worth more at the new location, whereas 8 per cent report a decline in value. However, among the downwardly mobile the comparable proportions are 23 per cent and 38 per cent respectively.

The businesses that moved to a better area also have the largest proportion of owners who are satisfied with the progress made at the new location. Among these establishments, two-thirds report a high level of satisfaction, but this declines to one-third of the non-mobile units and to only 15 per cent of the downwardly mobile. At the other extreme, the proportion dissatisfied ranges from a low of 9 per cent of those who moved to a better area to 38 per cent of those who moved to a worse area – which, of course, is more than a four-fold percentage point difference. Further inquiry shows that only one-fifth of the upwardly mobile claim that they would be better off if they had remained at the old location, but such a claim is made by more than two-thirds of those who have moved to a less attractive area. And while less than one-fourth of the latter feel that they would not be any better off at the old location, more than three-fifths of the former respond thusly.

The favorable reaction of the upwardly mobile is also evident in terms of their comparative evaluation of the present site as a place to do business. Two-thirds of these units prefer doing business at the present site, but the proportion drops to only 40 per cent of the non-mobile and to only 18 per cent of the downwardly mobile. Conversely, 68 per cent of the latter report that they liked doing business at the old location better, as compared with only 15 per cent of the upwardly mobile.

Increases in income following the move are reported nearly

five times as often by the upwardly mobile as by those who were downwardly mobile. Also we find that while only 32 per cent of the former experienced a loss in income following displacement, this increases to 54 per cent among the non-mobile and to 58 per cent of those who moved to an area that is in worse condition than the one occupied prior to displacement. Within each mobility status group, approximately one-third experienced no change in income. For approximately one unit in three, the amount of business and value of business also remained largely unchanged after relocation. It is evident that a substantial majority of the upwardly mobile have made a favorable economic adjustment after the move and are satisfied with the progress they have made. However, among the downwardly mobile, which includes one-fifth of the relocated businesses, only a small minority improved their economic position, whereas at least a substantial minority and, according to some measures, a majority have made an unfavorable economic adjustment. They express dissatisfaction with the present site. A large majority also state a preference for the old location as a place to do business. However, a majority of the businesses moved to a better area, and among these a majority report a favorable adjustment in respect to each of the variables analyzed. These data suggest that changes in the quality of the area are of more significance in respect to adjustment than changes in either space or age of the building occupied. It is among the businesses that moved to better areas that we find the largest proportions responding favorably to the move.

LENGTH OF TIME SINCE MOVE

In order to more fully evaluate the consequences of displacement and relocation, it is necessary to view the relative adjustment at the new location according to the length of time since the move. One would expect that there might be stress placed on the operation of a business during the early stages of trying to get established at a new location, which would imply a poor adjustment, but these may lessen or even disappear in time. Thus to attempt an assessment of the effects of relocation on businesses, without regard for length of time since the move, would be to lose what could be a significant difference between temporary and long-run consequences. For this reason, the following discussion is devoted to how adjustment changes over a period of time. In short, the question of concern is the extent to which relocation results only in a temporary disruption.[1] These data are presented in Table 5-7.

When we view changes in volume of business following the move, we find that the proportion reporting an increase varies directly with length of time since the move. Thus while only 25 per cent of those who had moved within the last two years report a larger volume of business at the present site, this proportion increases to 36 per cent of those who relocated from two to five years ago, and to 43 per cent of those who were displaced more than five years ago. However, the variation by length of time since the move is less marked than the range of difference already observed in respect to changes in the general quality of the area into which the business moved. Similarly, larger differences are found by changes in the amount of space in the building than by length of time since the move. The proportion reporting a decline in volume of business is highest for those who moved during the past two years, but it is noteworthy that even after five years since the move, three businesses out of ten are doing less business than they had done at the old location. Here again we find that there are more variations by changes in site characteristics, type of area served, and changes in tenure, as well as among age and educational categories, than there are by length of time since the move.

Changes in value of business appear to be even more closely related to length of time since the move. Among those who moved five years ago, three-fifths report that their business is worth more now than prior to displacement, whereas only one-third of those who moved during the past two years report such an increase.[2] Decline in value seems to be largely unrelated to

1 This can only be inferred, however, since our data are cross-sectional and not longitudinal.

2 It should be kept in mind here that those who moved within the last two years are comparing changes in value over a much shorter period of time than those who moved more than five years ago. Consequently some of the differences may be due to inflation.

TABLE 5-7

ADJUSTMENT FOLLOWING RELOCATION BY LENGTH OF TIME SINCE DISPLACEMENT

Adjustment	Length of Time Since Move		
	Under 2 Years	2 to 5 Years	5 Years and Over
Total Per Cent	100.0	100.0	100.0
Volume of Business			
More Here	25.2	36.2	43.0
About Same	34.7	36.2	26.4
Less Here	40.1	27.6	30.6
Value of Business			
Worth More Here	35.0	37.9	58.3
About Same	48.5	41.4	22.2
Worth Less Here	16.5	20.7	19.4
Satisfaction With Progress at New Location			
Very and Quite Satisfied	43.3	51.7	41.6
Satisfied	33.0	22.4	38.9
Very and Quite Dissatisfied	23.7	25.8	19.5
Would You Have Done Better at Old Location			
Yes	39.2	36.2	30.5
Uncertain	21.6	19.0	16.7
No	39.2	44.8	52.8
How Like Doing Business Here vs Old Location			
Better Here	45.4	41.3	62.3
Same	19.6	25.9	11.3
Better at Old Location	35.0	32.8	26.4
Change in Income			
Increased	15.5	20.7	35.2
Same	37.1	37.9	25.4
Decreased	47.4	41.4	39.4

length of time since the move. Similarly there seems to be little variation in level of satisfaction with progress made at the new location by length of time since the move. Again the base for comparison here is not a fixed one, in that progress is being measured over different time periods. But within these limits we find that more than four out of ten establishments express a high level of satisfaction with the progress made at the new site, and not more than one unit in four in any of the time categories expresses dissatisfaction.

That length of time since the move is an important factor, at least in assessing the new location, is suggested by the responses to the question on whether the business would have done better had it remained at the old location. The largest proportion who responded positively to this question is found among the establishments that moved within the last two years, and is lowest among those who relocated more than five years ago. More than half of the latter report that they would not be better off if they had remained at the old location. This declines to two-fifths of those who moved more recently. The business units that moved within the last two years also have the largest proportion who report that they liked doing business better at the old location that at the present site. Those who relocated more than five years ago have a significantly higher proportion who express a preference for the present site as a place to do business.

The proportion reporting a larger income following the move increases directly by length of time since relocation. There is a steady increase from 16 per cent among the more recent movers to 35 per cent among those in the five years or more category. The more recent movers have the largest proportion who report a decline in income following the move. Again it is noted that these findings are likely to be misleading, in that the base for comparison is not the same for each sub-group. In one case the comparison is with a period five years earlier, and in the other the period of reference is within the last two years. One cannot discern how much of the change is due to a more satisfactory adjustment because of length of time since the move, and how much should be attributed to changes in business conditions or to inflation. For this reason, the use of relative changes in economic data as a measure of adjustment over time is of very limited value. However, this limitation does not apply to the non-economic evaluations. Among the attitudinal variables, we find that those who moved more than five years ago have the largest proportion who respond favorably in terms of the present site. Apparently adjustment does improve with time. In all of the length of time categories, a substantial minority views the present site less favorably than the old location, but the proportion tends to decline with time.

DISTANCE MOVED[3]

The distance moved in relocation is also an important factor in the adjustment at the new site. Business units moving the longest distance report the most favorable adjustment. Stated differently, it is apparent that the units that gained the most through displacement are those that made the most distinct break with the past. On the other hand, units that attempted to minimize the consequences of the move by relocating in close proximity to the original location, and thus remain in or near to their established market area, are the businesses that seemed to have made the least favorable adjustment following relocation. This observation is supported by the data presented in Table 6-7.

Businesses moving into the most distant zone have the largest proportion who report an increase in volume of business after relocation, and the smallest proportion who report a decline. With the exception of Zone I, there is a steady increase in the proportion of establishments reporting an increase in volume of business as distance of move increases.[4] The range is from 28 per cent in Zone II to 45 per cent in Zone IV. On the other hand, the proportion reporting a decline decreases by distance moved. Again excluding Zone I, the range is from 43 per cent to 17 per cent. However, in each instance, those remaining in Zone I have a larger proportion reporting an increase in volume of business than is

3 For definitions of zones, see Chapter III.

4 The high proportion in Zone I is due in large part to the units in the Willard Center project that moved into a new cooperatively owned shopping center on the same site. This is discussed throughout Chapter V.

TABLE 6-7

ADJUSTMENT FOLLOWING RELOCATION BY DISTANCE MOVED

Adjustment	Distance Moved			
	I	II	III	IV
Total Per Cent	100.0	100.0	100.0	100.0
Volume of Business				
More Here	35.9	28.4	30.4	45.2
About Same	28.2	28.4	36.2	38.1
Less Here	35.9	43.2	33.4	16.7
Value of Business				
Worth More Here	40.0	39.2	42.9	53.5
About Same	42.5	37.8	35.7	41.9
Worth Less Here	17.5	23.0	21.4	4.6
Satisfaction With Progress at New Location				
Very and Quite Satisfied	30.0	36.6	44.3	74.5
Satisfied	45.0	32.4	32.9	18.6
Very and Quite Dissatisfied	25.0	31.0	22.8	6.9
Would You Have Done Better at Old Location				
Yes	42.5	43.3	37.2	14.4
Uncertain	12.5	18.9	21.4	21.4
No	45.0	37.8	41.4	64.2
How Like Doing Business Here vs Old Location				
Better Here	37.5	45.9	49.3	67.4
Same	20.0	14.9	23.2	16.3
Better at Old Location	42.5	39.2	27.5	16.3
Change in Income				
Increased	17.5	17.6	22.9	38.1
Same	35.0	31.1	32.9	38.1
Decreased	47.5	51.3	44.2	23.8

found among units moving into either Zones II or III, but less of an increase than is found among those moving to Zone IV. The same general pattern is observed in respect to changes in value of business. The establishments moving to Zone IV are particularly distinct in the proportion reporting an increase. While approximately two-fifths of those in the first three zones report an increase in value, more than half of the units in Zone IV report their business to be worth more now than before displacement. And while only 5 per cent in the latter zone report a decline in value, nearly one-fifth of those in the other three zones report a decline. However, those in Zone I are less likely to experience a decline than businesses moving to Zones II or III. But this is due to the atypical experiences of the kosher markets that relocated in Zone I.

Level of satisfaction with the progress made at the new location varies directly with distance moved. Whereas less than one-third of those in Zone I report a high level of satisfaction, the proportion increases to three-fourths of the establishments in Zone IV. The proportion dissatisfied is slightly lower in Zone I than in Zone II, but from that point on the proportion decreases with distance and reaches a low point of only 7 per cent in Zone IV, as compared with 31 per cent in Zone II.

Businesses in the more distant zones are the least likely to report that they would be better off if they had remained in the old location, whereas those in the first two zones have the largest proportion who respond thusly. Nearly two-thirds of the businesses that moved to Zone IV feel that they would not be better off if they had remained at the old location. This exceeds the proportion found in any other distance zone.

The units in the first zone have the smallest proportion who prefer the present site over the old location as a place to do business. The proportion increases steadily by distance and is largest among the establishments in the last zone. The range is from 37 per cent to 67 per cent. Nearly one unit in five in each distance zone states no preference, whereas the proportion who like the old location better is highest among those in Zone I and lowest in Zone IV. The range of difference is substantial, declining from a high of 43 per cent to a low of only 16 per cent. Thus it is evident that there is a consistent inverse relationship between the proportion who prefer the old location as a place to do business between and distance moved. It seems that the more distinct the break with the past, the higher the proportion that prefer doing business at the present site. The more distant zone is made up largely of businesses that moved to the suburbs. The more favorable adjustment is likely due in part to the area but also to the type of establishments that are in this zone.

In the last panel is shown the relative income at the new location, as compared with income prior to the move. The establishments in Zone IV have more than twice as many that report an increase in income, as compared to the businesses that remained in close proximity to the original location. This takes on added significance when we note than 80 per cent of those in Zone I report an income of less than $7,500 per year, as compared with less than 30 per cent of those in Zone IV. Nearly half of the businesses in the latter zone report an income of $10,000 or more, as compared with only 12 per cent of those in Zone I. Zone IV has the lowest proportion of units reporting a decline in income. It has less than half as many as are found in any other zone. Thus, in general, there is a direct relationship between distance moved and proportion of businesses that are better off at the new site. The units relocating within one-half mile of the original site have the lowest proportion with an increase in income and the largest proportion with a decline following the move.

In summary, we find the units moving the greater distances have the largest proportion who report a favorable adjustment measured in terms of increases in volume and value of business, as well as increases in income following the move. In terms of the attitudinal variables considered, the proportion responding favorably to the present site also tends to increase by distance moved. However, one must view these findings with caution since, as noted earlier, distance moved varies both by type and size of business as well as size of market area served at the old location. Each of these has been found to be an important variable closely related to adjustment at the new location. Also each is related to distance moved. For example three-fourths of the "neighborhood"-type businesses relocated within one-half mile of the original location, whereas only one in eight moved more than one and one-half miles, that is to Zone IV; however of the businesses serving a regional or national market, three-fourths of the units moved beyond the first two zones of the original location. The significance of this becomes apparent when we recall that neighborhood-type businesses have made the least favorable adjustment following the move. This likely accounts in part for the less favorable adjustment of the units remaining in close proximity to the original site.

On the other hand, three-fourths of the establishments serving a non-local market moved into the more distant zones. Generally speaking these are the kinds of businesses that made the most favorable adjustment following displacement. However, even when we control for area served, we still find that those that moved the greater distance are the ones that showed the most improvement after the move.

It is also noted that short distant moves were made predominantly by food-related retail and service establishments, whereas the longer moves were made disproportionately by manufacturing, wholesale, and construction units. Thus, since the former type of units tended to make the least favorable adjustment and the latter made the most favorable adjustment, it seems safe to conclude that at least part of the variations found by distance moved is likely due to differences in the composition of the movers in each distance zone. At any rate, it is the business establishments that moved the furthest that report the most favorable adjustment at the new site. Part of the more favorable adjustment in the more distant zone probably also reflects the advantages of a suburban location.

TYPE OF CUSTOMER SERVED

Displacement is likely to create special kinds of problems for businesses that catered predominantly to selected racial, cultural and/or ethnic groups, since the relationship with such customers is largely established through, and is dependent upon, a particular location. Consequently when the business is forced to move, this is likely to be unusually disruptive, since it would be difficult to relocate and still retain an effective relationship with the same group. Thus we would expect the adjustment following relocation to be less favorable for businesses that had served a particular racial or cultural group than for those that had served the general population.[5] In the present study, approximately one-fifth of the businesses had catered to special groups prior to displacement. This is the basis for classification in the present analysis. The groups from which these businesses attracted a disproportionate number of their customers were Negroes, Jews, or Italians. The latter accounted for nearly half of the businesses serving a particular group. Negroes and Jews each accounted for about one-fourth of the units that catered to a particular group. In most instances, these populations were living in close proximity to the business establishments. Consequently relocation would necessarily disrupt established patterns. This would have serious implications in the operation of the business. The extent to which adjustment at the new location differs by type of customer served prior to the move is shown by the data presented in Table 7-7.

Businesses serving the general population have only a slightly higher proportion reporting an increase in the volume of the business following displacement than is found among the establishments that had catered to a special group. However, the latter businesses were much more likely to report a decline. The proportion reporting less business at the new site is 44 per cent of those who had catered to a particular group, as compared to only 31 per cent of those who serve the general population. One-fourth of the former report no change, as compared with one-third of the latter. Much the same pattern of difference by type of customer served is found in respect to changes in value of business at the new site.

Large differences are found in the proportion reporting a high level of satisfaction with the progress made at the new location. The businesses serving a specialized population have the lowest proportion who report that they are very or quite satisfied. Only one-fourth of the establishments that catered predominant-

5 This was not found to be the case of kosher markets from one of the urban renewal projects. These units were able to maintain their usual customers even though the Jewish population no longer lived in the same general area. This is a very atypical experience, however, due to the highly specialized nature of the products involved, and the lack of alternative choices for their customers.

TABLE 7-7

ADJUSTMENT FOLLOWING RELOCATION BY TYPE OF CUSTOMER SERVED PRIOR TO DISPLACEMENT

Adjustment	Served a Particular Racial or Cultural Group		
	Yes	No	Total
Total Per Cent	100.0	100.0	100.0
Volume of Business			
More Here	28.9	34.6	33.4
About Same	26.7	34.1	32.6
Less Here	44.4	31.3	34.0
Value of Business			
Worth More Here	35.6	45.1	43.1
About Same	37.7	39.0	38.8
Worth Less Here	26.7	15.9	18.1
Satisfaction With Progress at New Location			
Very and Quite Satisfied	26.7	49.5	45.0
Satisfied	44.4	29.1	32.2
Very and Quite Dissatisfied	28.9	21.4	22.8
Would You Have Done Better at Old Location			
Yes	55.6	30.8	35.7
Uncertain	17.8	19.8	19.4
No	26.6	49.4	44.9
How Like Doing Business Here vs Old Location			
Better Here	34.1	52.8	49.6
Same	18.2	19.2	18.6
Better at Old Location	47.7	28.0	31.8
Change in Income			
Increased	17.8	24.3	23.0
Same	20.0	37.0	33.6
Decreased	62.2	38.7	43.4

ly to a particular racial or ethnic group express this level of satisfaction, as compared with one-half of the units that had served the general population. Dissatisfaction is more frequently reported by the units catering to a special subgroup, but the differences are less marked. Viewed somewhat differently, we find that the modal response of the units serving a particular group is the middle of the satisfaction scale, but for the remaining businesses the most frequent responses are at the top of the scale.

As expected, it is the businesses that catered to a particular type of customer that have the largest proportion who report that they would be better off if they could have continued at the old location. Among such units, we find that 56 per cent report that they would be better off at the former site, but this proportion drops to only 31 per cent of all of the other businesses. On the other hand, one-half of the latter but only one-fourth of the former report that they would not be better off had they remained at the original site. About one unit in five is uncertain as to whether or not the move was to its advantage or disadvantage.

Preference for the former site among those that had served a special group is further evident from the responses comparing how they like doing business at the present and former location. More than half of the businesses that catered to a non-specialized general population state a preference for the present site. But only one-third of those that had served a special group state a similar preference. On the other hand, 48 per cent of the latter businesses report they liked doing business at the old location better than at the present site. Among the other businesses, only 28 per cent respond thusly. Again we note that, for approximately one unit in five, location seems to be of little significance in that they do not state a preference for either location.

Relative income before and after the move also varies by type of customer served. Businesses that catered to particular groups are less likely to report an increase in income following the move and are much more likely than others to report a decline. Among the units that served a particular subgroup, nearly two-thirds report a decline in income following relocation, as compared with two-fifths of the establishments that served the general population. Among the latter, nearly two-fifths report no change in income, but only one-fifth of those who served a particular group report the same income after the move as they had prior to displacement. Those serving the general population were more likely to experience an increase at the new location than units which were primarily dependent on a particular type of customer.

A further indication that businesses that served particular subgroups faced special difficulties in relocation is found in the responses to the question on how the amount of business at the new location compared with expectations. While 18 per cent of the total group report doing more business than expected, this ranges from only 7 per cent of those who drew their customers predominantly from a particular racial or ethnic group at the former location to more than 20 per cent of the units whose customers were attracted from the general population. On the other hand, 39 per cent of those serving a subgroup report the amount of business to be less than expected, as compared to only 22 per cent of all other establishments. Unfortunately we cannot determine whether these differences are due to an inability to accurately assess business potential in a different kind of area, or whether the businesses did not fully appreciate their dependence on a particular kind of population for their business and thus did not accurately assess the consequences of the disruption. Apparently these businesses did not foresee the effects of the move as realistically as did the businesses that served the general population. At any rate, the differences by type of customer served between actual and expected are large.

In short, business establishments which predominantly served a particular type of population have made a less favorable economic adjustment at the new location. They were also more likely to express a preference for the previous location as a place to do business, and to feel that they would be better off if they had not been forced to vacate the former site. Although only a minority were dissatisfied with the progress made at the new site, they were much less likely than businesses serving the general population to report a high level of satisfaction with progress made. This is likely due, in part at least, to the larger proportion reporting a decline in volume of business and a decrease in income following displacement.

CHANGES IN INCOME AND SIZE OF INCOME

Up to this point in the present chapter we have used changes in income as an index of adjustment at the new site. In the present discussion, the focus of attention is shifted to the influence that changes in income and the actual size of income have on the level of adjustment reported following the move. These data are shown in Table 8-7. The size of income is a rough approximation of the relative success of a business operation, since this is traditionally the goal of a business. Thus we would expect that adjustment would vary directly with size of income and more particularly with the direction of changes in income following relocation. Our data on this are strikingly clear.

Even a casual inspection of Table 8-7 suggests that there are very marked and consistent variations in adjustment in relation to both size of income and changes in income. Thus the businesses in the higher income category have nearly four times as many reporting an increase in volume after the move as are found among those in the lowest income category. A similar but even more marked difference is found in respect to changes in value of business. Here we find that only 15 per cent of the owners with present incomes of less than $4,000 per year report that the value of their business increased after the move. But nearly two-thirds of those in the top income category report an increase.

Declines in value are reported by only 8 per cent of those in the top income group, but by 45 per cent of those with the lowest incomes. Among the latter a decline in volume is reported by three units out of four, but among the former, that is, those in the top category, only one establishment out of seven experienced a decline.

Changes in both volume and value of business are even more closely related to changes in income following the move. This, of course, is to be expected, in that they tend to be different dimensions of the same thing, but they need not vary together because of the many other variables involved. At any rate, changes in volume and value of business vary directly by changes in income. Of those that report an increase in income, nine out of ten also report an increase in volume of business and that

TABLE 8-7
ADJUSTMENT FOLLOWING RELOCATION BY CHANGES IN INCOME AND ACTUAL INCOME

Adjustment	Actual Income			Changes in Income		
	Under $4,000	$4,000-$7,500	$7,500 Plus	Increased	Same	Decreased
Total Per Cent	100.0	100.0	100.0	100.0	100.0	100.0
Volume of Business						
More Here	12.8	28.6	45.4	88.5	27.0	9.3
About Same	12.8	40.8	37.7	11.5	67.6	16.5
Less Here	74.4	30.6	16.9	....	5.4	74.2
Value of Business						
Worth More Here	14.9	36.0	61.5	88.5	34.2	25.5
About Same	40.4	50.0	30.8	11.5	61.9	35.7
Worth Less Here	44.7	14.0	7.7	....	3.9	38.8
Satisfaction With Progress at New Location						
Very and Quite Satisfied	12.8	40.0	62.8	80.8	52.6	19.4
Satisfied	25.5	40.0	29.5	19.2	47.4	27.6
Very and Quite Dissatisfied	61.7	20.0	7.7	....	....	53.0
Would You Have Done Better at Old Location						
Yes	70.3	36.0	15.4	1.9	18.4	67.3
Uncertain	10.6	28.0	19.2	13.5	28.9	17.3
No	19.1	36.0	65.4	84.6	52.7	15.4
How Like Doing Business Here vs Old Location						
Better Here	12.8	46.0	69.2	86.5	52.0	26.5
Same	12.8	28.0	14.1	9.7	28.0	17.3
Better at Old Location	74.4	26.0	16.7	3.8	20.0	56.2
Change in Income						
Increased	4.2	16.0	39.0	....	....	....
Same	14.9	40.0	36.3	....	....	....
Decreased	80.9	44.0	24.7	....	....	....

their business is worth more now than while at the former location. At the other extreme, we find that three-fourths of those that experienced a decline in income report a decrease in volume of business. The relationship is less distinct in reference to value, however. Less than two-fifths of the units reporting less income also report a decline in value. The point worthy of note, however, is that even among the owners who experienced a decline in income after the move, more than one-third report the value of their business to have remained the same, and one-fourth report that the value has increased.

However, of more significance than the interrelationship of economic variables are the differences in attitudes expressed by different income groups, and by those who have experienced changes in income after the move. It is abundantly evident that the higher income groups and those that experienced an increase in income are most likely to report favorable attitudes concerning the present location. The business establishments in the top income category have nearly five times as many in the high satisfaction category as are found among the low income businesses. The proportions range from only 13 per cent to 63 per cent. At the low end of the satisfaction scale, the range is even larger in the opposite direction. Of those that report an income of less than $4,000 per year, 62 per cent are dissatisfied with the progress they have made since the move, but among those whose income is over $7,500, only 8 per cent respond thusly. Variations in satisfaction vary directly with current income. As income increases, the proportion satisfied also increases. The differences are consistent and marked, ranging from a low of 38 per cent to a high of 92 per cent.

All of the businesses that report an increase or no change in income report that they are satisfied with the progress they have made at the new site. Eight units out of ten of those whose income increased are in the top satisfaction category, as compared with slightly more than half of those whose income remained the same and less than one-fifth of the units that experienced a decline. Among the latter, a majority (53 per cent) is dissatisfied with the progress they have made at the new site.

It is the lower income groups and those whose income declined after the move that have the largest proportion who report that they would have done better had they remained at the old location. Similarly these categories have the largest proportion who state that they liked doing business better at the old location. Among the top income businesses and those that experienced an increase in income, we find a distinct preference for the new location.

Among the top income businesses, only 15 per cent report that they would have done better at the old location, while 65 per cent stated that they would not have done so. The differences were even more marked among those that report an increase in income. Only 2 per cent said they would have done better had they not moved, while 85 per cent reported that they would not have done any better at the old location. But among those that experienced a decline in income, more than two-thirds said that they would have done better at the former site. A majority of these also reported that they liked doing business better at the old location. But among those that had an increase in income, only 4 per cent stated a preference for the former site. However, those in the lower income group respond quite differently. Here we find that a large majority state a preference for the old location as a place to do business. Three units out of four report that they liked doing business better at the original location, but this declined to approximately one unit in six at the top income level.

In short, the size of the income and the direction of change in income after the move seem to be important factors in the reaction to the new location. Those high in income and those who experienced an increase in income respond very favorably to the new location, but the opposite is found among those low in income and among those whose income declined after the move. Larger differences in adjustment following relocation are found in relation to both size of income and direction of change than are found in respect to any other variables included in our analysis. This is further support of the earlier observation that relocation has worked a hardship on the smaller more marginal businesses, but it may have worked to the advantage of larger establishments.

Lastly we find that changes in income following the move are closely related to size of current income. Thus the proportion reporting an increase in income ranges from a low of only 4 per cent of those in the bottom income category to 16 per cent of those in the middle group, and to 39 per cent of those in the highest income category. Thus the range represents nearly a tenfold difference. It is particularly noteworthy that 80 per cent of the businesses reporting an income of $4,000 or less experienced a decrease in income following relocation, whereas only 25 per cent of those whose income exceeds $7,500 report less income at the new location. In short, those units which could least afford a decrease have the largest proportion who experienced a decline. Actually those at the bottom income level were more than three times as likely to experience a decrease in income than those in the top income category.

SUMMARY

Following the move, the businesses seem to be nearly equally divided into three categories as far as changes in selected economic variables are concerned. Approximately one-third of the businesses appear to be in a more favorable position after the move than while at the old location. However, an equal proportion report that they are in a less favorable position, and for the remaining one-third the move seems to have had little or no effect, in that no changes are reported.

The adjustment, measured in terms of attitudinal variables, appears to be even more favorable for a larger proportion of the establishments. Nearly half of the units respond favorably in respect to all three variables, that is, they are very or quite satisfied with the progress made at the new site, they do not feel that they would have done any better if they had not moved, and they prefer the present site as a place to do business. On the other hand, one-third or less responded negatively to each of these questions.

For a majority of the relocated businesses, the reaction to the new location is not a negative one. Nor is the economic adjustment unfavorable. However, a substantial minority – approximately three units out of ten – respond negatively to the new location and report economic losses following the move.

Adjustment at the new location is found to vary markedly by a number of selected variables. The same pattern of difference is found for attitudinal responses as for economic changes. The least favorable adjustment has been made by the older persons, and those with limited education. The most favorable adjustment is reported by the younger owners and those on the high end of the educational scale. Neighborhood-type businesses also report a below-average adjustment. These businesses experienced disproportionate declines economically and have the largest proportion who are dissatisfied with the progress made at the new site. Also a distinct majority state a preference for the old location and feel that they would have done better had they not been forced to move. Declines in income are particularly marked for business that catered predominantly to a neighborhood market.

Businesses occupying their own building have made a better adjustment than tenants. It is among those moving from "own" to "rent" that we find the least favorable responses. And the most favorable responses are reported by those who owned at both locations, and more particularly among those who moved from "rent" to "own". Businesses moving to larger and newer buildings tend to respond favorably to the new location, but an even larger proportion of favorable responses are reported by the businesses that moved to a better quality area than the one from which they had been displaced. The poorest adjustment is reported by the businesses that relocated in areas which they judged to be worse than the ones from which they had been forced to move.

Adjustment varies directly with distance moved. However, much of the favorable reaction reported by those in the more distant moves is due to the advantages of a suburban location. At any rate, the more distinct the break with the past, the more favorable is the reaction to the present site. The least favorable adjustment is reported by the units that remained in close proximity to the original location.

Businesses that catered predominantly to a particular ethnic or racial group prior to displacement report a less favorable adjustment at the new site than businesses that served a nonspecialized market. Part of this variation, however, can be attributed to the size and type of businesses involved.

The most marked variations in adjustment are found in respect to size of income and changes in income following the move. The least favorable adjustment is made by the low income businesses and those that experienced a decline in income after the move. Conversely the most favorable adjustment is reported by the high income establishments and, more particularly, by those who experienced an increase in income at the new location. It is strikingly evident that the lower income groups have the largest proportion who experienced a decline in income following the move, whereas the higher income groups are most likely to increase their income at the new location.

CHAPTER 8

SUMMARY AND CONCLUSIONS

THIS study has been concerned with the ability of certain kinds of institutional structures to withstand the disruptive effects of change, and how these structures have adapted to changes in the community resulting from public improvement programs. Although the two improvement programs involved, that is, urban renewal and highway construction, differ in purpose, the common feature is that both displace the occupants of an area and disrupt established patterns of behavior. The study has been concerned not only with the problems of displacement and relocation from the point of view of the individual business establishments, but also attention has been focused on how displacements have changed the spatial distribution of these units. In a very general sense, we have been concerned with what happens to business establishments when they have been forced to vacate their established sites, and what this means particularly to the central city.

Our findings likely represent minimal consequences of displacement and relocation, since the study was undertaken in the very early stages of the rebuilding program. In actual fact, the major developments belong to the future, and thus the full implications of rehousing the displaced population as well as non-residential establishments are yet to be faced by the community. In assessing the magnitude of these problems, it is evident that they will reach serious proportions in the future. Such improvement programs are developing at a rapid pace and will continue to be of a magnitude to effect profound changes in our urban centers. Thus, for example, we can expect that the pressure for sites and space in the city will increase in the future as vacant units are occupied by previously displaced businesses and additional structures are demolished. As these public improvement programs proceed, there will be increased competition for available sites in the city. This is likely to hasten the tendency for displaced units to move out of the city, unless positive and effective steps are taken to prevent this movement. This aspect of the problem is considered more fully below.

The present analysis was based on the experiences of approximately 300 businesses that had been displaced through governmental action during the five-year period 1954 through 1959. The data were obtained through personal interviews. Completed interviews were obtained from 292 of the 311 establishments contacted. This represents a response rate of 94 per cent. Approximately one-third of the units had been displaced by urban renewal projects and the remaining two-thirds were from highway project areas. The general analysis did not distinguish the problems of displacement and relocation by type of project. But when attention was focused on aspects where the particular type of project was important, data were presented separately. However, the major focus throughout has been on the consequences of displacement and relocation, regardless of the specific type of public improvement program involved.

The displaced businesses in the present study were predominantly small establishments. Nearly one-fifth were owner-operated with no employees. Eight units out of ten employed fewer than ten workers. While the median for all of the displaced establishments was only 3.2 employees, this ranged from a low of only 1.4 for service establishments to 9.2 for manufacturing, wholesale, and construction units. Less than 9 per cent employed twenty or more workers. These businesses were apparently firmly established, in that more than 90 per cent had been in business for more than five years, and three-fourths for more than ten years. We also found that two-thirds of the establishments had been in operation in the same neighborhood for ten years or more. Further, it was observed that the owners were long-time residents of the Providence area. Less than 10 per cent had lived in the area less than 25 years, whereas half had lived in the area for 45 years or more. Thus it is evident that these are not fly-by-night or even temporary businesses. Rather, the establishments affected were units of long standing.

While the study was limited only to those businesses displaced within the central city, it is of particular interest to note that more than half of the owners did not live in the city. Thus it is apparent that the consequences of public improvement programs within the city reach beyond the corporate limits. In passing, it is noted that place of residence showed considerable selectivity. The owners who lived in the suburbs tended to be younger and better educated than those living in the city. They also owned the larger businesses, and they were more likely to own the non-food-related retail as well as manufacturing, wholesale, and construction establishments.

Urban renewal programs tended to displace different types of businesses than were displaced by highway projects. In the former, we found a disproportionately large number of food-related retail and service establishments. Renewal projects also contained smaller businesses than were displaced by the highway construction program. Among renewal projects, nearly seven units out of ten employed fewer than three workers, as compared with four out of ten in highway project areas. Owners of businesses in renewal areas tended to be older and less well educated. In these areas, businesses disproportionately catered to a neighborhood-type market and served a particular ethnic or racial group. Such businesses tended to be less well-to-do than the units displaced by the highway program.

Monthly rentals in renewal projects were found to be substantially lower than in highway project areas, as were sales also. Many of the businesses in renewal areas were small, marginal, neighborhood-type units, whereas those displaced by the highway were larger and were more firmly established economically. This explains in part why units from renewal areas responded more negatively to the move than businesses displaced by the highway. The latter were in a better financial position to absorb the disruptive effects of the move, whereas the former were less able to tolerate the costs and the temporary losses resulting from such a change. This observation finds support in the differences in the proportion of establishments that successfully relocated from each type of project.

Since it was not possible to locate all of the displaced establishments, we have expressed business losses to the community in two ways, that is, as "known" losses and as "probable" losses. The known losses were computed on the basis of actual data gathered through interviews with the owners, whereas the probable losses were inferred from the best available evidence. In the latter instances, we could find no evidence that would even suggest to us that the business was still in operation. Actually when all efforts failed to find any trace of these units it seemed safe to conclude that they were probably no longer in business in the area. On this assumption, an analysis of our data showed that the loss rate was slightly higher among units displaced from urban renewal areas. Approximately 40 per cent of these establishments discontinued in business, as compared with 30 per cent of those displaced from highway project areas. Thus the loss rate is one-third higher in renewal areas. Without regard to type of project, the loss rate was highest among food-related retail units and lowest among the establishments in the manufacturing, wholesale, and construction category. In short, the types of units least likely to survive displacement were predominantly those businesses that had a close and frequent relationship with their customers. Such units largely served a neighborhood-type market. The owners tended to know most of their customers who came disproportionately from a particular ethnic or racial group. Because of this closer and apparently more recurrent relationship with their customers, who tended to live in close proximity, these establishments were much more sensitive to the disruptive effects of the move. Such customer relationships were most likely to obtain in renewal areas.

As expected, the smaller establishments had the lowest survival rate. One-third of the non-survivors had no employees and more than three out of four had less than three workers. But among the survivors, only four out of ten were in this size class.

Viewed differently, the proportion that did not survive the move ranged from a low of 10 per cent among those with ten or more workers to a high of 40 per cent among those with no employees. Thus it is evident that displacement worked a particular hardship on the smaller establishments. Such units were likely marginal even prior to the move. Displacement jeopardized this minimal balance. These businesses could not survive the change. Although the loss of such units actually means little to the commercial and industrial structure of the city, the losses, nonetheless, are of crucial consequence to the owners of individual business establishments.

The relationship between average monthly sales and rate of survival was found to be a marked one, but further analysis proved it to be much more involved than appeared at first blush. Median monthly sales of the survivors prior to the move were 3.5 times higher than sales of the non-survivors. This ratio obtained within each type of project. Although median sales varied markedly by type of project, there was a comparable relative difference between survivors and non-survivors within each type of project. Urban renewal businesses while at the original location clearly operated at a much lower level than those displaced by the highway. Of particular interest, however, is that the median monthly sales of the survivors in renewal areas were lower than the sales of the non-survivors from highway projects. Also the median sales of the non-survivors from highway project areas were 2.5 times larger than the sales reported by the non-survivors from renewal areas. The apparent inconsistencies here are due largely to differences in rent levels. The rent-to-sales ratio in both types of projects is much higher among the non-survivors. The lower sales in renewal areas were more than compensated for by much lower rentals. Thus the median monthly sales of the survivors from renewal areas were slightly lower than the sales of the non-survivors displaced by highway projects, but rents varied markedly. Consequently the rent burden at the original location among the latter units was nearly double that of the former. The proportions of sales devoted to rents were 4.3 per cent and 2.4 per cent respectively. Apparently the lower operating costs in the renewal areas made these businesses less marginal, and placed them in a better position financially to survive the disruptive effects of the move.[1] Not to be overlooked here also is that different types of businesses were displaced from the renewal areas; thus the absolute dollar value of sales may have a different meaning than for the types of businesses in highway project areas that did not survive the move. It may be that the "break point" varies according to the quality of the area from which the businesses are moved, as well as by the type and size of business displaced.

As we pursued our analysis further, we found that even though many of the non-survivors were operating close to a subsistence level prior to displacement, nearly all expressed the opinion that they would have continued in business indefinitely had they not been forced to move out of the area. It may well be that they could have done so, since many had no employees and either owned the building occupied or paid low rentals. Operating costs were apparently minimal. It is worthy of note that 94 per cent of the non-survivors had been in business for more than five years, and 91 per cent had occupied the same location for five years or more. Actually one unit in three that did not survive the move had been at the same location for more than fifteen years. Of particular interest is the very low proportion of non-survivors that had entered business during the war years, and the very high proportion that entered business during the early postwar period.

It should be noted that not all non-survivals were business failures in the traditional sense. Some used displacement as an opportunity to discontinue in business, which they had vague plans to do anyway. The move provided the external stimulus which was needed in order to reach a definite decision. In other instances, the business was discontinued because the owner had a "more attractive" job offer. However, a majority of the owners would have preferred to remain in business, but did not do so for a variety of reasons.

Following displacement, approximately one-fifth of the non-

1 Part of the differential ability to survive displacement may have been due to different policies and practices concerning compensation for the cost of the move. In highway project areas, the cost of the move was the responsibility of the owner – which may well have been too much of a burden for businesses operating at this level. A comparable burden was not faced by such businesses in renewal areas.

survivors entered the ranks of the unemployed, but this probably represented a temporary condition. Although a majority of the non-survivors reported that they were through with business, some still hoped to re-enter business at some future but largely unspecified date. At any rate, for a substantial minority unemployment was at least a temporary condition in the transition from business to some other position in the labor force. A similar proportion went into retirement after closing down their business. However, this was not always voluntary nor was it without problems, in that many were probably not covered by any formal retirement system. Accordingly, their present and future income would be severely limited. The fact that many resented retirement and sought in vain for "something to do with their time," was probably not peculiar to this group, in that it frequently occurs at this stage of the life cycle. Many went into retirement because they felt that they were too old to start over. Also they were too old to find other employment. Thus, in effect, when they closed down their business they were forced out of the labor market. The harmful effects for the unemployed and, to a lesser extent, the retired, are readily apparent.

But a majority of the non-survivors entered the labor market in different functional positions. More than half of those employed entered white collar occupations, while one-fourth hold jobs at the craftsman level. About one in five was engaged at the semi-skilled operative level. In general the level at which the former business owners entered the labor market was closely related to the size of their business prior to displacement. Thus those who employed three or more workers were nearly five times as likely to enter white collar occupations as those who had no employees. Conversely, the latter disproportionately entered manual-type jobs or retired. The owners of the smaller establishments were also more likely to enter the ranks of the unemployed.

It is of particular interest to note that a substantial majority of those who are currently working entered the same line of work as they were engaged in while in business. We also found that the business experience apparently prepared the former owners for better jobs than they had held prior to entering business. At least they had higher status positions in the labor force at the time of the study than the positions from which they had originally entered business. Our data showed that while none had entered business from the professional-managerial level, nearly one-fifth of those who are currently working moved into such positions after closing down their businesses. On the other hand, approximately three out of five entered business from blue collar work, but we found only one in five engaged in work at this level. To what extent this upward mobility was due to the business experience as such, and how much was due merely to the passing of time, cannot be determined.

The present income of the non-survivors is in the aggregate substantially lower than that reported by those who continued in business. This, of course, is to be expected because of the large number of unemployed and retired. However, the point of particular interest is that nearly nine out of ten of the non-survivors experienced a decrease in income. Although changes in income vary by type of activity entered, in no occupational category was a decline reported by less than seven former owners out of ten.

There was general agreement among the non-survivors that they would have been better off if they had not been displaced. They also felt that if the government is going to force businesses to move, owners who do not relocate should be compensated not only for their property but also should be compensated for the "worth of the business" as well. The general feeling among the non-survivors was that displacement had deprived them of their source of livelihood, and they should have been compensated accordingly.

In addition to the losses due to the non-survivors, there were also losses to the central city (but not to the community) resulting from some of the establishments moving beyond the corporate limits of the city. From the point of view of the city, this type of movement has practically the same effect as "going out of business," for the economic contribution of such establishments is lost to the city. Not only are the jobs lost, but the tax base is accordingly decreased. This type of movement represented less of a numerical loss of establishments but more of an absolute loss to the city than did the non-survivors, for the suburban movement was selective of different-type establishments.

In the process of displacement and relocation, the central city tended to retain a high disproportionate number of the smaller establishments, whereas the larger units were more likely to move to the suburbs. The latter areas seemed to attract the businesses that wanted to own the building they occupied. The types of business that were overrepresented in the suburbanization movement were those in non-food-related retail and those in the manufacturing, wholesale, and construction category. The latter, more so than any other type of business, tended to move to the suburbs. The city, however, retained the food-related retail and service establishments. Jewelry manufacturing firms also relocated in the city. This they did because of the advantages of being in the jewelry district. There seems to be general agreement among owners of jewelry manufacturing firms that the suburbs would not offer any advantages for these units. On the contrary, the suburbs were thought to be too inaccessible, especially for buyers when they come to the area to place their orders. Also such a location would cut the units off from other jewelry establishments with whom they were likely to be functionally related.

In general the proportion of units moving to the suburbs varied directly and consistently by size of business. The median-sized business that relocated in the city employed 3.8 workers at the time of displacement, while those moving to the suburbs averaged 7.2 workers. This, of course, means that the suburbanization of "jobs" far exceeded the suburbanization of establishments. Of particular interest is the fact that the losses to the city through businesses moving to the suburbs following displacement far exceeded the losses due to units going out of business, even though the number of establishments that did not survive the move nearly doubled the number of units that relocated in the suburbs. A comparison of the losses showed that the median-size units that moved to the suburbs were more than four times larger than the units that went out of business. The aggregate job opportunities lost through the suburbanization of businesses were more than double the number of jobs lost, including the positions of the owners themselves, through units closing down their business operations. It is noted further that while the non-survivors were largely small food-related retail, neighborhood-type businesses, the units that moved to the suburbs were predominantly those in the manufacturing, wholesale, and construction category.

Unquestionably units going out of business cause serious losses for the individual owners, but from the point of view of the city, as far as the tax base is concerned, the losses due to businesses moving out of the city are of more importance. This was abundantly evident from a comparison of rental and sales prior to displacement. The median monthly rent paid by the non-survivors at the old location was $80, whereas those that continued in business and moved to the suburbs paid more than $200. Differences in median monthly sales were even more marked. While the non-survivors reported median sales of less than $1,700 per month prior to displacement, the businesses that moved to the suburbs had median sales in excess of $8,200. This represents nearly a five-fold difference in average monthly sales. Although less than one unit in five relocated in the suburbs, the movement out was such that the loss to the city of jobs and volume of business far exceeded the proportionate movement of establishments. The significance of this type of loss to the city needs no elaboration.

Movement to the suburbs seems to have been influenced by the place of residence of the owner. Our data showed that a substantial number of those who moved to the suburbs moved closer to home than they were prior to displacement. Persons who lived in the suburbs were more than five times as likely to move their business to the suburbs as were those who lived in the city. When viewed from a different perspective, we found that nearly nine out of ten owners who moved their business to the suburbs lived in the suburbs, as compared with less than half of those who relocated in the city. Thus not only does the influence of public improvement programs extend beyond the corporate limits of the city, but the changing distribution of population from city to suburbs portends a change in the distribution of commercial and industrial functions also.

It may be that we have observed the early stages of a new rationale for an even more widespread settlement pattern in urban centers than has developed to date. Owners of businesses apparently now have a greater amount of freedom and wider range of choice in the selection of a site because of the marked improvements in transportation and the general reliance on the private automobile as the predominant mode of travel. The problem of space in the traditional sense seems to have lost much of its meaning in the local community setting, even though owners continue to report accessibility as a very important factor in selecting a site. Because of the higher incomes and higher levels of living in general, workers and customers alike appear to be willing and able to overcome the costs of distance. Thus, in the modern context, with the widespread ownership of private automobile and adequate highways, nearly any location is readily accessible. Employers seem to be no longer dependent on workers living in close proximity. Also businesses can more effectively attract customers from greater distances. Consequently business owners in relocation have been able to select sites largely in relation to their own place of residence. Under present conditions, it is possible for owners to live and have their place of business away from the densely settled areas of the city. Many businesses seem no longer to be as dependent upon a specific location. This suggests that the time-cost variable may have lost much of its original significance as a limiting factor influencing either residential locations, places of employment, or the sites for many commercial establishments. At any rate, our data indicate that many owners located their businesses for their own convenience, with little or no regard for the time-cost factor for either their workers or their customers. We would infer from this that, as transportation facilities are improved, this more widespread pattern of settlement of commercial and industrial establishments is likely to develop further. This obviously works to the disadvantage of the city.

Businesses moving to the suburbs seem to occupy more attractive sites than businesses that relocated in the city. At least a larger proportion of the units that relocated in the suburbs moved to newer, better buildings with more space than they had previously occupied. As compared with those that remained in the city, businesses in the suburbs occupied much larger buildings. Also they were more likely to occupy newly constructed structures. Improvements in parking facilities were observed in both areas, but such improvements were more marked among the units that moved to the suburbs.

Following relocation the units that moved to the suburbs

seemed to have made a more favorable adjustment than the businesses that remained in the city. This is reflected not only in respect to the economic variables considered, but also in general reaction to the new location. Suburban businesses had a larger proportion who were satisfied with the progress they had made at the new site, and they were more certain they would not have done any better had they remained at the original site. Suburban units also had a larger proportion who stated a preference for doing business at the present location.

The more favorable reaction among the businesses in the suburbs was to be expected, in the light of the selective movement originally, and in terms of what happened to these units economically since the move. While the units that remained in the city experienced an increase in rent and a substantial decline in sales after the move, the opposite was found in the suburbs. Rentals declined slightly, but sales increased by approximately the same proportion that they had declined in the city. Consequently the rent-to-sales ratio in the suburbs declined by 20 per cent following the move, but increased by 49 per cent among the businesses that remained in the city. In short, the suburbs not only attracted the bigger and better establishments but also proved to be an attractive location for such businesses.

There was a marked improvement in parking facilities following the move. Less than half reported off-street parking at the original site, but this increased to two-thirds at the new location. Prior to the move, less than 40 per cent of the businesses reported parking to be adequate, but after the move this increased to more than 70 per cent. All types of businesses reported more adequate parking at the new location, but it was the non-food-related retail, manufacturing, wholesale, and construction establishments that were most likely to report adequate facilities at the new site. This was due in large part to the larger proportion of units that moved to the suburbs. Jewelry firms, service establishments, and food-related retail firms, other than those that relocated in a new shopping center, had the largest proportions reporting that parking was inadequate at the new site. This, of course, was due to the type of areas into which these businesses moved. They tended to remain in, or at least near to, the original location. Thus they relocated in the old built-up part of the city where space for parking was more limited. But even among these units, there was a substantial improvement in parking accommodations following relocation.

The changes observed by size of business were even more marked. Prior to the move it was the large units that had the largest proportion with inadequate facilities, but after the move these units were the most likely to report facilities to be adequate. While the proportion of small units reporting adequate parking increased by only 25 per cent, the increase among the large units exceeded 200 per cent. Thus one of the apparent consequences of the move was that parking facilities were much improved. This improvement, however, was not shared equally by all types of businesses. Nonetheless the ever-present problem of providing adequate parking facilities was apparently successfully resolved by a majority of the businesses.

For the individual business establishment, the cost of the move is of crucial significance. Particularly is this the case in highway project areas where no compensation is available. However, it is important also in renewal areas, for frequently the amount paid by the government is insufficient to cover the full costs. The median costs of the move for all of the units that relocated was approximately $1,000. This ranged only slightly by type of project. However, on closer inspection we found the median to be somewhat deceptive, since the businesses displaced by highway projects tended to be concentrated disproportionately in the top costs category. The modal costs for renewal projects were between $1,000 and $3,000, but were more than $3,000 for the units displaced by the highway. This difference takes on added significance when we note that only in renewal areas were any legislative provisions made for covering the costs of the move. But even in these projects, there were instances where costs would not be covered through some technicality. Also, compensation could not exceed a specified upper limit. At any rate, less than half of the units from renewal areas, and none of those from highway project areas, report that all of the costs of the move were covered. Thus while a heavy financial burden for moving was placed on many businesses, the full impact of the burden fell on those units displaced by the highway program.[2]

2 Under more recent legislation, states may adopt legislation which would provide compensation for covering the costs of the move up to a maximum of $3,000, when displaced by highway construction projects.

Costs of the move were found to vary by type and size of business. This was to be expected; thus the question on which attention was focused pertained to the relative costs of the move for selected subgroups. When costs were computed in terms of per-employee costs or as a ratio to median monthly sales, significant differences were found by a number of important subgroups. Although service units showed the lowest median costs, they had the largest relative costs by both measures. Jewelry manufacturing units also had a disproportionately high relative burden. These units also had the largest median costs. The relative burden was least for the non-food-related retail and those in the manufacturing, wholesale and construction category. The median costs of the move ranged from only $300 for small establishments (those with less than two employees) to more than $3,800 among the large units (eight or more workers). However, the relative costs varied inversely with size. The burden of the small units exceeds the large ones two-fold. However, the smaller units (in renewal areas) were more likely to have the costs of the move covered, since the costs would not exceed the upper limits, but in highway project areas this was not the case, in that the full burden fell on the individual business concern. While the absolute costs of the move varied directly by size, the relative burden, in terms of ability to absorb such costs, was inversely related to size of business. Service units and, to a lesser extent, jewelry firms carried a disproportionate burden also. The latter units, in particular, were displaced by the highway program. Thus among these businesses the unit costs were high and there were no provisions for covering the costs of the move.

We found that in some instances procedures were followed which indirectly helped to ease the burden relative to the costs of the move. That is, some owners seem to feel that at least part of the cost of the move was covered indirectly through the price received for their property. This practice was reflected in the proportion of owners who reported that they had been treated fairly as far as the cost of the move was concerned. Owners, particularly of the larger businesses, were much more likely to report fair treatment than renters of equal-size establishments. The larger owners seemed to have been in a better position to negotiate a more favorable price for their building. This apparently served to absorb at least part of the expense of moving. Even though the law technically did not make any provisions for covering any part of the costs of the move, we found that nearly one-fifth of the owners reported that they have received some compensation, and even in renewal areas where provisions were made to cover the costs of the move, owners were more likely than renters to report that the full costs had been covered, whereas renters disproportionately reported only partial coverage. Apparently when the costs exceeded the upper limits for renters, no adjustments were possible, but for owners a higher price could be agreed on for the property involved. At any rate, in both types of projects, owners who reported that they had received a "fair price" for their property were the ones most likely to report that they had been treated fairly in respect to the costs of the move.

It is particularly noteworthy that nearly half of the owners displaced by highway projects who reported that they had received a fair price for their building reported that they had been treated fairly as far as the cost of the move is concerned. This seems to be a very high proportion of such responses when we recall that no direct compensations were made to defray the costs of moving. That nearly half would respond thusly under the circumstances, when technically the whole burden of the move had to be absorbed by the individual business, is strong presumptive evidence, at least to the writer, that some indirect help had been provided through some adjustment in the price received for their property. The possible abuses arising out of such practices are as obvious as they are dangerous. Also, such practices do not provide any adjustments that can be offered to renters, and thus place a differential burden on tenants. That this was a rather common practice was evident from reading over the case materials. It was explicitly stated by many. Although more prevalent in highway project settlements, it was also evident in renewal projects, especially when the costs of the move exceeded the legislative upper limits. But here too the practice discriminated against tenants. Failures to pay the costs of moving directly, or even to cover the costs indirectly, were aspects of the displacement process which were frequently and bitterly criticized particularly by tenants and by owners of small establishments.

There was a considerable amount of change in tenure following the move. One-fourth of those who owned prior to displacement moved to rented quarters, while one-fifth of the renters became owners. The net result was a slight increase in the proportion of businesses that owned the building they occupied. However, a majority of the establishments continued to be tenants at the new location. Thus an analysis of rentals served as a rough index of the relative costs of doing business for a majority of the businesses following the move, as compared with the original location.

Rentals increased substantially at the new locations. The increases, however, were more marked among the units displaced from renewal areas than from highway project areas. Rentals in the latter area were nearly double those in the former area prior to the move, but after the move the rent excess was only slightly more than 50 per cent. The major shifts in rentals occurred in the extremes, particularly among the business displaced from renewal areas. The proportion paying less than $50 declined from 47 per cent to only 27 per cent. Among the highway units, the major shift occurred in the top rental category. Whereas only 12 per cent had paid $300 or more per month prior to the move, this increased to 27 per cent after relocation. The proportionate increase in rentals among units displaced from renewal areas was three times the increase among units from highway project areas. The rent increases were 45 per cent and 15 per cent respectively. This, of course, was due to the fact that in the deteriorated areas needing renewal the original rent levels were much lower. Our data clearly showed that one of the consequences of displacement was that rentals costs increased for a majority of the units. Nearly six units out of ten reported present rents to be higher than rents paid prior to the move.

A point particularly worthy of note is that the relative rent burden exceeded the absolute increase, since sales declined after the move. Rent, as a per cent of sales, increased by 24 per cent. The increased burden varied markedly by a number of subgroups. Service units in particular carried a heavy rent burden in relation to sales even prior to the move, but at the new location the burden increased and the differential was more marked. Similarly, the small units and those serving predominantly neighborhood markets carried a disproportionately heavy rent burden at both locations. These units also showed above-average per cent increases following the move. Again this was due in large part to the type of areas from which they had been displaced. At both locations, their median rent levels were much lower than for businesses in other subgroups, but the proportionate increase in rentals following the move exceeded the other sub-categories. While rents increased, median sales declined at the new location, thus placing an increased rent burden on these units. In most other sub-categories, rents also increased and sales declined, but the proportionate changes were less marked. Thus while the large units experienced a larger absolute and per cent increase in rents following the move than smaller units, sales declined less. Consequently the rent burden did not increase proportionately.

It is to be expected that rents and even the rent burden would increase following the move, for most of the businesses are in a much more favorable environment, that is, a majority moved to newer, better buildings in better areas. These improvements were reported with approximately equal frequency by businesses displaced by the highway as well as those from renewal areas. In only a minority of the cases did the quality of the site decline. And this occurred predominantly when the business relocated in close proximity to the original location. The smaller establishments, and those serving a neighborhood area, were most likely to show a decline, since they tended to remain in the same general area, whereas the large businesses were most likely to move to more distant zones and more attractive areas. Rent differentials changed accordingly.

Displacement and relocation create special problems for businesses that depend primarily on a neighborhood market. Yet these are the types of businesses that are most likely to be located in areas in need of renewal. In the present study approximately one-third of the displaced businesses served a local neighborhood market area. This varied markedly by type of project, however, ranging from more than half of the businesses from renewal areas to less than one-fifth of those displaced by highway construction programs. But, regardless of the cause of displacement, the disruptive effects were similar. A major difference by type of project pertained to the type of customer ordinarily served prior to the move. Businesses in renewal areas were four times as likely to serve a particular ethnic or racial group. This is to be expected since it is in such areas that minority groups live. It is this dependence on a particular type of customer and on a recurrent type of relationship that makes the small businesses and those serving a small geographical area distinct from other-type businesses in the problems encountered in relocation.

The non-survival rates were found to be substantially higher for neighborhood-type businesses than for those serving a larger area. Since such units were dependent on a small local population, displacement was particularly disruptive. To remain in the same general neighborhood was not a solution, since many of their former customers had also been displaced from the area. Nonetheless this was the type of move made by many such businesses. More than one-third of the neighborhood-type businesses moved one-tenth mile or less, and three-fourths moved within a radius of one-half mile of the original site. The median distance moved was only one-fourth mile. While the median costs of the move were less than for other types of businesses, the relative costs in relation to sales exceed those of businesses that served a larger market area. This is particularly meaningful in highway project areas where none of the costs were covered. In such cases, the brunt of the burden fell on the small neighborhood businesses which were likely to be marginal units at best and least likely to be able to afford such a burden. Also these units, more so than other-type businesses, experienced declines in sales following relocation. At the same time, rents increased. The net result was that they experienced more of a relative increase in rent burden than any other sub-group. The rent burden as a proportion of sales increased 80 per cent following the move. While median rents increased by more than one-fifth, median monthly sales declined by nearly one-third. The consequences of these changes need no further elaboration.

The negative consequences of relocation were most severe for neighborhood-type businesses. More than half of these units reported a decline in sales. This was approximately double the proportion found among businesses that served a larger market area.

Thus it is not surprising that owners of neighborhood-type establishments were much less satisfied with the progress made since the move. They stated a distinct preference for the former location as a place to do business, and a substantial majority reported that they would have done better had they not moved. The proportion of such responses exceeded by two and one-half times comparable responses found in any other market area category. Among the businesses that served a larger market area, a majority reported that they would not have been any better off if they had not moved. The latter, quite generally, responded favorably to the move. The rather negative evaluation of the neighborhood-type businesses which are predominantly food-related retail and service establishments is understandable, in view of the changes in income following relocation. A substantial majority reported a decrease.

Considering all of the relocated businesses, the adjustment following the move was predominantly favorable, even though selected subgroups experienced substantial losses. In our analysis we focused on two dimensions of adjustment; the one pertained to the objective changes measured economically, while the second was expressed psychologically in attitudinal evaluations regarding the new location. In respect to both dimensions a majority of the relocated businesses appeared to have responded favorably to the move. This, however, varied significantly by a number of sub-groups, as was clearly shown in our discussion of neighborhood-type businesses where we observed significant economic losses. Consistent with this was a marked negative reaction on the part of these businesses to the whole relocation process. This, of course, suggests that in order to properly assess the consequences of relocation, attention must be focused on specific sub-categories. Thus our analysis proceeded accordingly.

When our attention was focused on economic variables, we found that the relocated businesses fell evenly into three groups as far as changes in volume of business are concerned. Approximately one-third reported more business than prior to the move. An equal proportion reported no change, while the remaining one-third experienced a decline. More favorable responses were found in their evaluations regarding changes in the value of their businesses following the move. The most frequent response was that the business had increased in value. Only a small minority reported a decline. A less favorable response was reported with respect to changes in income. However, even here a substantial minority (nearly one unit in four) reported an increase, while one-third reported no change. This, of course, means that a majority either held their own or improved their income following the move. But for a substantial number (43 per cent), income declined at the new location. This decline, however, was largely due to small neighborhood-type businesses. Declines were reported disproportionately by food-related retail and service establishments. These businesses, as we have noted several times, were predominantly dependent on a recurrent relationship with customers living in close proximity. Movement out of an established area proved to be particularly disruptive for such businesses. Many were unable to survive displacement and, of those that did relocate, many experienced rather severe economic losses. Food-related retail and service establishments were the types of businesses that had the largest proportion that reported a decline in sales following the move. Jewelry manufacturing firms also had an above-average proportion reporting a decline, but it was generally agreed that this change was quite independent of the move. Rather, the owners attributed the decline to the overall depressed condition of the jewelry market at the time of the study.

Small businesses encountered much more difficulty in moving to a new location than did the larger establishments. Nearly half experienced a decline in volume of business and a substantial majority (60 per cent) reported a decline in income. This is nearly 50 per cent higher than the proportion for all businesses. Small units could ill afford such a decline, in that their median income at the new location was less than $4,000. However, a distinct majority of the businesses in the median and large-size categories made a favorable economic adjustment. They were able to either maintain the same business volume or to show an improvement. Similarly, for a majority, income remained the same or increased. Approximately one-third of the median and large units were better off after the move than prior to displacement. In many instances, the move gave them an opportunity to expand their business which was not possible at the old location. This was evident from remarks such as: "We were slowly strangling down in that area – that place was too small – the area was too congested for our business – we have been able to expand here because of more space but we couldn't have expanded at the old location – we were glad to leave – we wanted to expand and the move gave us the push forward we needed – we were blocked at the old location because of the poor condition of the building – we were growing and sooner or later would have to find a larger place – it was a good thing that it happened to us – moving shook the businesses up and in five years they will be in much better shape than if they hadn't moved." In these instances the consequences of displacement were to their advantage.

At the time of displacement, the reaction seemed to have been predominantly negative. Highly emotional and angry responses were frequent. Much of the unfavorable reaction, however, was found to be due to uncertainty as to what would happen to their businesses. Owners were suspicious that the move would be harmful, and thus the change was viewed with considerable apprehension. This view proved to be justified, at least in part, for approximately one-third of the establishments went out of business. There was general consensus among these owners that they had been badly handled. The reaction of the non-survivors to the whole displacement program was distinctly negative. A substantial majority expressed the opinion that they would be better off if they had not been forced to move. The owners of nearly all of these establishments reported that they would have continued in business indefinitely at the old site if they had not been displaced. With few exceptions, the non-survivors experienced a decline in income, even though a majority entered the labor force in some other capacity. Clearly displacement worked a real hardship for this group.

Later developments also showed that many of those that relocated were also justified in being apprehensive concerning the consequences of displacement, for many experienced economic losses as a result of the move. But such losses were reported by less than a majority. If we focus on the non-survivors and on those who experienced economic losses, the reaction to the move would, of course, be negative, but when attention is focused only on the establishments that continued in business, we find the appraisal of the move to be favorable. However, it is not overwhelmingly so. Nonetheless we found that only one-third of the units reported that they would have done better if they had not moved, and an equally small proportion stated a preference for the old location as a place to do business. Less than one-fourth expressed dissatisfaction with the progress made at the new site. Thus in respect to all three questions a majority either made no evaluative distinction between the old and new location or responded more favorably toward the new site. It is noteworthy that nearly half of the owners who relocated reported that they would not have done any better if they had not moved. A similar high proportion preferred the present location as a place to do business. A nearly equal number were found in the top satisfaction category when asked to evaluate the progress they had made at the new site. These reactions, however, varied markedly by a number of selected subgroups.

A favorable reaction to the move was reported by a majority of the owners of non-food-related retail establishments and those in the manufacturing, wholesale and construction category. Similarly favorable responses were reported by the owners of the larger businesses and those serving a non-local market area. Businesses that moved to the suburbs responded much more favorably to the move than those that remained in the city. This was not unrelated, however, to the type of selectivity that occurred in this movement. Also it was due in part to differences in site characteristics in the two areas. The suburbs attracted the kinds of establishments the owners of which responded most favorably to the move, that is, the younger, better educated owners who were concentrated in the higher income categories. Owners possessing these characteristics accounted for a disproportionately large part of the favorable reactions to the new locations.

On the negative side, it was the food-related retail and service units and the small neighborhood-type establishments that responded least favorably to displacement and relocation. Their more negative reaction was due to their greater dependence on a recurrent relationship with customers living in close proximity, many of whom came from a particular ethnic or racial group. Consequently such units were very sensitive to a change in location. For the most part, these units were not satisfied with the progress they had made since the move, and disproportionately they reported that they would have done better had they remained at the old location. They also stated a preference for the original location as a place to do business. In short, our analysis has shown that the reaction to the new location varies consistently and significantly by a number of important variables. Accordingly, to understand the consequences of displacement and relocation, as already noted, full attention must be focused on sub-groupings.

As far as the city is concerned, the displacement of commercial and industrial establishments results in considerable losses.[3] Part of the loss to the city is due to a changing distribution of these functions in the community, resulting from public improvement programs which disrupt established patterns. Not only do many of the displaced establishments go out of business, but other establishments move out of the city to the nearby suburban areas. This movement was found to be of more significance than would be implied from the relative number of units that leave the city, since from the point of view of volume of business and jobs the suburban movement was more costly to the city than losses experienced through establishments going out of business. We would expect that, as programs resulting in displacements become more extensive as well as accumulative, as they will in the future, the suburban movement is likely to increase, since fewer sites may be available in the city. It is readily apparent that the pressure for sites is certain to increase as more and more commercial structures are demolished. To lose such businesses to the suburbs is to decrease the number of jobs in the city and to detract accordingly from the tax base. This, cities can ill afford.

It would seem that, from the point of view of the welfare of the city, public improvement programs should be phased in such a way as to minimize the opportunities for such losses. This could be done, for example, by scheduling improvement projects in such a way as to provide space and accommodations for the es-

3 This is not a net loss, however, since no account has been taken of any gains that may have been realized in rebuilding the cleared areas. Nor has any attempt been made to measure what effect the new highways have on attracting new businesses to specific areas. This is only an account of what happens to the existing establishments at the time of displacement. Also we have not assessed what the long-range costs would be to the city if these public improvement programs had not been undertaken.

tablishments that are to be forced to move prior to their displacement. This suggests that clearance should be used to provide industrial and commercial spaces not only to attract new businesses and industry and thus add to the employment and tax base of the city, but also to house displaced establishments from other project areas in order to keep them in the city. The carrying out of such programs would represent gains for the city insofar as they would successfully prevent units moving from the city in order to find adequate sites. The present system is driving many of the more attractive businesses out of the city; thus, from the point of view of the city, the current programs are realizing less than their full potential.[4]

The programs for rebuilding cities are effectively eliminating the small marginal businesses. For such units, relocation is frequently not feasible. These businesses tend to be owned by older persons and those with very limited financial resources. Displacement in such cases has the effect of depriving the owners of their usual livelihood, meager as it may have been prior to the disruption. For the most part, the owner received no compensation for his loss, even though he had been forced to vacate his site. In some instances where they happened to own the building that they occupied, some minor adjustments may have been made in the price paid for the property which would make the loss less severe. But no such even token adjustments were possible in the case of renters. However, regardless of tenure, the move was most costly for the particular types of businesses that could least afford the loss.

To date, renewal and other public improvement programs, including highway construction, are efficient in the physical clearance of built-up areas, but they have not been able to accommodate the very small businesses that traditionally have been dependent upon sites in deteriorated areas where rents are low. These businesses are at best marginal. They operate at minimal levels; nonetheless, in their operations they provide at least a very small return to the owner. The business provides him with a job as well as an income. The owners of such units, however, are unable to ab-

4 It is noted, however, that such phasing of public improvement programs would likely not effectively resolve the typical relocation problems faced by small neighborhood-type businesses.

sorb the disruptive effects of the move, and thus close down their business. Although the loss of such units means little, if anything, to the city, the consequences represent real hardships for the individual owners. Perhaps it is incumbent upon the responsible governmental agencies to make equitable adjustments when public improvement programs are such as to make continuance in business economically unfeasible for individual owners. Such cases are limited, for, as we have found, only certain kinds of businesses are particularly sensitive to the disruptive effects of dislocation. However, these units account for a disproportionate number that suffer economic losses as a result of the move, and they also account for a disproportionate amount of the negative reactions that are expressed concerning the forced moves.

Neighborhood-type businesses constitute one type that pays a heavy price when displaced. Not only do they lose their business site but they are largely deprived of their market area as well. Consequently business failures and other economic losses are frequent. Closely related to this are the similar heavy costs that must be borne by food-related retail and service establishments. Few of these units gained from the move and, when they did, it was found to be due to a combination of atypical circumstances. Among such units that relocated, a substantial number experienced declines in sales while at the same time they experienced increases in rents. As a consequence of these changes, they were in a less favorable position after the move.

If we are to continue to rebuild our cities through extensive urban renewal programs and through the construction of modern highways, it is evident that we need to know more about the consequences of that expense and effort. The really basic question seems to be whether the aggregate gains are worth not only the aggregate social and economic costs, but worth the individual costs as well. This study has attempted to assess some of these costs.

In our analysis of the experiences of approximately 300 business establishments, we have presented ample evidence to show that, in many instances, the individual costs were high. The costs to the city were also substantial. Losses resulted either from the discontinuance of the business or through movement of the business to the suburbs. However, at the same time we found that there were real gains realized by many of the displaced businesses. Thus to emphasize only the negative effects and reactions to the move would be to give a false impression of the consequences of displacement. For instance, only a few of the larger businesses (those employing eight or more workers) were hurt by displacement. A much larger proportion was better off after the move than while at the original location.

Our findings are abundantly clear. One of the apparent changes wrought by these programs is the changing distribution of these functions. Displacements are hastening the suburbanization movement of commercial and industrial establishments. Also the problems resulting from displacements tend to be most severe among small business establishments and those largely dependent on a particular neighborhood market area, as well as on those units owned by persons who are perhaps too old to start over again. Many of these businesses may well be marginal in the larger economic system, but to the owners their business operation is a way of life as well as a means of making a living. Neither dimension can be easily ignored when individual costs are measured.

INDEX

INDEX

■